First Stop
on Reading Street

PEARSON

Glenview, Illinois • Boston, Massachusetts • Chandler, Arizona
Shoreview, Minnesota • Upper Saddle River, New Jersey

Any Path, Any Pace

"Welcome to Reading Street! Bienvenidos too."

Find Your Place on Reading Street!

Who leads the way on

YOU ARE HERE!

UNIT 1 UNIT 2 UNIT 3 UNIT 4 UNIT 5 UNIT 6

SCOTT FORESMAN
READING STREET

FIRST**STOP**

GRADE
5

My Teaching Library
PEARSON

Any Path, Any Pace

My Teaching Library
The ultimate find-your-place case! It stores all your Teacher's Editions in one space.

First Stop on Reading Street
It's your how-to guide, coach, and roadmap.
Find your place on *Reading Street*.

- Research into Practice
- Teacher Resources
- Professional Development
- Pacing Charts
- Reteach Lessons (and more!)

"Start here, go there, you see a chicken anywhere?"

Print • Online • CD/DVD • School to Home • English/Spanish

Reading Street?
Teachers Do.

How can something be slim and chunky?
The Teacher's Edition is slim, so it won't weigh you down. It's chunky, because it "chunks" the curriculum in manageable, three-week increments.

It's a Snap!
Snap-in tab to bookmark DIFFERENTIATING INSTRUCTION

Three Weekly Lessons
Considerate design that's manageable and doable

Where are all my teaching resources?
On disk or online—all the time!

Customize Literacy
Mini skill lessons to use with a variety of text sets

Customize Writing
21st Century Writing Projects and Writing Process lessons

Any Path, Any Pace

Who thrives on

All Children.

Every Child.

Every Single One.

"Hey, what about chickens?
You didn't mention chickens!"

PEARSON

SCOTT FORESMAN

Print • Online • CD/DVD • School to Home • English/Spanish

Reading Street?

★ Let's read it and write it and think it and do it! ★

Let's Go Digital
See It! Hear It! Do It!

Let's Write
Weekly Writing

Let's Learn
Application and Transfer

SCOTT FORESMAN
READING STREET
1ST

"Oh, Chicky wicky, don't be so picky."

Let's Listen
Phonemic Awareness

Let's Talk
Oral Vocabulary/
Amazing Words

Let's Envision
Visual Skills and Strategies

Let's Think
Personalized Reading Coach

Any Path, Any Pace

What makes Reading Stree

A day, a week, a unit, and a year!
Connect and scaffold learning

On *Reading Street* everything is neat. The unit concepts connect the curriculum from start to finish, scaffolding children's prior knowledge. Sustained concept and language development accelerates children's ability to comprehend, discuss, and write about what they're reading. Neat? *Sweeeeet.*

"A sweet, humble Cow. Now that's a WOW! So long, Chicky."

"Build your unit around one idea with power, an idea that helps learners make sense of otherwise isolated content."

Grant Wiggins
Coauthor with Jay McTighe of
Understanding by Design
Exclusive Pearson Consulting Author

PEARSON Rules!

strong?

Sustained Concept and Language Development.

Big Ideas
Consider big questions

Language
Hear and use sophisticated language

Envision It
Envision new ways of thinking

Team Talk
Share information every day

Unit Concept

Writing
Write to share what you know

Text Sets
Read related text sets

Science and Social Studies
Transfer concepts and language to content areas

Print • Online • CD/DVD • School to Home • English/Spanish   **Any Path, Any Pace**

What makes Reading Street

PRIORITY SKILL	SUCCESS PREDICTOR
PHONEMIC AWARENESS	Blending and Segmenting
PHONICS	Word Reading
FLUENCY	Words Correct per Minute
VOCABULARY	Word Knowledge
COMPREHENSION	Retelling

Don't Wait Until Friday!
Prevent misunderstandings right away with on-the-spot reteaching and prescriptions.

Monitor Progress with Success Predictors
Check students' progress of each priority skill with research-based predictors of reading success.

Print • Online • CD/DVD • School to Home • English/Spanish

work?

The Right Skills at the Right Time.

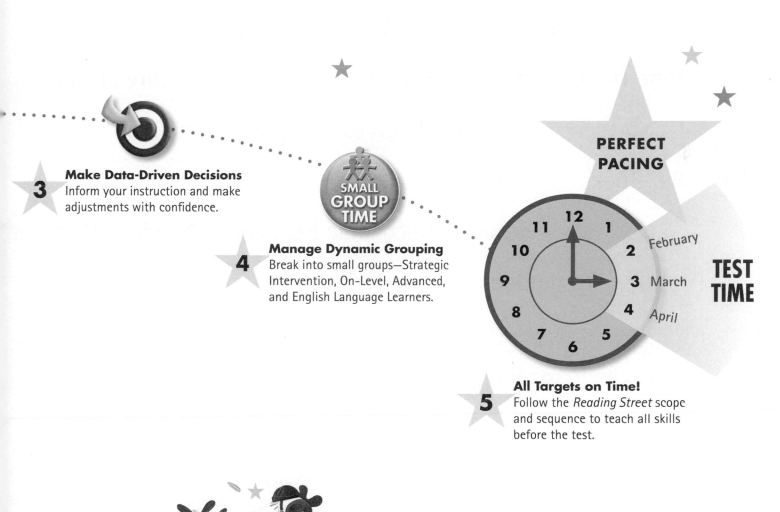

Make Data-Driven Decisions
3 Inform your instruction and make adjustments with confidence.

SMALL GROUP TIME

Manage Dynamic Grouping
4 Break into small groups—Strategic Intervention, On-Level, Advanced, and English Language Learners.

PERFECT PACING

February
March
April

TEST TIME

All Targets on Time!
5 Follow the *Reading Street* scope and sequence to teach all skills before the test.

"Sure a cow can talk the talk, but can a cow ride a bike?"

PEARSON

SCOTT FORESMAN

Any Path, Any Pace

What do readers read

Funny Stories   Myths   Caldecott Winners   Classic Literature

Multicultural Literature   E-mails   Big Books

Online Directories   Trucktown Readers   Adventure Stories

Nonfiction   Online Sources   Informational Text

Little Big Books   Concept Literacy Readers   Biographies

Narrative Fiction   Decodable Readers   Newbery Winners

Poetry   Trade Books   Mysteries   Realistic Fiction

English Language Development Readers   Historical Fiction   Blogs

Legends   Recipes   Search Engines   News Stories

Pourquoi Tales   Fables   Tall Tales   Fantasy Stories

Nursery Rhymes   Web Sites   Drama   Trickster Tales

"I prefer doggy stories over chicky stories."

Print • Online • CD/DVD • School to Home • English/Spanish

on Reading Street?

Grade 2 Literature Selections

● **Main Selection**

● Paired Selection

"I like horse stories. Say, Chicky,
do you have any spare hay?"

Any Path, Any Pace

What do writers write

Narrative Poems   Invitations   Research Papers

Blogs   Classroom Newsletters   Realistic Stories

Adventure Stories   Compare and Contrast Essays   Lists

Friendly Letters   Online Journals   Online Forums

Persuasive Essays   Formal Letters   Steps in a Process

Expository Compositions   Podcasts   Captions

Personal Narratives   Multi-paragraph Essays

Drama Scenes   E-mail Pen Pals

Fiction   Peer Revisions   Responses to Prompts

"A writer notices things. Now where's that chicken?"

Print • Online • CD/DVD • School to Home • English/Spanish

on Reading Street?

Customize Your Writing

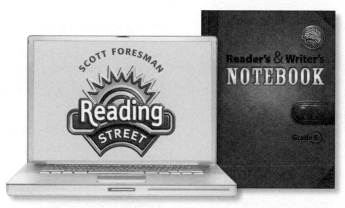

21st Century Writing Projects
The writing section in your Teacher's Edition also provides collaborative writing projects that use the Internet to develop new literacies. Go digital! You choose.

Writing Process
Turn to the writing tab in your Teacher's Edition. A writing process lesson helps children learn the process of writing. Use as a Writing Workshop or customize to your needs.

The Internet Guy
Donald Leu, Ph.D.

The Write Guy
Jeff Anderson, M.Ed.

"Chicken stories are for the birds. I'll write about acorns."

Any Path, Any Pace

Who said so?

The Leading Researchers,

Program Authors

Peter Afflerbach, Ph.D.
Professor
Department of Curriculum
and Instruction
University of Maryland
at College Park

Camille L. Z. Blachowicz, Ph.D.
Professor of Education
National-Louis University

Candy Dawson Boyd, Ph.D.
Professor
School of Education
Saint Mary's College of California

Elena Izquierdo, Ph.D.
Associate Professor
University of Texas at El Paso

Connie Juel, Ph.D.
Professor of Education
School of Education
Stanford University

Edward J. Kame'enui, Ph.D.
*Dean-Knight Professor of
Education and Director*
Institute for the Development of
Educational Achievement and
the Center on Teaching and Learning
College of Education
University of Oregon

Donald J. Leu, Ph.D.
*John and Maria Neag Endowed
Chair in Literacy and Technology
Director, The New Literacies
Research Lab*
University of Connecticut

Jeanne R. Paratore, Ed.D.
Associate Professor of Education
Department of Literacy and
Language Development
Boston University

P. David Pearson, Ph.D.
Professor and Dean
Graduate School of Education
University of California, Berkeley

Sam L. Sebesta, Ed.D.
Professor Emeritus
College of Education
University of Washington, Seattle

Deborah Simmons, Ph.D.
Professor
College of Education and
Human Development
Texas A&M University

Alfred W. Tatum, Ph.D.
*Associate Professor and Director
of the UIC Reading Clinic*
University of Illinois at Chicago

Sharon Vaughn, Ph.D.
*H. E. Hartfelder/Southland
Corporation Regents Professor
Director, Meadows Center for
Preventing Educational Risk*
University of Texas

Susan Watts Taffe, Ph.D.
*Associate Professor in Literacy
Division of Teacher Education*
University of Cincinnati

Karen Kring Wixson, Ph.D.
Professor of Education
University of Michigan

Consulting Authors

Jeff Anderson, M.Ed.
Author and Consultant
San Antonio, Texas

Jim Cummins, Ph.D.
Professor
Department of Curriculum,
Teaching and Learning
University of Toronto

Lily Wong Fillmore, Ph.D.
Professor Emerita
Graduate School of Education
University of California, Berkeley

Georgia Earnest García, Ph.D.
Professor
Language and Literacy Division
Department of Curriculum
and Instruction
University of Illinois at
Urbana-Champaign

George A. González, Ph.D.
Professor (Retired)
School of Education
University of Texas-Pan American,
Edinburg

Valerie Ooka Pang, Ph.D.
Professor
School of Teacher Education
San Diego State University

Sally M. Reis, Ph.D.
*Board of Trustees Distinguished
Professor*
Department of Educational
Psychology
University of Connecticut

Jon Scieszka, M.F.A.
*Children's Book Author
Founder of GUYS READ
Named First National Ambassador
for Young People's Literature 2008*

Grant Wiggins, Ed.D.
Educational Consultant
Authentic Education
Concept Development

Lee Wright, M.Ed.
Pearland, Texas

Practitioners, and Authors.

Consultant

Sharroky Hollie, Ph.D.
Assistant Professor
California State University
Dominguez Hills, CA

Teacher Reviewers

Dr. Bettyann Brugger
*Educational Support Coordinator—
Reading Office*
Milwaukee Public Schools
Milwaukee, WI

Kathleen Burke
K–12 Reading Coordinator
Peoria Public Schools, Peoria, IL

Darci Burns, M.S.Ed.
University of Oregon

Bridget Cantrell
District Intervention Specialist
Blackburn Elementary School
Independence, MO

**Tahira DuPree Chase,
M.A., M.S.Ed.**
*Administrator of Elementary
English Language Arts*
Mount Vernon City School District
Mount Vernon, NY

Michele Conner
Director, Elementary Education
Aiken County School District
Aiken, SC

Georgia Coulombe
*K–6 Regional Trainer/
Literacy Specialist*
Regional Center for Training and
Learning (RCTL), Reno, NV

Kelly Dalmas
Third Grade Teacher
Avery's Creek Elementary, Arden, NC

Seely Dillard
First Grade Teacher
Laurel Hill Primary School
Mt. Pleasant, SC

Jodi Dodds-Kinner
Director of Elementary Reading
Chicago Public Schools, Chicago, IL

Dr. Ann Wild Evenson
District Instructional Coach
Osseo Area Schools, Maple Grove, MN

Stephanie Fascitelli
Principal
Apache Elementary, Albuquerque
Public Schools, Albuquerque, NM

Alice Franklin
*Elementary Coordinator, Language
Arts & Reading*
Spokane Public Schools, Spokane, WA

Laureen Fromberg
Assistant Principal
PS 100, Queens, NY

Kimberly Gibson
First Grade Teacher
Edgar B. Davis Community School
Brockton, MA

Kristen Gray
Lead Teacher
A.T. Allen Elementary School
Concord, NC

Mary Ellen Hazen
State Pre-K Teacher
Rockford Public Schools #205
Rockford, IL

Patrick M. Johnson
Elementary Instructional Director
Seattle Public Schools, Seattle, WA

Theresa Jaramillo Jones
Principal
Highland Elementary School
Las Cruces, NM

Sophie Kowzun
*Program Supervisor, Reading/
Language Arts, PreK-5*
Montgomery County Public Schools
Rockville, MD

David W. Matthews
Sixth Grade Teacher
Easton Area Middle School
Easton, Pennsylvania

Ana Nuncio
Editor and Independent Publisher
Salem, MA

Joseph Peila
Principal
Chappell Elementary School
Chicago, IL

Ivana Reimer
Literacy Coordinator
PS 100, Queens, NY

Sally Riley
Curriculum Coordinator
Rochester Public Schools
Rochester, NH

Dyan M. Smiley
*English Language Arts Program
Director, Grades K-5*
Boston Public Schools, Literacy
Department, Boston, MA

Michael J. Swiatowiec
Lead Literacy Teacher
Graham Elementary School
Chicago, IL

Dr. Helen Taylor
Director of Reading/English Education
Portsmouth City Public Schools
Portsmouth, VA

Carol Thompson
Teaching and Learning Coach
Independence School District
Independence, MO

Erinn Zeitlin
Kindergarten Teacher
Carderock Springs Elementary School
Bethesda, MD

Any Path, Any Pace

Any Path, Any Pace

Reading STREET

CALLE de la Lectura

Find Your Place on Reading Street!

"On Reading Street, you can do anything and go anywhere."

PEARSON

SCOTT FORESMAN

"Tell me and I forget. Teach me and I remember. Involve me and I learn."

—Benjamin Franklin

Welcome! You've arrived on Reading Street

You're about to take your class on a rich instructional journey. As children explore the world that reading opens to them, they will look to you for guidance and support. You, as their teacher, can make the difference in their literacy experience. To help you, *Scott Foresman Reading Street* has paved the way with solid, research-based instruction. This support will be your clear path to success.

Now it's time to discover what you can expect in the materials and professional support that *Reading Street* offers. It's time to make your *First Stop on Reading Street!*

First Stop on
Reading Street: Grade 2

From Our Authors...

Dear Second-Grade Teacher,

Greetings. You may be well acquainted with the wild and wonderful ways of second graders. These children are a unique group, not only because they are about seven years old (give or take a few uncomplaining months), they have successfully negotiated first grade, and they are beginning to develop a sense of humor about the giddiness of human beings, but also because they generally arrive in second grade with the radiant feeling that they *CAN* read! In fact, their appetite for reading fully and imaginatively—like most giddy adults—is hard to satisfy. They are literally empowered by the confidence of last year's experience. They now know the "secret code."

They are entering the expansive, always provocative, world of words and ideas.

As second graders, children can read stories—like *Miss Nelson Is Missing*—that have rhetorical depth, with a problem, a resolution or two, and a theme, or message. This new reading agility affords them a workable (and growing) lexicon, as well as sufficient story experience (e.g., the *Magic Tree House* and *Junie B. Jones* series) to use in creating and writing their own stories. Second graders are beginning to engage and apply their newly acquired "reading brain"—a brain that was not *born* to read but must learn *how* to read in an alphabetic writing system. In doing so, second graders are also just beginning the often treacherous transition from learning to read to reading to learn. They are entering the expansive, always provocative, world of words and ideas.

So, expect second-grade readers to exercise their ability to read fluently, automatically, and with agility when deciphering the code. In doing so, second graders will gain access to millions of new words as they become independent readers. Importantly, in doing so, they will also gain access to interesting ideas as they build a mental dictionary of new words that give expression to their world and the fascinating human beings and creatures in it.

Edward J. Kame'enui, Ph.D.

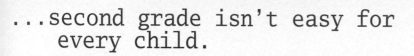

...second grade isn't easy for every child.

However, it is worth considering that second grade isn't easy for every child. For some, keeping their heads above water will require your diligent and strategic support. In order for "seconds" to get to be "thirds," they will need your best instruction and the faithful implementation of this program and its support materials. Your attention to the details of instruction is essential, along with frequent monitoring of reading progress, and anticipation of necessary instructional changes. These children will likely need your explicit guidance and scaffolding on complex second-grade strategies. Your expert teaching and commitment make an acute difference. Thank you.

Welcome back to second grade.

Edward J. Kame'enui

Edward J. Kame'enui, Ph.D.
Dean-Knight Professor of Education
College of Education
University of Oregon

Research into Practice
on Reading Street

Section 1 is your tour of the daily lesson on
Scott Foresman Reading Street. When you make each of these stops, your second grade instruction is successful.

• Get Ready to Read

• Read and Comprehend

• Language Arts

• Wrap Up Your Day

Along the way, you'll learn more about Oral Language, Phonemic Awareness, and other research building blocks of literacy. You'll discover that every activity and routine in the daily lesson is there because research has shown that it's important for your teaching practice.

This Research into Practice section presents a representative sample of lesson pages for one week of instruction. Where pages from the Teacher's Edition are not shown for a given unit, those pages are listed with references to research supporting the instruction.

The Building Blocks of Research in Literacy

- Oral Language
- Phonemic Awareness
- Phonics
- Decodable Text
- Fluency
- Oral Vocabulary
- Language Arts
- Reading Vocabulary
- Comprehension
- Academic Vocabulary
- Informational Text
- 21st Century Skills
- Writing
- Differentiated Instruction
- English Language Learners
- Success Predictors

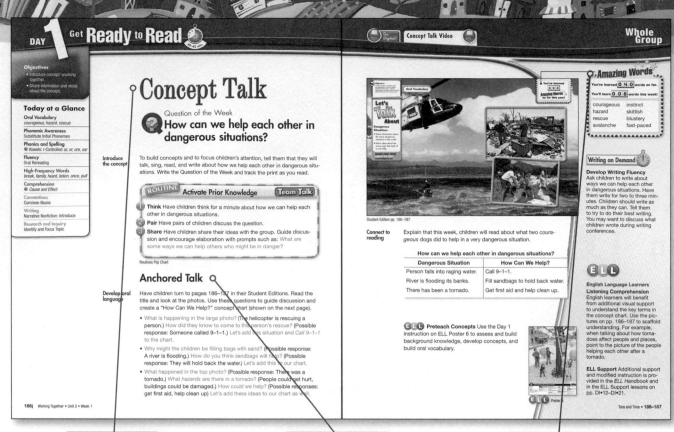

ORAL LANGUAGE

In Reading Street

Concept Talk To begin each day, children come together for a brief, whole-class, rich, oral language experience. Discussion of the Question of the Week guides children to activate prior knowledge and develop new knowledge and understanding of the unit concept. Each Concept Talk throughout the week includes opportunities for reviewing skills.

Because Research Says

Reading instruction builds especially on oral language. If this foundation is weak, progress in reading will be slow and uncertain. Children must have at least a basic vocabulary, a reasonable range of knowledge of the world around them, and the ability to talk about their knowledge. These abilities form the basis for comprehending text. —(Anderson, Hiebert, Scott, and Wilkinson, 1985)

ORAL LANGUAGE

In Reading Street

Anchored Talk During the week, the class creates a concept map to build comprehension of the week's concept. The map first takes shape as students explore their prior knowledge and discuss visual cues. Throughout the week, students add related concepts based on their reading and their life experiences.

Because Research Says

Semantic maps address the relationships between words and concepts. Relational charts allow students to generate new information based on their reading and learning. —(Blachowicz and Fisher, 2002)

Text discussions should go beyond answering comprehension questions. Discussing text with students requires that teachers understand that meaning is not in text per se, but is to be found in the text and the experiences the reader brings to it. —(Tatum, 2005)

ORAL VOCABULARY

In Reading Street

Amazing Words Each week children learn a set of conceptually related Amazing Words, generally beyond their reading ability, selected from shared songs and literature. Throughout the week children use the words in multiple contexts: in conversations about text, in retelling a story or summarizing a text, in their daily writing, and in the end-of-day discussions.

Because Research Says

A robust approach to vocabulary involves directly explaining the meanings of words along with thought-provoking, playful, and interactive follow-up. —(Beck, McKeown, and Kucan, 2002)

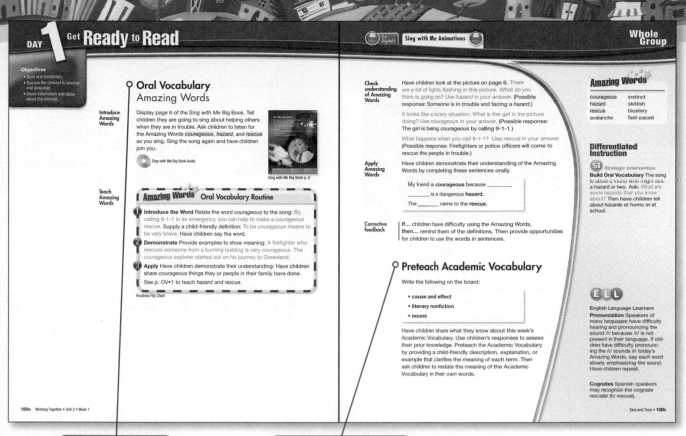

In Reading Street

Oral Vocabulary Daily shared literature offers exposure to new oral vocabulary and frequent opportunities for discussion. On Day 1, children learn a song from the *Sing with Me* Big Book. Using the Oral Vocabulary Routine, the teacher introduces each word, supplies word meaning, provides multiple contexts for the word, and has children practice using the word.

Because Research Says

Although a great deal of vocabulary is learned indirectly through shared storybook reading, teachers need to provide more explicit vocabulary instruction. It is important to provide multiple exposures of target words and carefully scheduled review and practice.
—(Armbruster and Osborn, 2001; Coyne, Simmons, and Kame'enui, 2004)

In Reading Street

Academic Vocabulary During the week, the teacher directly teaches a limited number of academic vocabulary words related to reading and language arts concepts. Lessons also offer multiple strategies for developing an understanding of this academic vocabulary.

Because Research Says

When choosing words for direct instruction, include those that lead to conceptual understanding. Students need to understand these words beyond the sense of the general concept and be able to provide precision and specificity in describing the concept. The most productive direct vocabulary instruction aims at words that are of high frequency for mature language users and are found across a variety of domains. —(Beck, McKeown, and Kucan, 2002)

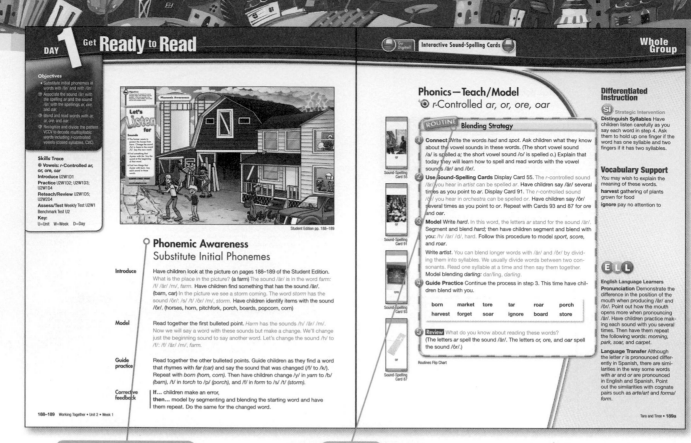

····· PHONEMIC AWARENESS ·····

In Reading Street

Phonemic Awareness Each phonemic awareness lesson ties to phonics instruction. Lessons focused on blending and segmenting words with certain vowels prepare children for the phonics lesson that follows.

Because Research Says

▶ Learning to break the code of written text is partly dependent on phonemic awareness, or the realization that words are composed of sequences of meaningless and somewhat distinct sounds (i.e., phonemes). Phonics instruction attempts to explicitly map phonemes to graphemes (i.e., letters in English), but is not effective unless children have some phonemic awareness. —(Juel, 1988)

····· PHONICS ·····

In Reading Street

Blending Strategy This routine provides explicit instruction for sound-spellings and word parts. Children develop an understanding of the alphabetic principle as they are led to use and point to letters as words are written, and then to blend, or decode, words.

Because Research Says

▶ Segmenting words into phonemes and blending phonemes into words contributes more to learning to read than any other phonological awareness skills. —(Vaughn and Linan-Thompson, 2004)

Pages 190–190a are based on the same research as page 189a.

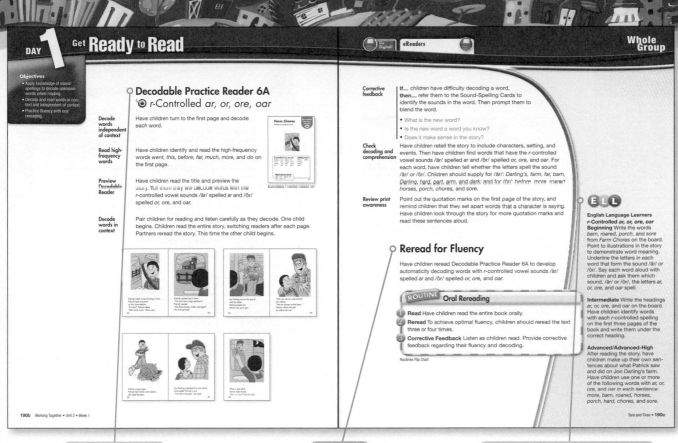

eReaders

Whole Group

Objectives
- Apply knowledge of sound-spellings to decode unknown words when reading.
- Decode and read words in context and independent of context.
- Practice fluency with oral rereading.

Decodable Practice Reader 6A
r-Controlled *ar, or, ore, oar*

Decode words independent of context
Have children turn to the first page and decode each word.

Read high-frequency words
Have children identify and read the high-frequency words *went, this, before, far, much, more,* and *do* on the first page.

Preview Decodable Reader
Have children read the title and preview the story. Tell them they will decode words with the *r*-controlled vowel sounds /är/ spelled *ar* and /ôr/ spelled *or, ore,* and *oar.*

Decode words in context
Pair children for reading and listen carefully as they decode. One child begins. Children read the entire story, switching readers after each page. Partners reread the story. This time the other child begins.

Corrective feedback
If... children have difficulty decoding a word, **then...** refer them to the Sound-Spelling Cards to identify the sounds in the word. Then prompt them to blend the word.
- What is the new word?
- Is the new word a word you know?
- Does it make sense in the story?

Check decoding and comprehension
Have children retell the story to include characters, setting, and events. Then have children find words that have the *r*-controlled vowel sounds /är/ spelled *ar* and /ôr/ spelled *or, ore,* and *oar.* For each word, have children tell whether the letters spell the sound /är/ or /ôr/. Children should supply for /är/: *Darling's, farm, far, barn, Darling, hard, part, arm,* and *dark;* and for /ôr/: *before, more, roared, horses, porch, chores,* and *sore.*

Review print awareness
Point out the quotation marks on the first page of the story, and remind children that they set apart words that a character is saying. Have children look through the story for more quotation marks and read these sentences aloud.

Reread for Fluency
Have children reread Decodable Practice Reader 6A to develop automaticity decoding words with *r*-controlled vowel sounds /är/ spelled *ar* and /ôr/ spelled *or, ore,* and *oar.*

ROUTINE Oral Rereading
1. **Read** Have children read the entire book orally.
2. **Reread** To achieve optimal fluency, children should reread the text three or four times.
3. **Corrective Feedback** Listen as children read. Provide corrective feedback regarding their fluency and decoding.

Routines Flip Chart

ELL
English Language Learners
r-Controlled *ar, or, ore, oar*
Beginning Write the words *barn, roared, porch,* and *sore* from *Farm Chores* on the board. Point to illustrations in the story to demonstrate word meaning. Underline the letters in each word that form the sound /är/ or /ôr/. Say each word aloud with children and ask them which sound, /är/ or /ôr/, the letters *ar, or, ore,* and *oar* spell.

Intermediate Write the headings *ar, or, ore,* and *oar* on the board. Have children identify words with each *r*-controlled spelling on the first three pages of the book and write them under the correct heading.

Advanced/Advanced-High After reading the story, have children make up their own sentences about what Patrick saw and did on Jon Darling's farm. Have children use one or more of the following words with *ar, or, ore,* and *oar* in each sentence: *more, barn, roared, horses, porch, hard, chores,* and *sore.*

190b Working Together • Unit 2 • Week 1

Tara and Tiree • 190c

DECODABLE TEXT

In Reading Street

Decodable Practice Readers
Children use readers to practice the weekly target phonics skills. Children can read these texts with a high potential for accuracy because they are at least 80 percent decodable—that is, at least 80 percent of all words are based on previously taught phonics elements. The remaining words in the readers are previously taught sight words.

Because Research Says
Learning letter-sound relationships in isolation is necessary, but not enough. Children must know how to apply their knowledge to reading text. They should begin by reading decodable text comprised largely of words containing previously taught letter-sound relationships and gradually move to less controlled text as their ability and confidence grow. —(Vaughn and Linan-Thompson, 2004)

FLUENCY

In Reading Street

Reread for Fluency Children have opportunities to reread the same text orally several times throughout the week. In the Routine for Oral Rereading, children engage in repeated oral reading as the teacher monitors fluency and provides guidance and feedback.

Because Research Says
Perhaps the best known of the strategies designed to support fluency development is that of repeated readings. Generally, the children involved in using this strategy enjoy seeing the gains they make through their tracking of the changes in their reading and experience gratification when making visible improvement over a short period of time. —(Kuhn, 2003)

ENGLISH LANGUAGE LEARNERS

In Reading Street

Support for English Learners
Throughout the lesson, teachers are offered strategies and activities that help scaffold and support English learners in reading, writing, listening, and speaking at all levels of English proficiency.

Because Research Says
All the preliteracy skills, such as the development of concepts about print, alphabet knowledge, phonemic awareness, writing, and environmental print, are important for ELL children to be exposed to and to learn. —(Tabors, 1997)

Page 190d is based on the same research as page 192d. Page 191 is based on the same research as page 192e.

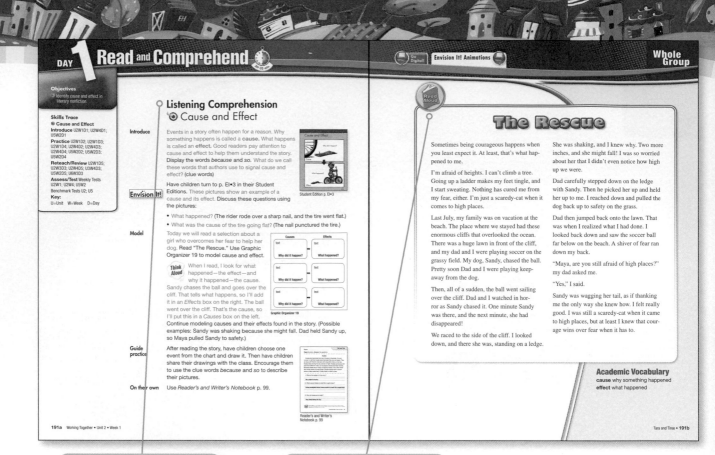

Objectives
- Identify cause and effect in literary nonfiction.

Skills Trace
Cause and Effect
Introduce U2W1D1; U2W4D1; U5W2D1
Practice U2W1D2; U2W1D3; U2W1D4; U2W4D2; U2W4D3; U2W4D4; U5W2D2; U5W2D3; U5W2D4
Reteach/Review U2W1D5; U2W3D3; U2W4D5; U3W4D3; U5W2D5; U6W3D3
Assess/Test Weekly Tests U2W1; U2W4; U5W2
Benchmark Tests U2; U5
Key:
U=Unit W=Week D=Day

Listening Comprehension
Cause and Effect

Introduce
Events in a story often happen for a reason. Why something happens is called a **cause**. What happens is called an **effect**. Good readers pay attention to cause and effect to help them understand the story. Display the words *because* and *so*. What do we call these words that authors use to signal cause and effect? (clue words)

Envision It!
Have children turn to p. EI•3 in their Student Editions. These pictures show an example of a cause and its effect. Discuss these questions using the pictures:

Student Edition p. EI•3

- What happened? (The rider rode over a sharp nail, and the tire went flat.)
- What was the cause of the tire going flat? (The nail punctured the tire.)

Model
Today we will read a selection about a girl who overcomes her fear to help her dog. Read "The Rescue." Use Graphic Organizer 19 to model cause and effect.

Think Aloud When I read, I look for what happened—the effect—and why it happened—the cause.
Sandy chases the ball and goes over the cliff. That tells what happens, so I'll add it in an *Effects* box on the right. The ball went over the cliff. That's the cause, so I'll put this in a *Causes* box on the left.
Continue modeling causes and their effects found in the story. (Possible examples: Sandy was shaking because she might fall. Dad held Sandy up, so Maya pulled Sandy to safety.)

Graphic Organizer 19

Guide practice
After reading the story, have children choose one event from the chart and draw it. Then have children share their drawings with the class. Encourage them to use the clue words *because* and *so* to describe their pictures.

On their own
Use *Reader's and Writer's Notebook* p. 99.

Reader's and Writer's Notebook p. 99

191a Working Together • Unit 2 • Week 1

Read Aloud

The Rescue

Sometimes being courageous happens when you least expect it. At least, that's what happened to me.

I'm afraid of heights. I can't climb a tree. Going up a ladder makes my feet tingle, and I start sweating. Nothing has cured me from my fear, either. I'm just a scaredy-cat when it comes to high places.

Last July, my family was on vacation at the beach. The place where we stayed had these enormous cliffs that overlooked the ocean. There was a huge lawn in front of the cliff, and my dad and I were playing soccer on the grassy field. My dog, Sandy, chased the ball. Pretty soon Dad and I were playing keep-away from the dog.

Then, all of a sudden, the ball went sailing over the cliff. Dad and I watched in horror as Sandy chased it. One minute Sandy was there, and the next minute, she had disappeared!

We raced to the side of the cliff. I looked down, and there she was, standing on a ledge.

She was shaking, and I knew why. Two more inches, and she might fall! I was so worried about her that I didn't even notice how high up we were.

Dad carefully stepped down on the ledge with Sandy. Then he picked her up and held her up to me. I reached down and pulled the dog back up to safety on the grass.

Dad then jumped back onto the lawn. That was when I realized what I had done. I looked back down and saw the soccer ball far below on the beach. A shiver of fear ran down my back.

"Maya, are you still afraid of high places?" my dad asked me.

"Yes," I said.

Sandy was wagging her tail, as if thanking me the only way she knew how. I felt really good. I was still a scaredy-cat when it came to high places, but at least I knew that courage wins over fear when it has to.

Academic Vocabulary
cause why something happened
effect what happened

Tara and Tiree • 191b

COMPREHENSION

In Reading Street

Listening Comprehension
Using an explicit model of instruction, teachers introduce and model a target comprehension skill through a read-aloud. Then children recall a previously read story or selection and apply the skill to it. Teachers monitor children's listening comprehension as they apply skills and strategies to new texts.

Because Research Says
Teacher read-alouds can be a good starting point for introducing critical strategies for comprehension. That is, just by listening first, children can focus on the strategy being introduced without actually having to read. —(Ivey, 2002)

COMPREHENSION

In Reading Street

Read Aloud Children develop comprehension skills and strategies through listening to literature, both fiction and non-fiction. The read-aloud relates to the concept of the week and provides strong examples of the target comprehension skill.

Because Research Says
Read-alouds are especially beneficial to children who have had few experiences with story-book reading prior to coming to school. When teachers and other adults read to children, they (1) hear fluent reading; (2) develop listening skills; (3) increase their exposure to new and interesting words and concepts; and (4) increase their background knowledge. —(Paratore and McCormack, 2005)

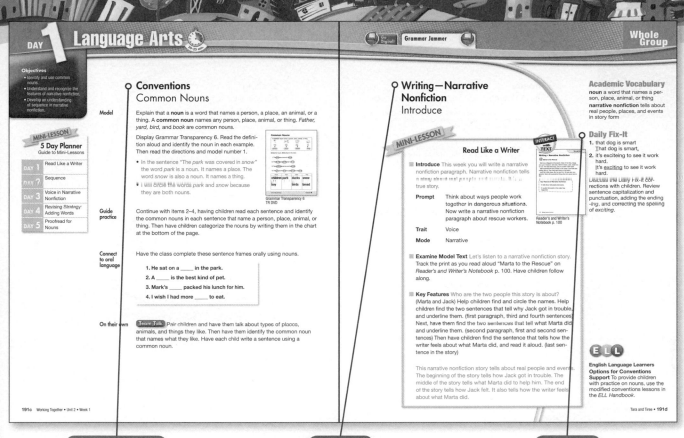

Grammar Jammer

Whole Group

Objectives
• Identify and use common nouns.
• Understand and recognize the features of narrative nonfiction.
• Develop an understanding of sequence in narrative nonfiction.

MINI-LESSON
5 Day Planner
Guide to Mini-Lessons

DAY 1	Read Like a Writer
DAY 2	Sequence
DAY 3	Voice in Narrative Nonfiction
DAY 4	Revising Strategy: Adding Words
DAY 5	Proofread for Nouns

Conventions
Common Nouns

Model Explain that a **noun** is a word that names a person, a place, an animal, or a thing. A **common noun** names any person, place, animal, or thing. *Father, yard, bird,* and *book* are common nouns.

Display Grammar Transparency 6. Read the definition aloud and identify the noun in each example. Then read the directions and model number 1.

• In the sentence "The *park* was covered in *snow*" the word *park* is a noun. It names a place. The word *snow* is also a noun. It names a thing.
• I will circle the words *park* and *snow* because they are both nouns.

Grammar Transparency 6
TR DVD

Guide practice Continue with items 2–4, having children read each sentence and identify the common nouns in each sentence that name a person, a place, an animal, or a thing. Then have children categorize the nouns by writing them in the chart at the bottom of the page.

Connect to oral language Have the class complete these sentence frames orally using nouns.

1. He sat on a _____ in the park.
2. A _____ is the best kind of pet.
3. Mark's _____ packed his lunch for him.
4. I wish I had more _____ to eat.

On their own **Team Talk** Pair children and have them talk about types of places, animals, and things they like. Then have them identify the common noun that names what they like. Have each child write a sentence using a common noun.

191c Working Together • Unit 2 • Week 1

Writing—Narrative Nonfiction
Introduce

MINI-LESSON

INTERACT with TEXT

Read Like a Writer

■ **Introduce** This week you will write a narrative nonfiction paragraph. Narrative nonfiction tells a story about real people and events. It's a true story.

Prompt Think about ways people work together in dangerous situations. Now write a narrative nonfiction paragraph about rescue workers.

Trait Voice

Mode Narrative

Reader's and Writer's Notebook p. 100

■ **Examine Model Text** Let's listen to a narrative nonfiction story. Track the print as you read aloud "Marta to the Rescue" on *Reader's and Writer's Notebook* p. 100. Have children follow along.

■ **Key Features** Who are the two people this story is about? (Marta and Jack) Help children find and circle the names. Help children find the two sentences that tell why Jack got in trouble, and underline them. (first paragraph, third and fourth sentences) Next, have them find the two sentences that tell what Marta did and underline them. (second paragraph, first and second sentences) Then have children find the sentence that tells how the writer feels about what Marta did, and read it aloud. (last sentence in the story)

This narrative nonfiction story tells about real people and events. The beginning of the story tells how Jack got in trouble. The middle of the story tells what Marta did to help him. The end of the story tells how Jack felt. It also tells how the writer feels about what Marta did.

English Language Learners Options for Conventions Support To provide children with practice on nouns, use the modified conventions lessons in the *ELL Handbook*.

Academic Vocabulary
noun a word that names a person, place, animal, or thing
narrative nonfiction tells about real people, places, and events in story form

Daily Fix-It
1. that dog is smart
   That dog is smart.
2. it's exciting to see it work hard.
   It's *exciting* to see it work hard.

Discuss the Daily Fix-It corrections with children. Review sentence capitalization and punctuation, adding the ending *-ing*, and correcting the spelling of *exciting*.

Tara and Tiree • 191d

LANGUAGE ARTS

In Reading Street

Conventions Children learn a new grammar skill each week. The skill is introduced on Day 1 with the Grammar Transparency and tied to reading and writing activities throughout the week.

Because Research Says

▶ The study of grammar will help people become better users of the language, that is, more effective as listeners and speakers, and especially as readers and writers. —(Weaver, 1996)

WRITING

In Reading Street

Writing Writing lessons are organized around a weekly writing routine that encourages connections with reading. Each week, writing focuses on a product or form. Lessons incorporate the use of mentor text and mini-lessons on writing traits and writer's craft. Children then apply the lessons to their own writing.

Because Research Says

▶ Writing has a central role in early reading development. Increasingly, we see the synergistic relationship between learning to write and learning to read. —(National Writing Project and Nagin, 2003)

WRITING

In Reading Street

Daily Fix-It Practice sentences provide opportunities for reviewing conventions, such as spelling, grammar, and punctuation. Each sentence contains errors in previously taught skills.

Because Research Says

▶ Instead of formally teaching children grammar, we need to give them plenty of structured and unstructured opportunities to deal with language directly. —(Weaver, 1979)

Pages 191e–191f are based on the same research as pages 191d, 207d, and 207f. Pages 192a–192b are based on the same research as pages 186j and 186–187.

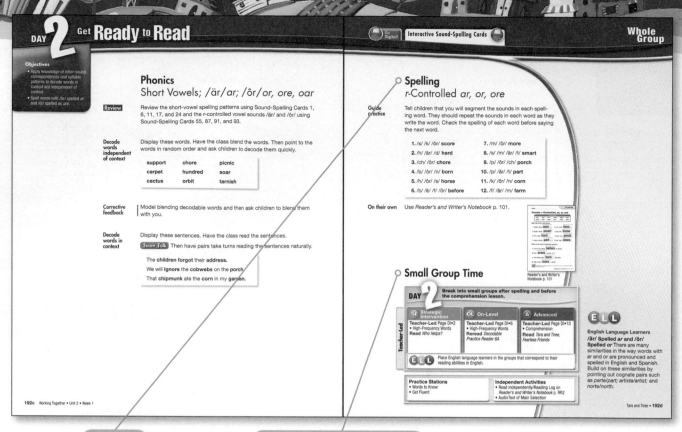

PHONICS

In Reading Street

Spelling Instruction in spelling and phonics are interconnected because both rely on knowledge of the alphabetic system. Spelling instruction begins at the sound level, moves to the structure level (word endings, prefixes, suffixes), and finally moves to the meaning level (compound words, homophones, word origins).

Because Research Says

Grapheme-phoneme knowledge, also referred to as alphabetic knowledge, is essential for literacy acquisition to reach a mature state. It is important to include spelling as well as reading in this picture, because learning to read and learning to spell words in English depend on processes that are tightly interconnected. —(Ehri, 1992)

DIFFERENTIATED INSTRUCTION

In Reading Street

Small Group Time Group instruction is based on the 3-Tier Reading Model developed at the University of Texas. At the start of the school year, teachers use the Baseline Group Test to make initial instructional decisions: Children with below-level performance are given Strategic Intervention instruction, those performing at grade level are placed in the On-Level group, and those who perform above grade level are given Advanced instruction.

Because Research Says

The components of effective reading instruction are the same whether the focus is prevention or intervention. By coordinating research evidence from effective classroom reading instruction with effective small-group and one-on-one reading instruction, teachers can meet the literacy needs of all children. —(Foorman and Torgesen, 2001)

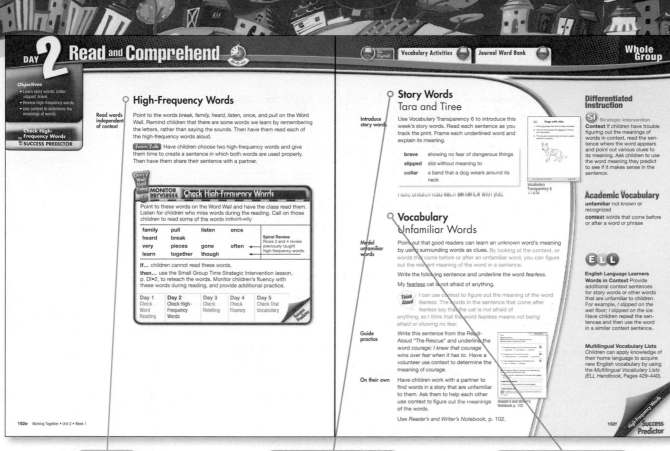

Objectives
- Learn story words: collar, slipped, brave.
- Review high-frequency words.
- Use context to determine the meanings of words.

Check High-Frequency Words
SUCCESS PREDICTOR

High-Frequency Words

Read words independent of context

Point to the words *break, family, heard, listen, once,* and *pull* on the Word Wall. Remind children that there are some words we learn by remembering the letters, rather than saying the sounds. Then have them read each of the high-frequency words aloud.

Team Talk Have children choose two high-frequency words and give them time to create a sentence in which both words are used properly. Then have them share their sentence with a partner.

Don't Wait Until Friday
MONITOR PROGRESS **Check High-Frequency Words**

Point to these words on the Word Wall and have the class read them. Listen for children who miss words during the reading. Call on those children to read some of the words individually

family	pull	listen	once	
heard	break			Spiral Review
very	pieces	gone	often	Rows 3 and 4 review previously taught
learn	together	though		high-frequency words.

If... children cannot read these words,
then... use the Small Group Time Strategic Intervention lesson, p. DI•2, to reteach the words. Monitor children's fluency with these words during reading, and provide additional practice.

Day 1	Day 2	Day 3	Day 4	Day 5
Check Word Reading	Check High-Frequency Words	Check Retelling	Check Fluency	Check Oral Vocabulary

Story Words
Tara and Tiree

Introduce story words

Use Vocabulary Transparency 6 to introduce this week's story words. Read each sentence as you track the print. Frame each underlined word and explain its meaning.

brave	showing no fear of dangerous things
slipped	slid without meaning to
collar	a band that a dog wears around its neck

Have children read each sentence with you.

Vocabulary
Unfamiliar Words

Model unfamiliar words

Point out that good readers can learn an unknown word's meaning by using surrounding words as clues. By looking at the context, or words that come before or after an unfamiliar word, you can figure out the relevant meaning of the word in a sentence.

Write the following sentence and underline the word *fearless*.

My <u>fearless</u> cat is not afraid of anything.

Think Aloud — I can use context to figure out the meaning of the word *fearless*. The words in the sentence that come after *fearless* say that the cat is not afraid of anything, so I think that the word *fearless* means *not being afraid or showing no fear.*

Guide practice

Write this sentence from the Read-Aloud "The Rescue" and underline the word *courage: I knew that courage wins over fear when it has to.* Have a volunteer use context to determine the meaning of *courage.*

On their own

Have children work with a partner to find words in a story that are unfamiliar to them. Ask them to help each other use context to figure out the meanings of the words.

Use *Reader's and Writer's Notebook,* p. 102.

Reader's and Writer's Notebook, p. 102

Differentiated Instruction

SI Strategic Intervention
Context If children have trouble figuring out the meanings of words in context, read the sentence where the word appears and point out various clues to its meaning. Ask children to use the word meaning they predict to see if it makes sense in the sentence.

Academic Vocabulary
unfamiliar not known or recognized
context words that come before or after a word or phrase

ELL

English Language Learners
Words in Context Provide additional context sentences for story words or other words that are unfamiliar to children. For example, *I slipped on the wet floor; I slipped on the ice.* Have children repeat the sentences and then use the word in a similar context sentence.

Multilingual Vocabulary Lists Children can apply knowledge of their home language to acquire new English vocabulary by using the *Multilingual Vocabulary Lists (ELL Handbook,* Pages 429–440).

192e Working Together • Unit 2 • Week 1

192f Success Predictor

PHONICS

In Reading Street

High-Frequency Words
Children learn three to seven high-frequency words each week. The words are presented individually and in connected text. The teacher guides children to say and spell each word and demonstrate meaning. Additional practice opportunities help children read the words fluently.

Because Research Says

Not all words can be read through decoding. For example, in irregular words, some or all of the letters do not represent their most commonly used sound. Children should encounter some of these words in texts for beginning readers, and will need to identify them by sight or automatically. To help children learn these words, teachers should introduce them in a reasonable order, and cumulatively review the ones that have been taught. —(Vaughn and Linan-Thompson, 2004)

READING VOCABULARY

In Reading Street

Story Words Nondecodable story words are pretaught before children read the main selection. These words are carefully chosen to help understand the text and for their utility in discussing the text. Story words are taught directly through strategies that engage readers in constructing word meanings.

Because Research Says

Pre-instruction of vocabulary prior to reading can facilitate both vocabulary acquisition and comprehension. —(National Reading Panel, 1999)

When choosing vocabulary to use for reading strategy instruction, focus on words that are important to the selection. Directly teach those words that are important for understanding the text. —(Blachowicz and Fisher, 2002; Armbruster, Lehr, and Osborn, 2001)

READING VOCABULARY

In Reading Street

Vocabulary Skill This activity helps to expand children's word knowledge by introducing them to word-learning strategies and concepts such as synonyms and antonyms. Using words from the selection, the teacher explains the concept. Then children provide additional examples.

Because Research Says

Effective vocabulary teaching in the early years should make children curious about words. To be a good word learner, one must be hungry for words. Learning (and using) new words can be exciting because a new word not only is a sign of growing up, but it also is a sign of greater control and understanding about one's world. —(Stahl and Stahl, 2004)

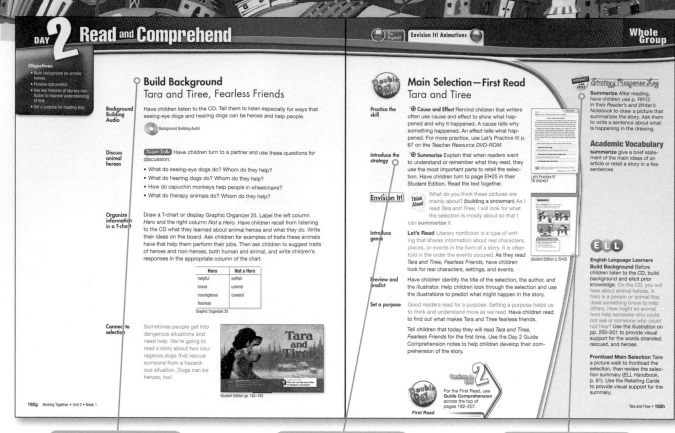

COMPREHENSION

In Reading Street

Build Background Every week, children listen to audio CDs that provide background knowledge through sounds, conversations, music, and other audio realia. Children then discuss what they learned from the audio and how it relates to key concepts in the selection.

Because Research Says

▶ Children's understanding of what they read is based on their experiences and knowledge; thus, teachers must do whatever they can to help children fill the gaps in their background knowledge. —(Gaskins, 2001)

▶ For optimum learning to occur, children should think about what they already know about a topic and gather new information to facilitate their understanding of new ideas that will be encountered in the text. —(Duke and Pearson, 2002)

COMPREHENSION

In Reading Street

Comprehension Strategies Children are instructed in comprehension strategies practiced with a variety of literature. Each week the teacher models a comprehension strategy through the use of the suggested think-aloud before the selection is read the first time.

Because Research Says

▶ Strategies need to be practiced with narrative and expository texts. Readers benefit from explicit instruction in activating prior knowledge, making predictions, recognizing informational text structure, story structure, using graphic and semantic organizers, visualizing, summarizing, answering questions, generating clarifying questions, and self-monitoring to resolve difficulties in meaning. —(Armbruster, Lehr, and Osborn, 2001; Pearson, Roehler, Dole, and Duffy, 1992; Duke and Pearson, 2002; Pressley, 2002; Pressley and Block, 2002)

COMPREHENSION

In Reading Street

Strategy Response Log Students keep a Strategy Response Log to record their use of a specific strategy and do a mid-selection self-check on their use of the strategy. The teacher monitors their progress on how and when they apply the strategy and coaches them as necessary. After reading, students do a strategy self-check, looking back on how and when they applied the strategy.

Because Research Says

▶ Comprehension processes instruction is about encouraging young readers to be cognitively active as they read, just the way that mature, excellent readers are active cognitively. —(Block and Pressley, 2003)

Objectives
- Summarize important ideas.
- Identify cause and effect in literary nonfiction.
- Determine word meaning and use newly acquired vocabulary.
- Discuss ideas related to, but not expressed in the literature.

DAY 2

Guide Comprehension
Skills and Strategies

Connect to Concept
Working Together Look at the picture on pages 192 and 193. Based on the title, these dogs must be Tara and Tiree. How might these dogs work together? (They are "fearless friends," so maybe they work together in a courageous way.)

Amazing Words
Have children continue discussing the concept using the Amazing Words *courageous, hazard,* and *rescue* as they read.

Strategies
⊛ **Summarize** Remind children that good readers stop frequently and put what is happening into their own words. Have children summarize by telling what happened on pages 194 and 195.

If... children have difficulty summarizing, **then...** model how to retell what is happening on these pages. *All his life, Jim loved dogs. He loved them so much that when he grew up, he became a dog trainer.*

Student Edition pp. 192–193

Student Edition pp. 194–195

DAY 3

Extend Thinking
Think Critically

Higher-Order Thinking Skills
Analysis Illustrations often provide clues about a story setting. Explain when and where you think this story takes place.

If... children cannot explain where and when this story takes place, **then...** ask them to identify what time of year snow falls and describe where they might see buildings and landscapes that look like those in the illustration.

Review Fact and Opinion
Analysis Reread the first sentence on page 194. Is this sentence a fact or an opinion? How do you know? (It's a fact because it could be proved.) Read the first sentence in the last paragraph on page 194. Is this sentence a fact or an opinion? How do you know? (It's an opinion because it is what Jim believes to be true about dogs.)

Higher-Order Thinking Skills
Synthesis Do you conclude that the dogs shown in the pictures on pages 194 and 195 are, or are not, Tara and Tiree? Explain. (They are not Tara and Tiree because they look different from the dogs shown on pages 192–193. The text tells you that these are the dogs Jim had as a boy.)

192–193 Working Together • Unit 2 • Week 1

Tara and Tiree • 194–195

COMPREHENSION

In Reading Street

Guide Comprehension During the first read of the selection on Day 2, children respond to questions that address a target skill or strategy in context. If children have difficulty answering the question, the teacher models a response, and then guides children through a quick activity in which children's ability to apply the skill or strategy is assessed.

Because Research Says

Good comprehenders have learned that they have control of the reading process. They actively construct meaning as they read by directing their own comprehension using basic strategies. They know reading works because they have knowledge about how sounds, letters, and print work; they know what strategies to use to help them understand; and they know when to use which strategies.
—(Blachowicz and Ogle, 2001)

COMPREHENSION

In Reading Street

Extend Thinking During the second read of the selection on Day 3, children respond to questions that require using the higher-order thinking skills of analysis, synthesis, and evaluation.

Because Research Says

More effective teachers engage children in more higher-level responses to text (both in discussions and written assignments) as part of what the researchers labeled a framework of instruction promoting cognitive engagement during reading.
—(Taylor, Pearson, Peterson, and Rodriguez, 2005)

Pages 196–207 are based on the same research as pages 192–195.

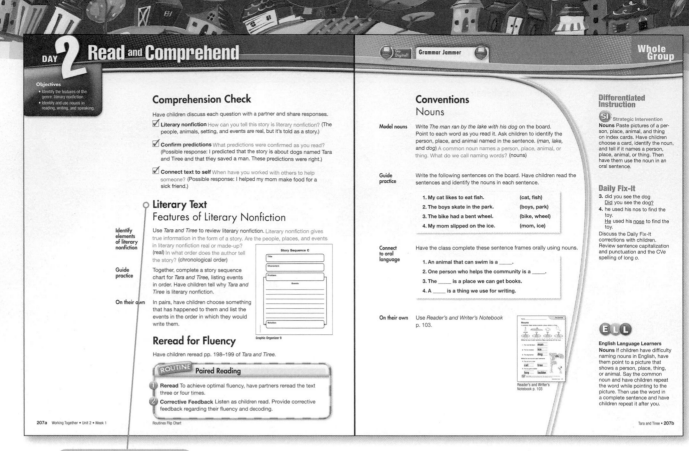

Objectives
• Identify the features of the genre: literary nonfiction.
• Identify and use nouns in reading, writing, and speaking.

Comprehension Check

Have children discuss each question with a partner and share responses.

☑ **Literary nonfiction** How can you tell this story is literary nonfiction? (The people, animals, setting, and events are real, but it's told as a story.)

☑ **Confirm predictions** What predictions were confirmed as you read? (Possible response: I predicted that the story is about dogs named Tara and Tiree and that they saved a man. These predictions were right.)

☑ **Connect text to self** When have you worked with others to help someone? (Possible response: I helped my mom make food for a sick friend.)

Literary Text
Features of Literary Nonfiction

Identify elements of literary nonfiction

Use *Tara and Tiree* to review literary nonfiction. Literary nonfiction gives true information in the form of a story. Are the people, places, and events in literary nonfiction real or made-up? (real) In what order does the author tell the story? (chronological order)

Guide practice

Together, complete a story sequence chart for *Tara and Tiree*, listing events in order. Have children tell why *Tara and Tiree* is literary nonfiction.

On their own

In pairs, have children choose something that has happened to them and list the events in the order in which they would write them.

Story Sequence C

Title
Characters
Problem

Events

Solution

Graphic Organizer 9

Reread for Fluency

Have children reread pp. 198–199 of *Tara and Tiree*.

ROUTINE **Paired Reading**

1 **Reread** To achieve optimal fluency, have partners reread the text three or four times.
2 **Corrective Feedback** Listen as children read. Provide corrective feedback regarding their fluency and decoding.

207a Working Together • Unit 2 • Week 1   Routines Flip Chart

---

Grammar Jammer   **Whole Group**

Conventions
Nouns

Model nouns

Write *The man ran by the lake with his dog* on the board. Point to each word as you read it. Ask children to identify the person, place, and animal named in the sentence. (*man*, *lake*, and *dog*) A common noun names a person, place, animal, or thing. What do we call naming words? (nouns)

Guide practice

Write the following sentences on the board. Have children read the sentences and identify the nouns in each sentence.

1. My cat likes to eat fish.   (cat, fish)
2. The boys skate in the park.   (boys, park)
3. The bike had a bent wheel.   (bike, wheel)
4. My mom slipped on the ice.   (mom, ice)

Connect to oral language

Have the class complete these sentence frames orally using nouns.

1. An animal that can swim is a _____.
2. One person who helps the community is a _____.
3. The _____ is a place we can get books.
4. A _____ is a thing we use for writing.

On their own

Use *Reader's and Writer's Notebook* p. 103.

Reader's and Writer's Notebook p. 103

Tara and Tiree • 207b

Differentiated Instruction

SI Strategic Intervention

Nouns Paste pictures of a person, place, animal, and thing on index cards. Have children choose a card, identify the noun, and tell if it names a person, place, animal, or thing. Then have them use the noun in an oral sentence.

Daily Fix-It

3. did you see the dog
   Did you see the dog?
4. he used his nos to find the toy.
   He used his nose to find the toy.

Discuss the Daily Fix-It corrections with children. Review sentence capitalization and punctuation and the CVe spelling of long o.

ELL

English Language Learners

Nouns If children have difficulty naming nouns in English, have them point to a picture that shows a person, place, thing, or animal. Say the common noun and have children repeat the word while pointing to the picture. Then use the word in a complete sentence and have children repeat it after you.

COMPREHENSION

In Reading Street

Literary Text This instruction provides children the opportunity to analyze what they have read, focusing on text structure, literary concepts, and story elements.

Because Research Says

Comprehension improves when teachers design and implement activities that support the understanding of the texts that children will read in their classes. —(Pearson and Duke, 2002)

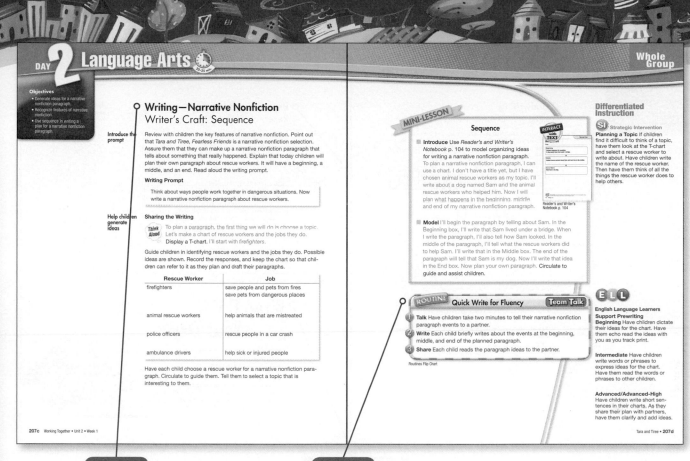

Objectives
- Generate ideas for a narrative nonfiction paragraph.
- Recognize features of narrative nonfiction.
- Use sequence in writing a plan for a narrative nonfiction paragraph.

Writing—Narrative Nonfiction
Writer's Craft: Sequence

Introduce the prompt

Review with children the key features of narrative nonfiction. Point out that *Tara and Tiree, Fearless Friends* is a narrative nonfiction selection. Assure them that they can make up a narrative nonfiction paragraph that tells about something that really happened. Explain that today children will plan their own paragraph about rescue workers. It will have a beginning, a middle, and an end. Read aloud the writing prompt.

Writing Prompt

Think about ways people work together in dangerous situations. Now write a narrative nonfiction paragraph about rescue workers.

Help children generate ideas

Sharing the Writing

Think Aloud To plan a paragraph, the first thing we will do is choose a topic. Let's make a chart of rescue workers and the jobs they do. Display a T-chart. I'll start with *firefighters*.

Guide children in identifying rescue workers and the jobs they do. Possible ideas are shown. Record the responses, and keep the chart so that children can refer to it as they plan and draft their paragraphs.

Rescue Worker	Job
firefighters	save people and pets from fires save pets from dangerous places
animal rescue workers	help animals that are mistreated
police officers	rescue people in a car crash
ambulance drivers	help sick or injured people

Have each child choose a rescue worker for a narrative nonfiction paragraph. Circulate to guide them. Tell them to select a topic that is interesting to them.

207c Working Together • Unit 2 • Week 1

MINI-LESSON

Sequence

Introduce Use *Reader's and Writer's Notebook* p. 104 to model organizing ideas for writing a narrative nonfiction paragraph. To plan a narrative nonfiction paragraph, I can use a chart. I don't have a title yet, but I have chosen animal rescue workers as my topic. I'll write about a dog named Sam and the animal rescue workers who helped him. Now I will plan what happens in the beginning, middle, and end of my narrative nonfiction paragraph.

Model I'll begin the paragraph by telling about Sam. In the Beginning box, I'll write that Sam lived under a bridge. When I write the paragraph, I'll also tell how Sam looked. In the middle of the paragraph, I'll tell what the rescue workers did to help Sam. I'll write that in the Middle box. The end of the paragraph will tell that Sam is my dog. Now I'll write that idea in the End box. Now plan your own paragraph. Circulate to guide and assist children.

INTERACT with TEXT

Reader's and Writer's Notebook p. 104

ROUTINE Quick Write for Fluency Team Talk

1 **Talk** Have children take two minutes to tell their narrative nonfiction paragraph events to a partner.
2 **Write** Each child briefly writes about the events at the beginning, middle, and end of the planned paragraph.
3 **Share** Each child reads the paragraph ideas to the partner.

Routines Flip Chart

Differentiated Instruction

SI Strategic Intervention
Planning a Topic If children find it difficult to think of a topic, have them look at the T-chart and select a rescue worker to write about. Have children write the name of the rescue worker. Then have them think of all the things the rescue worker does to help others.

ELL English Language Learners
Support Prewriting
Beginning Have children dictate their ideas for the chart. Have them echo read the ideas with you as you track print.

Intermediate Have children write words or phrases to express ideas for the chart. Have them read the words or phrases to other children.

Advanced/Advanced-High Have children write short sentences in their charts. As they share their plan with partners, have them clarify and add ideas.

Tara and Tiree • 207d

WRITING

In Reading Street

Writing Daily mini-lessons focus on the traits and craft of writing. Following the 5–10 minute mini-lesson, children apply the trait or craft in their own writing.

Because Research Says

Learning to write should include composing staged across various phases of rumination, investigation, consultation with others, drafting, feedback, revision, and perfecting. —(National Writing Project and Nagin, 2003)

WRITING

In Reading Street

Quick Write for Fluency In Grades 1 through 5, children engage in daily writing activities to develop language, grammar, and writing skills.

Because Research Says

Writing has to be learned in school very much the same way that it is practiced out of school. This means that the writer has a reason to write, an intended audience, and control of subject and form. —(National Writing Project and Nagin, 2003)

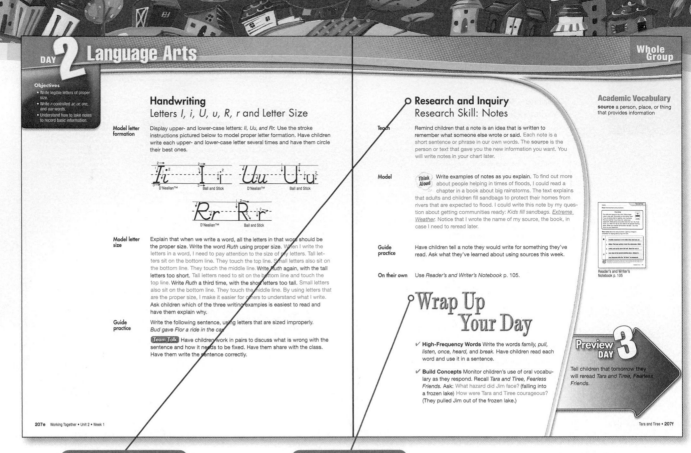

Objectives
- Write legible letters of proper size.
- Write r-controlled ar, or, ore, and oar words.
- Understand how to take notes to record basic information.

Handwriting
Letters I, i, U, u, R, r and Letter Size

Model letter formation Display upper- and lower-case letters: Ii, Uu, and Rr. Use the stroke instructions pictured below to model proper letter formation. Have children write each upper- and lower-case letter several times and have them circle their best ones.

Model letter size Explain that when we write a word, all the letters in that word should be the proper size. Write the word Ruth using proper size. When I write the letters in a word, I need to pay attention to the size of my letters. Tall letters sit on the bottom line. They touch the top line. Small letters also sit on the bottom line. They touch the middle line. Write Ruth again, with the tall letters too short. Tall letters need to sit on the bottom line and touch the top line. Write Ruth a third time, with the short letters too tall. Small letters also sit on the bottom line. They touch the middle line. By using letters that are the proper size, I make it easier for others to understand what I write. Ask children which of the three writing examples is easiest to read and have them explain why.

Guide practice Write the following sentence, using letters that are sized improperly. Bud gave Flor a ride in the car.
Team Talk Have children work in pairs to discuss what is wrong with the sentence and how it needs to be fixed. Have them share with the class. Have them write the sentence correctly.

207e Working Together • Unit 2 • Week 1

Research and Inquiry
Research Skill: Notes

Teach Remind children that a note is an idea that is written to remember what someone else wrote or said. Each note is a short sentence or phrase in our own words. The source is the person or text that gave you the new information you want. You will write notes in your chart later.

Model Think Aloud Write examples of notes as you explain. To find out more about people helping in times of floods, I could read a chapter in a book about big rainstorms. The text explains that adults and children fill sandbags to protect their homes from rivers that are expected to flood. I could write this note by my question about getting communities ready: Kids fill sandbags. Extreme Weather. Notice that I wrote the name of my source, the book, in case I need to reread later.

Guide practice Have children tell a note they would write for something they've read. Ask what they've learned about using sources this week.

On their own Use Reader's and Writer's Notebook p. 105.

Wrap Up Your Day

✔ **High-Frequency Words** Write the words family, pull, listen, once, heard, and break. Have children read each word and use it in a sentence.

✔ **Build Concepts** Monitor children's use of oral vocabulary as they respond. Recall Tara and Tiree, Fearless Friends. Ask: What hazard did Jim face? (falling into a frozen lake) How were Tara and Tiree courageous? (They pulled Jim out of the frozen lake.)

Academic Vocabulary
source a person, place, or thing that provides information

Reader's and Writer's Notebook p. 105

Preview DAY 3 Tell children that tomorrow they will reread Tara and Tiree, Fearless Friends.

Tara and Tiree • 207f

21ST CENTURY SKILLS

In Reading Street

Research and Inquiry Children conduct a 5-day inquiry project connected to the weekly concept. Daily step-by-step instruction focuses on identifying and focusing a research topic, exploring relevant sources, gathering and recording information, revising the topic, analyzing and synthesizing information, and communicating ideas.

Because Research Says

To be newly literate means to take advantage of the information resources available on the Internet. To use information and communication technologies, readers and writers must be able to identify important questions, locate information, critically evaluate the usefulness of that information, synthesize information to answer those questions, and then communicate the answers to others. —(Leu, Kinzer, Coiro, and Cammack, 2004)

ORAL LANGUAGE

In Reading Street

Wrap Up Your Day This end-of-the-day routine reviews the day's skill instruction, encourages discussion about shared literature and the week's concepts, and previews what's to come.

Because Research Says

For children to develop rich vocabularies, they need to have many interactions with adults. It is from these interactions that they will develop the words they need to negotiate their world. —(Stahl and Stahl, 2004)

Pages 208a–208b are based on the same research as pages 186j and 186–187.

Objectives
- Blend and read words with the sounds /är/ spelled *ar* and /ôr/ spelled *or*, *ore*, and *oar*.
- Decode words in context and independent of context.

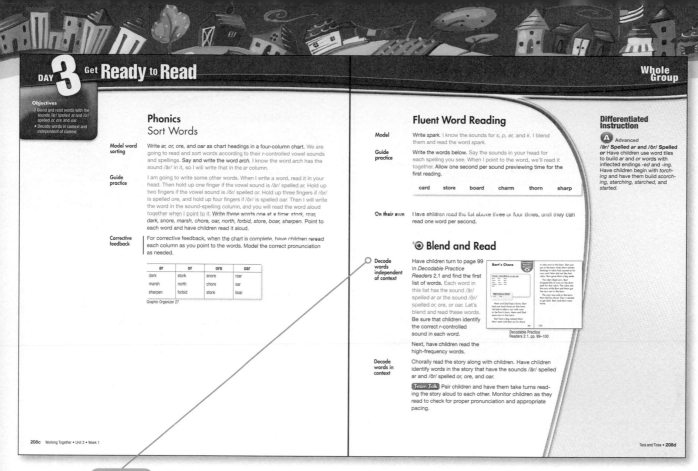

Phonics
Sort Words

Model word sorting
Write *ar*, *or*, *ore*, and *oar* as chart headings in a four-column chart. We are going to read and sort words according to their *r*-controlled vowel sounds and spellings. **Say and write the word *arch*.** I know the word *arch* has the sound /är/ in it, so I will write that in the *ar* column.

Guide practice
I am going to write some other words. When I write a word, read it in your head. Then hold up one finger if the vowel sound is /är/ spelled *ar*. Hold up two fingers if the vowel sound is /ôr/ spelled *or*. Hold up three fingers if /ôr/ is spelled *ore*, and hold up four fingers if /ôr/ is spelled *oar*. Then I will write the word in the sound-spelling column, and you will read the word aloud together when I point to it. Write these words one at a time: *stork, roar, dark, snore, marsh, chore, oar, north, forbid, store, boar, sharpen.* Point to each word and have children read it aloud.

Corrective feedback
For corrective feedback, when the chart is complete, have children reread each column as you point to the words. Model the correct pronunciation as needed.

ar	or	ore	oar
dark	stork	snore	roar
marsh	north	chore	oar
sharpen	forbid	store	boar

Graphic Organizer 27

Fluent Word Reading

Model
Write *spark*. I know the sounds for *s, p, ar,* and *k*. I blend them and read the word *spark*.

Guide practice
Write the words below. Say the sounds in your head for each spelling you see. When I point to the word, we'll read it together. Allow one second per sound previewing time for the first reading.

card	store	board	charm	thorn	sharp

On their own
Have children read the list above three or four times, until they can read one word per second.

⦿ Blend and Read

Decode words independent of context
Have children turn to page 99 in *Decodable Practice Readers* 2.1 and find the first list of words. Each word in this list has the sound /är/ spelled *ar* or the sound /ôr/ spelled *or*, *ore*, or *oar*. Let's blend and read these words. Be sure that children identify the correct *r*-controlled sound in each word.

Next, have children read the high-frequency words.

Decode words in context
Chorally read the story along with children. Have children identify words in the story that have the sounds /är/ spelled *ar* and /ôr/ spelled *or*, *ore*, and *oar*.

Team Talk Pair children and have them take turns reading the story aloud to each other. Monitor children as they read to check for proper pronunciation and appropriate pacing.

Decodable Practice Readers 2.1, pp. 99–100

Differentiated Instruction

Ⓐ Advanced
/är/ Spelled *ar* and /ôr/ Spelled *or* Have children use word tiles to build *ar* and *or* words with inflected endings *-ed* and *-ing*. Have children begin with *torching* and have them build *scorching, starching, starched,* and *started*.

208c Working Together • Unit 2 • Week 1

Tara and Tiree • 208d

PHONICS

In Reading Street

Decoding Strategy This activity encourages children to preview, or think about, all the sounds or word parts in a word before they read the word aloud.

Because Research Says

Decoding is a strategy for reading unknown words. It is the process of reading letters or letter patterns in a word to determine the meaning of the word. Once children develop this skill, they can apply it to reading words automatically and effortlessly. This allows them to focus on getting meaning from what they read. —(Vaughn and Linan-Thompson, 2004)

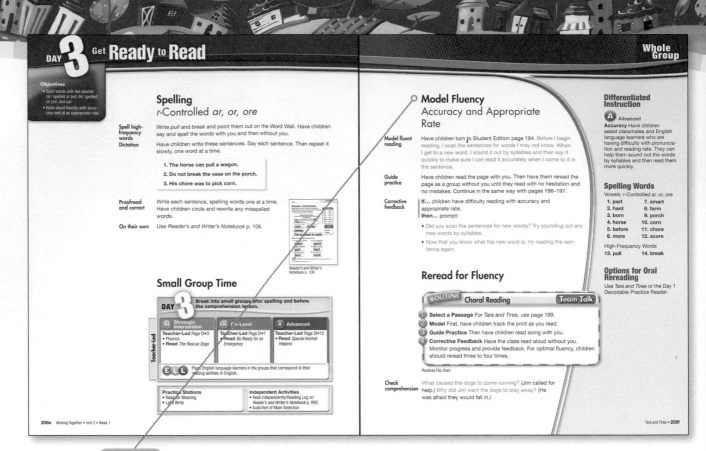

Objectives
- Spell words with the sounds /är/ spelled ar and /ôr/ spelled or, ore, and uar.
- Read aloud fluently with accuracy and at an appropriate rate.

Spelling
r-Controlled ar, or, ore

Spell high-frequency words Dictation
Write *pull* and *break* and point them out on the Word Wall. Have children say and spell the words with you and then without you.

Have children write these sentences. Say each sentence. Then repeat it slowly, one word at a time.

1. The horse can pull a wagon.
2. Do not break the vase on the porch.
3. His chore was to pick corn.

Proofread and correct
Write each sentence, spelling words one at a time. Have children circle and rewrite any misspelled words.

On their own
Use *Reader's and Writer's Notebook* p. 106.

Reader's and Writer's Notebook p. 106

Small Group Time

DAY 3 Break into small groups after spelling and before the comprehension lesson.

Teacher-Led

SI Strategic Intervention
Teacher-Led Page DI•3
- Phonics
- **Read** *The Rescue Dogs*

OL On-Level
Teacher-Led Page DI•7
- **Read** *Be Ready for an Emergency*

A Advanced
Teacher-Led Page DI•10
- **Read** *Special Animal Helpers*

ELL Place English language learners in the groups that correspond to their reading abilities in English.

Practice Stations
- Read for Meaning
- Let's Write

Independent Activities
- Read independently/Reading Log on *Reader's and Writer's Notebook* p. RR2
- AudioText of Main Selection

208e Working Together • Unit 2 • Week 1

Model Fluency
Accuracy and Appropriate Rate

Model fluent reading
Have children turn to Student Edition page 194. Before I begin reading, I scan the sentences for words I may not know. When I get to a new word, I sound it out by syllables and then say it quickly to make sure I can read it accurately when I come to it in the sentence.

Guide practice
Have children read the page with you. Then have them reread the page as a group without you until they read with no hesitation and no mistakes. Continue in the same way with pages 196–197.

Corrective feedback
If... children have difficulty reading with accuracy and appropriate rate,
then... prompt:
- Did you scan the sentences for new words? Try sounding out any new words by syllables.
- Now that you know what the new word is, try reading the sentence again.

Reread for Fluency

ROUTINE Choral Reading **Team Talk**

1. **Select a Passage** For *Tara and Tiree*, use page 199.
2. **Model** First, have children track the print as you read.
3. **Guide Practice** Then have children read along with you.
4. **Corrective Feedback** Have the class read aloud without you. Monitor progress and provide feedback. For optimal fluency, children should reread three to four times.

Routines Flip Chart

Check comprehension
What caused the dogs to come running? (Jim called for help.) Why did Jim want the dogs to stay away? (He was afraid they would fall in.)

Tara and Tiree • 208f

Differentiated Instruction

A Advanced

Accuracy Have children assist classmates and English language learners who are having difficulty with pronunciation and reading rate. They can help them sound out the words by syllables and then read them more quickly.

Spelling Words
Vowels: r-Controlled ar, or, ore

1. part	7. smart
2. hard	8. farm
3. born	9. porch
4. horse	10. corn
5. before	11. chore
6. more	12. score

High-Frequency Words
13. pull   14. break

Options for Oral Rereading
Use *Tara and Tiree* or the Day 1 Decodable Practice Reader.

.... FLUENCY ....

In Reading Street

Model Fluency Teachers model expressive oral reading with a new fluency skill each week. Skills include reading with accuracy, appropriate rate, attending to punctuation, and expression introduced each week. After listening to the teacher model the skill, students engage in guided oral reading practice with feedback.

Because Research Says

Repeated reading practice produces significant improvement in reading speed, word recognition, and oral reading expression. Repeated reading and assisted readings may enable children to read more difficult material than they might otherwise be able to read. —(Samuels, 2002; Kuhn and Stahl, 2003; National Reading Panel, 1999)

Pages 208g–208h are based on the same research as pages 192f and 192h.

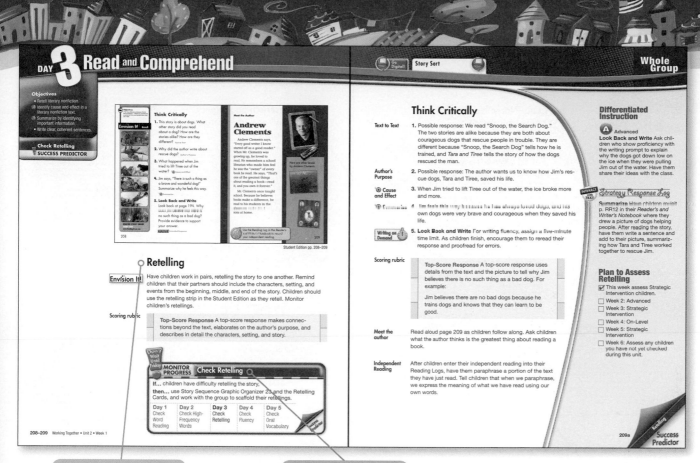

Student Edition pp. 208–209

Objectives
- Retell literary nonfiction.
- Identify cause and effect in a literary nonfiction text.
- Summarize by identifying important information.
- Write clear, coherent sentences.

Check Retelling
SUCCESS PREDICTOR

Retelling

Envision It!

Have children work in pairs, retelling the story to one another. Remind children that their partners should include the characters, setting, and events from the beginning, middle, and end of the story. Children should use the retelling strip in the Student Edition as they retell. Monitor children's retellings.

Scoring rubric

Top-Score Response A top-score response makes connections beyond the text, elaborates on the author's purpose, and describes in detail the characters, setting, and story.

Don't Wait Until Friday

MONITOR PROGRESS **Check Retelling**

If... children have difficulty retelling the story,
then... use Story Sequence Graphic Organizer 23 and the Retelling Cards, and work with the group to scaffold their retellings.

Day 1	Day 2	**Day 3**	Day 4	Day 5
Check Word Reading	Check High-Frequency Words	**Check Retelling**	Check Fluency	Check Oral Vocabulary

208–209 Working Together • Unit 2 • Week 1

Think Critically

Text to Text 1. Possible response: We read "Snoop, the Search Dog." The two stories are alike because they are both about courageous dogs that rescue people in trouble. They are different because "Snoop, the Search Dog" tells how he is trained, and *Tara and Tiree* tells the story of how the dogs rescued the man.

Author's Purpose 2. Possible response: The author wants us to know how Jim's rescue dogs, Tara and Tiree, saved his life.

Cause and Effect 3. When Jim tried to lift Tiree out of the water, the ice broke more and more.

Summarize 4. Jim feels this way because he has always loved dogs, and his own dogs were very brave and courageous when they saved his life.

Writing on Demand 5. **Look Back and Write** For writing fluency, assign a five-minute time limit. As children finish, encourage them to reread their response and proofread for errors.

Scoring rubric

Top-Score Response A top-score response uses details from the text and the picture to tell why Jim believes there is no such thing as a bad dog. For example:

Jim believes there are no bad dogs because he trains dogs and knows that they can learn to be good.

Meet the author Read aloud page 209 as children follow along. Ask children what the author thinks is the greatest thing about reading a book.

Independent Reading After children enter their independent reading into their Reading Logs, have them paraphrase a portion of the text they have just read. Tell children that when we paraphrase, we express the meaning of what we have read using our own words.

Differentiated Instruction

A Advanced
Look Back and Write Ask children who show proficiency with the writing prompt to explain why the dogs got down low on the ice when they were pulling Jim out of the water. Have them share their ideas with the class.

Strategy Response Log
Summarize Have children revisit p. RR12 in their *Reader's and Writer's Notebook* where they drew a picture of dogs helping people. After reading the story, have them write a sentence and add to their picture, summarizing how Tara and Tiree worked together to rescue Jim.

Plan to Assess Retelling
- ☑ This week assess Strategic Intervention children.
- ☐ Week 2: Advanced
- ☐ Week 3: Strategic Intervention
- ☐ Week 4: On-Level
- ☐ Week 5: Strategic Intervention
- ☐ Week 6: Assess any children you have not yet checked during this unit.

209a   Success Predictor

COMPREHENSION

In Reading Street

Retelling With the assistance of the retelling strip in the Student Edition, children retell narrative text or summarize expository text.

Because Research Says

▶ Oral retelling provides information as a process and a product. It allows teachers to assess what students remember about what they read without direct questioning or support from a teacher. —(Paratore and McCormack, 2005)

▶ Practice, guidance, and evaluation of stories retold and rewritten have been found to improve children's written and oral original stories. —(Morrow, 1996)

SUCCESS PREDICTORS

In Reading Street

Monitor Progress Throughout the week, teachers do quick checks in the context of classroom instruction to monitor children's progress in five core areas of reading instruction: phonics, high-frequency words, fluency, retelling or summarizing, and vocabulary. Don't Wait Until Friday/Monitor Progress features provide *if..., then...* statements to help teachers evaluate the skills and respond to children's difficulties on the spot.

Because Research Says

▶ Comprehension instruction should be accompanied by ongoing assessment. Teachers should monitor students' use of comprehension strategies and their success at understanding what they read. Results of this monitoring should, in turn, inform the teacher's instruction. —(Duke and Pearson, 2002)

Pages 209b–211 are based on the same research as pages 191c–191d.

Objectives
• Write a draft of a narrative nonfiction paragraph.
• Use voice in writing.
• Gather information about a topic.

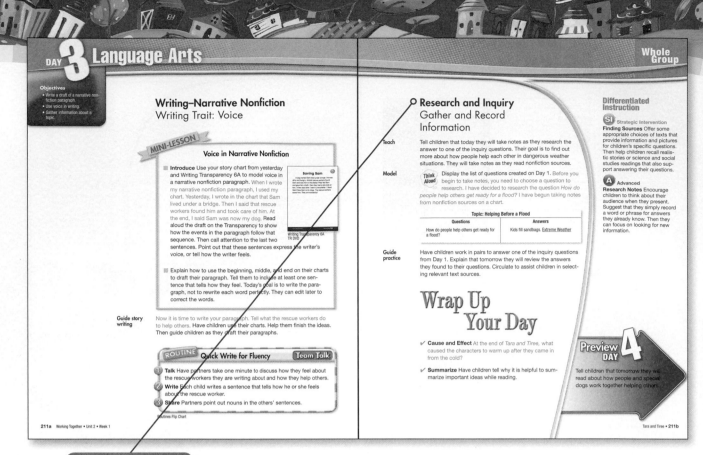

Writing–Narrative Nonfiction
Writing Trait: Voice

MINI-LESSON

Voice in Narrative Nonfiction

■ **Introduce** Use your story chart from yesterday and Writing Transparency 6A to model voice in a narrative nonfiction paragraph. When I wrote my narrative nonfiction paragraph, I used my chart. Yesterday, I wrote in the chart that Sam lived under a bridge. Then I said that rescue workers found him and took care of him. At the end, I said Sam was now my dog. **Read aloud the draft on the Transparency to show how the events in the paragraph follow that sequence.** Then call attention to the last two sentences. Point out that these sentences express the writer's voice, or tell how the writer feels.

Writing Transparency 6A TR DVD

■ Explain how to use the beginning, middle, and end on their charts to draft their paragraph. Tell them to include at least one sentence that tells how they feel. Today's goal is to write the paragraph, not to rewrite each word perfectly. They can edit later to correct the words.

Guide story writing Now it is time to write your paragraph. Tell what the rescue workers do to help others. **Have children use their charts.** Help them finish the ideas. Then guide children as they draft their paragraphs.

ROUTINE Quick Write for Fluency   Team Talk

1. **Talk** Have partners take one minute to discuss how they feel about the rescue workers they are writing about and how they help others.
2. **Write** Each child writes a sentence that tells how he or she feels about the rescue worker.
3. **Share** Partners point out nouns in the others' sentences.

Routines Flip Chart

211a Working Together • Unit 2 • Week 1

Research and Inquiry
Gather and Record Information

Teach Tell children that today they will take notes as they research the answer to one of the inquiry questions. Their goal is to find out more about how people help each other in dangerous weather situations. They will take notes as they read nonfiction sources.

Model Think Aloud Display the list of questions created on Day 1. Before you begin to take notes, you need to choose a question to research. I have decided to research the question *How do people help others get ready for a flood?* I have begun taking notes from nonfiction sources on a chart.

Topic: Helping Before a Flood	
Questions	**Answers**
How do people help others get ready for a flood?	Kids fill sandbags. Extreme Weather

Guide practice Have children work in pairs to answer one of the inquiry questions from Day 1. Explain that tomorrow they will review the answers they found to their questions. Circulate to assist children in selecting relevant text sources.

Wrap Up Your Day

✔ **Cause and Effect** At the end of *Tara and Tiree*, what caused the characters to warm up after they came in from the cold?

✔ **Summarize** Have children tell why it is helpful to summarize important ideas while reading.

Preview DAY 4
Tell children that tomorrow they will read about how people and special dogs work together helping others.

Tara and Tiree • 211b

Differentiated Instruction

SI Strategic Intervention
Finding Sources Offer some appropriate choices of texts that provide information and pictures for children's specific questions. Then help children recall realistic stories or science and social studies readings that also support answering their questions.

A Advanced
Research Notes Encourage children to think about their audience when they present. Suggest that they simply record a word or phrase for answers they already know. Then they can focus on looking for new information.

····· **21ST CENTURY SKILLS** ·····

In Reading Street

Research and Inquiry Each day, activities provide step-by-step instructions for identifying and focusing a research topic, exploring relevant sources, gathering and recording information, revising the topic, analyzing and synthesizing information, and communicating ideas.

Because Research Says

To be newly literate means to take advantage of the information resources available on the Internet. To use information and communication technologies, readers and writers must be able to identify important questions, locate information, critically evaluate the usefulness of that information, synthesize information to answer those questions, and then communicate the answers to others. –(Leu, Kinzer, Coiro, and Cammack, 2004)

Pages 212a–212b are based on the same research as pages 186j and 186–187. Pages 212c–212d are based on the same research as page 192c. Pages 212e–212f are based on the same research as pages 190b–190c.

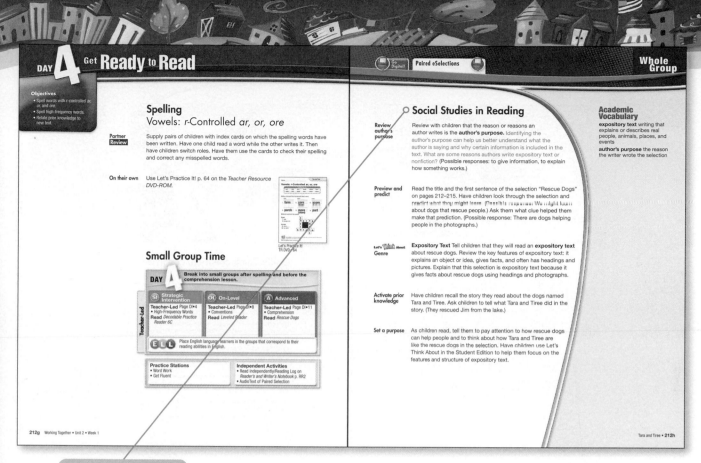

Objectives
- Spell words with r-controlled ar, or, and ore.
- Spell high-frequency words.
- Relate prior knowledge to new text.

Spelling
Vowels: r-Controlled *ar, or, ore*

Partner Review
Supply pairs of children with index cards on which the spelling words have been written. Have one child read a word while the other writes it. Then have children switch roles. Have them use the cards to check their spelling and correct any misspelled words.

On their own
Use Let's Practice It! p. 64 on the *Teacher Resource DVD-ROM*.

Let's Practice It!
TR DVD p. 64

Small Group Time

DAY 4 Break into small groups after spelling and before the comprehension lesson.

SI Strategic Intervention	OL On-Level	A Advanced
Teacher-Led Page DI•4 • High-Frequency Words Read *Decodable Practice Reader 6C*	Teacher-Led Page DI•8 • Conventions Read *Leveled Reader*	Teacher-Led Page DI•11 • Comprehension Read *Rescue Dogs*

ELL Place English language learners in the groups that correspond to their reading abilities in English.

Practice Stations
- Word Work
- Get Fluent

Independent Activities
- Read Independently/Reading Log on *Reader's and Writer's Notebook* p. RR2
- AudioText of Paired Selection

○ Social Studies in Reading

Review author's purpose
Review with children that the reason or reasons an author writes is the **author's purpose.** Identifying the author's purpose can help us better understand what the author is saying and why certain information is included in the text. What are some reasons authors write expository text or nonfiction? (Possible responses: to give information, to explain how something works.)

Preview and predict
Read the title and the first sentence of the selection "Rescue Dogs" on pages 212–215. Have children look through the selection and predict what they might learn. (Possible response: We might learn about dogs that rescue people.) Ask them what clue helped them make that prediction. (Possible response: There are dogs helping people in the photographs.)

Let's Think About Genre
Expository Text Tell children that they will read an **expository text** about rescue dogs. Review the key features of expository text: it explains an object or idea, gives facts, and often has headings and pictures. Explain that this selection is expository text because it gives facts about rescue dogs using headings and photographs.

Activate prior knowledge
Have children recall the story they read about the dogs named Tara and Tiree. Ask children to tell what Tara and Tiree did in the story. (They rescued Jim from the lake.)

Set a purpose
As children read, tell them to pay attention to how rescue dogs can help people and to think about how Tara and Tiree are like the rescue dogs in the selection. Have children use Let's Think About in the Student Edition to help them focus on the features and structure of expository text.

Academic Vocabulary
expository text writing that explains or describes real people, animals, places, and events
author's purpose the reason the writer wrote the selection

212g Working Together • Unit 2 • Week 1

Tara and Tiree • 212h

In Reading Street

Social Studies in Reading
Each week's concept emphasizes either science or social studies comments. As children read the paired selection, they have additional opportunities to make connections to science and social studies concepts.

Because Research Says
Many young children show a high degree of interest in nonfiction texts, suggesting not only that they can interact successfully with such text but also that they should be given opportunities to do so. Informational text can play a role in building children's knowledge about the world around them, in developing their vocabulary, and in motivating them to read. —(Duke and Tower, 2004)

DAY 4 Read and Comprehend 40–45 min.

Objectives
• Summarize important ideas.
• Monitor comprehension and clarify during reading.
• Analyze the author's purpose.

Go Digital! | Paired eSelections

Whole Group

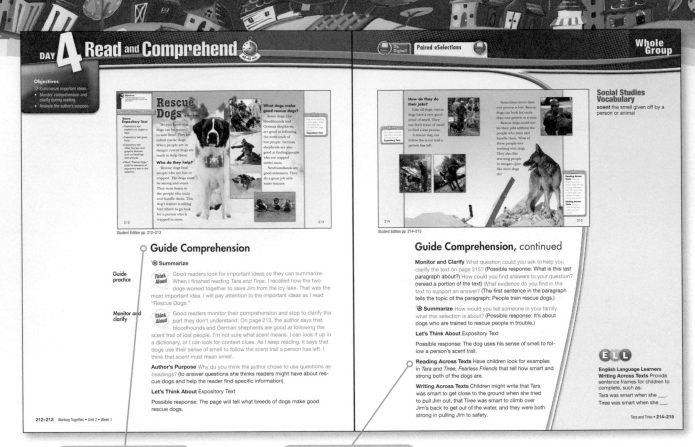

Student Edition pp. 212–213

Student Edition pp. 214–215

Guide Comprehension

Summarize

Think Aloud Good readers look for important ideas so they can summarize. When I finished reading *Tara and Tiree*, I recalled how the two dogs worked together to save Jim from the icy lake. That was the most important idea. I will pay attention to the important ideas as I read "Rescue Dogs."

Monitor and clarify

Think Aloud Good readers monitor their comprehension and stop to clarify the part they don't understand. On page 213, the author says that bloodhounds and German shepherds are good at following the scent trail of lost people. I'm not sure what *scent* means. I can look it up in a dictionary, or I can look for context clues. As I keep reading, it says that dogs use their sense of smell to follow the scent trail a person has left. I think that *scent* must mean *smell*.

Author's Purpose Why do you think the author chose to use questions as headings? (to answer questions she thinks readers might have about rescue dogs and help the reader find specific information)

Let's Think About Expository Text

Possible response: The page will tell what breeds of dogs make good rescue dogs.

212–213 Working Together • Unit 2 • Week 1

Guide Comprehension, continued

Monitor and Clarify What question could you ask to help you clarify the text on page 215? (Possible response: What is this last paragraph about?) How could you find answers to your question? (reread a portion of the text) What evidence do you find in the text to support an answer? (The first sentence in the paragraph tells the topic of the paragraph: People train rescue dogs.)

Summarize How would you tell someone in your family what this selection is about? (Possible response: It's about dogs who are trained to rescue people in trouble.)

Let's Think About Expository Text

Possible response: The dog uses his sense of smell to follow a person's scent trail.

Reading Across Texts Have children look for examples in *Tara and Tiree, Fearless Friends* that tell how smart and strong both of the dogs are.

Writing Across Texts Children might write that Tara was smart to get close to the ground when she tried to pull Jim out, that Tiree was smart to climb over Jim's back to get out of the water, and they were both strong in pulling Jim to safety.

Social Studies Vocabulary
scent the smell given off by a person or animal

ELL

English Language Learners
Writing Across Texts Provide sentence frames for children to complete, such as:
Tara was smart when she ___.
Tiree was smart when she ___.

Tara and Tiree • 214–215

COMPREHENSION

In Reading Street

Guide Comprehension During the reading of the paired selection on Day 4, children respond to questions that address a target skill or strategy in context. If children have difficulty answering the question, the teacher models a response.

Because Research Says

▶ Good comprehenders have learned that they have control of the reading process. They actively construct meaning as they read by directing their own comprehension using basic strategies. They know reading works because they have knowledge about how sounds, letters, and print work; they know what strategies to use to help them understand; and they know when to use which strategies.
—(Blachowicz and Ogle, 2001)

COMPREHENSION

In Reading Street

Extend Thinking Children respond to guiding comprehension questions about the paired reading that provide opportunities for discussion. These questions engage the higher-order thinking skills of analysis, synthesis, and evaluation.

Because Research Says

▶ More effective teachers engage children in more higher-level responses to text (both in discussions and written assignments) as part of what the researchers labeled a framework of instruction promoting cognitive engagement during reading.
—(Taylor, Pearson, Peterson, and Rodriguez, 2005)

Pages 215a–215b are based on the same research as pages 208f and 191c. Pages 215c–215d are based on the same research as pages 207c–207d.

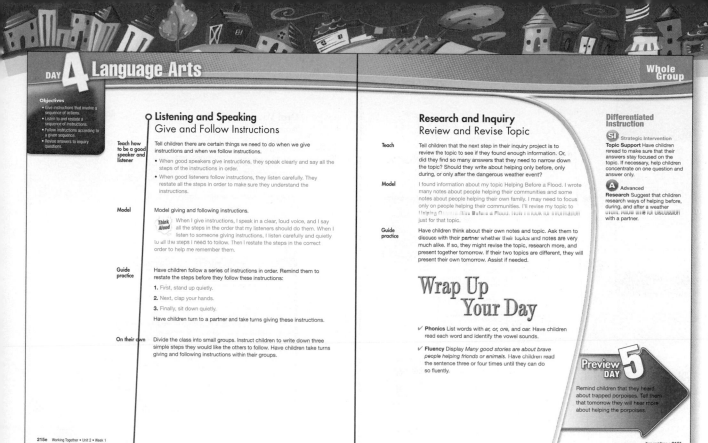

Objectives
- Give instructions that involve a sequence of actions.
- Listen to and restate a sequence of instructions.
- Follow instructions according to a given sequence.
- Revise answers to inquiry questions.

Listening and Speaking
Give and Follow Instructions

Teach how to be a good speaker and listener

Tell children there are certain things we need to do when we give instructions and when we follow instructions.

- When good speakers give instructions, they speak clearly and say all the steps of the instructions in order.
- When good listeners follow instructions, they listen carefully. They restate all the steps in order to make sure they understand the instructions.

Model

Model giving and following instructions.

Think Aloud When I give instructions, I speak in a clear, loud voice, and I say all the steps in the order that my listeners should do them. When I listen to someone giving instructions, I listen carefully and quietly to all the steps I need to follow. Then I restate the steps in the correct order to help me remember them.

Guide practice

Have children follow a series of instructions in order. Remind them to restate the steps before they follow these instructions:

1. First, stand up quietly.
2. Next, clap your hands.
3. Finally, sit down quietly.

Have children turn to a partner and take turns giving these instructions.

On their own

Divide the class into small groups. Instruct children to write down three simple steps they would like the others to follow. Have children take turns giving and following instructions within their groups.

Research and Inquiry
Review and Revise Topic

Teach

Tell children that the next step in their inquiry project is to review the topic to see if they found enough information. Or, did they find so many answers that they need to narrow down the topic? Should they write about helping only before, only during, or only after the dangerous weather event?

Model

I found information about my topic Helping Before a Flood. I wrote many notes about people helping their communities and some notes about people helping their own family. I may need to focus only on people helping their communities. I'll revise my topic to Helping Communities Before a Flood. Now I'll look for information just for that topic.

Guide practice

Have children think about their own notes and topic. Ask them to discuss with their partner whether their topics and notes are very much alike. If so, they might revise the topic, research more, and present together tomorrow. If their two topics are different, they will present their own tomorrow. Assist if needed.

Wrap Up Your Day

✔ **Phonics** List words with *ar, or, ore,* and *oar.* Have children read each word and identify the vowel sounds.

✔ **Fluency** Display *Many good stories are about brave people helping friends or animals.* Have children read the sentence three or four times until they can do so fluently.

Preview DAY 5

Remind children that they heard about trapped porpoises. Tell them that tomorrow they will hear more about helping the porpoises.

Differentiated Instruction

SI Strategic Intervention
Topic Support Have children reread to make sure that their answers stay focused on the topic. If necessary, help children concentrate on one question and answer only.

A Advanced
Research Suggest that children research ways of helping before, during, and after a weather event. Allow time for discussion with a partner.

.... LANGUAGE ARTS ....

In Reading Street

Listening and Speaking Each week children practice an important listening or speaking behavior while relating their own personal experiences. The teacher models the behavior, and then children apply the behavior during a classroom or partner activity.

Because Research Says

In order to learn language, children need opportunities to talk and be heard. Listening is not a natural, innate ability. Instead, it is learned through the guidance and teaching of parents, teachers, and other people in young children's environment.
—(Seefeldt and Wasik, 2006)

Objectives
• Review the concept: helping each other in dangerous situations.
• Build oral vocabulary.
• Identify details in text.

Today at a Glance

Oral Vocabulary
Review

Phonics
⊙ Review Vowels: r-Controlled ar, or, ore, oar

Comprehension
⊙ Cause and Effect

High-Frequency Words
Review

Story Words
Review

Conventions
Nouns

Writing
Narrative Nonfiction: Edit

Research and Inquiry
Communicate

Check Oral Vocabulary
▤ SUCCESS PREDICTOR

Concept Wrap Up

Question of the Week
How can we help each other in dangerous situations?

Review Concept

This week we have read and listened to selections about how we help others in danger. Today you will find out how the children continued to help the porpoises after they were rescued. **Read the story.**

• After the rescue of the porpoises, what did Owen and Diana do? (They splashed the porpoises with water to keep them cool, wet, and calm.)

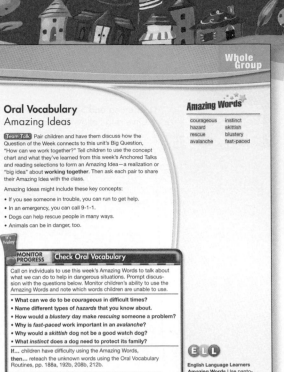
Read Aloud Anthology
"Porpoise Savers"

Review Amazing Words

Review the meaning of this week's Amazing Words. Then display this week's concept chart. Have children use Amazing Words and the chart to answer the question, "How can we help each other in dangerous situations?"

How can we help each other in dangerous situations?

Dangerous Situation	How Can We Help?
Person falls into raging water.	Call 911.
A river is flooding its banks.	Fill sandbags to hold back water.
There has been a tornado.	Get first aid and help clean up.
A friend is in trouble.	Get help.
Sandy falls off a cliff onto a ledge.	Maya helps her dad rescue Sandy.
Jim falls into the freezing lake.	Tiree and Tara pull Jim out.
Porpoises caught in fishing weirs.	Owen and Diana help free the porpoises.

ⒺⓁⓁ **Check Concepts and Language** Use the Day 5 instruction on Poster 6 to monitor children's understanding of the lesson concept.

ⒺⓁⓁ Poster 6

216a Working Together • Unit 2 • Week 1

Oral Vocabulary
Amazing Ideas

Connect to the Big Question

Team Talk Pair children and have them discuss how the Question of the Week connects to this unit's Big Question, "How can we work together?" Tell children to use the concept chart and what they've learned from this week's Anchored Talks and reading selections to form an Amazing Idea—a realization or "big idea" about **working together**. Then ask each pair to share their Amazing Idea with the class.

Amazing Ideas might include these key concepts:

• If you see someone in trouble, you can run to get help.
• In an emergency, you can call 9-1-1.
• Dogs can help rescue people in many ways.
• Animals can be in danger, too.

It's Friday

MONITOR PROGRESS | Check Oral Vocabulary

Call on individuals to use this week's Amazing Words to talk about what we can do to help in dangerous situations. Prompt discussion with the questions below. Monitor children's ability to use the Amazing Words and note which words children are unable to use.

• What can we do to be *courageous* in difficult times?
• Name different types of *hazards* that you know about.
• How would a *blustery* day make *rescuing* someone a problem?
• Why is *fast-paced* work important in an *avalanche*?
• Why would a *skittish* dog not be a good watch dog?
• What *instinct* does a dog need to protect its family?

If… children have difficulty using the Amazing Words,
then… reteach the unknown words using the Oral Vocabulary Routines, pp. 188a, 192b, 208b, 212b.

Day 1	Day 2	Day 3	Day 4	Day 5
Check Word Reading	Check High-Frequency Words	Check Retelling	Check Fluency	Check Oral Vocabulary

Success Predictor

Amazing Words ⭐

courageous	instinct
hazard	skittish
rescue	blustery
avalanche	fast-paced

ⒺⓁⓁ
English Language Learners
Amazing Words Use pantomime or gesture to give children clues as you review the Amazing Words.

216b
Oral Vocabulary
Success Predictor

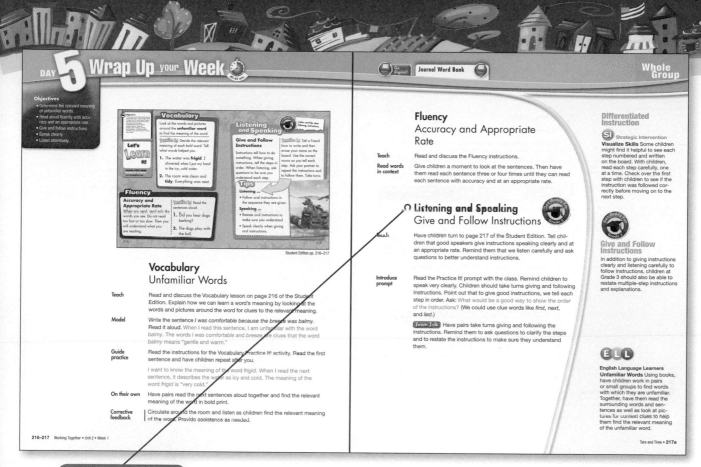

Student Edition pp. 216–217

Go Digital! Journal Word Bank

Whole Group

Vocabulary
Unfamiliar Words

Teach
Read and discuss the Vocabulary lesson on page 216 of the Student Edition. Explain how we can learn a word's meaning by looking at the words and pictures around the word for clues to the relevant meaning.

Model
Write the sentence *I was comfortable because the breeze was balmy.* Read it aloud. When I read this sentence, I am unfamiliar with the word *balmy.* The words *I was comfortable* and *breeze* are clues that the word *balmy* means "gentle and warm."

Guide practice
Read the instructions for the Vocabulary Practice It! activity. Read the first sentence and have children repeat after you.

I want to know the meaning of the word *frigid.* When I read the next sentence, it describes the water as icy and cold. The meaning of the word *frigid* is "very cold."

On their own
Have pairs read the next sentences aloud together and find the relevant meaning of the word in bold print.

Corrective feedback
Circulate around the room and listen as children find the relevant meaning of the word. Provide assistance as needed.

216–217 Working Together • Unit 2 • Week 1

Fluency
Accuracy and Appropriate Rate

Teach
Read and discuss the Fluency instructions.

Read words in context
Give children a moment to look at the sentences. Then have them read each sentence three or four times until they can read each sentence with accuracy and at an appropriate rate.

Listening and Speaking
Give and Follow Instructions

Teach
Have children turn to page 217 of the Student Edition. Tell children that good speakers give instructions speaking clearly and at an appropriate rate. Remind them that we listen carefully and ask questions to better understand instructions.

Introduce prompt
Read the Practice It! prompt with the class. Remind children to speak very clearly. Children should take turns giving and following instructions. Point out that to give good instructions, we tell each step in order. Ask: What would be a good way to show the order of the instructions? (We could use clue words like *first, next,* and *last.*)

Team Talk Have pairs take turns giving and following the instructions. Remind them to ask questions to clarify the steps and to restate the instructions to make sure they understand them.

Tara and Tiree • 217a

Differentiated Instruction

SI Strategic Intervention
Visualize Skills Some children might find it helpful to see each step numbered and written on the board. With children, read each step carefully, one at a time. Check over the first step with children to see if the instruction was followed correctly before moving on to the next step.

Get Ready
Give and Follow Instructions
In addition to giving instructions clearly and listening carefully to follow instructions, children at Grade 3 should also be able to restate multiple-step instructions and explanations.

ELL
English Language Learners
Unfamiliar Words Using books, have children work in pairs or small groups to find words with which they are unfamiliar. Together, have them read the surrounding words and sentences as well as look at pictures for context clues to help them find the relevant meaning of the unfamiliar word.

In Reading Street

Listening and Speaking
Each week children have direct instruction for the listening and speaking skills needed to perform and be an audience for brief oral presentations. Children demonstrate these skills with others during Team Talk activities.

Because Research Says
Social learning strategies will become increasingly important. Helping children learn effective literacy strategies from one another will prepare them for their futures where workplaces require these collaborative learning skills. —(Leu and Kinzer, 2000)

Page 217b is based on the same research as pages 191a and 192e–192f. Page 217c is based on the same research as 207a.

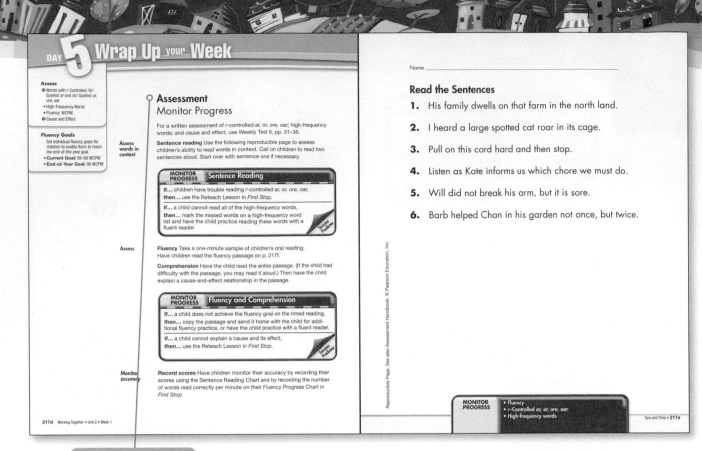

Assess
- Words with *r*-Controlled /är/ Spelled *ar* and /ôr/ Spelled *or, ore, oar*
- High-Frequency Words
- Fluency: WCPM
- Cause and Effect

Fluency Goals
Set individual fluency goals for children to enable them to reach the end-of-the-year goal.
- Current Goal: 58–68 WCPM
- End-of-Year Goal: 90 WCPM

Assess words in context

○ **Assessment**
Monitor Progress

For a written assessment of *r*-controlled *ar, or, ore, oar*; high-frequency words; and cause and effect, use Weekly Test 6, pp. 31–36.

Sentence reading Use the following reproducible page to assess children's ability to read words in context. Call on children to read two sentences aloud. Start over with sentence one if necessary.

MONITOR PROGRESS	Sentence Reading

If... children have trouble reading *r*-controlled *ar, or, ore, oar*,
then... use the Reteach Lesson in *First Stop.*

If... a child cannot read all of the high-frequency words,
then... mark the missed words on a high-frequency word list and have the child practice reading these words with a fluent reader.

Assess

Fluency Take a one-minute sample of children's oral reading. Have children read the fluency passage on p. 217f.

Comprehension Have the child read the entire passage. (If the child had difficulty with the passage, you may read it aloud.) Then have the child explain a cause-and-effect relationship in the passage.

MONITOR PROGRESS	Fluency and Comprehension

If... a child does not achieve the fluency goal on the timed reading,
then... copy the passage and send it home with the child for additional fluency practice, or have the child practice with a fluent reader.

If... a child cannot explain a cause and its effect,
then... use the Reteach Lesson in *First Stop.*

Monitor accuracy

Record scores Have children monitor their accuracy by recording their scores using the Sentence Reading Chart and by recording the number of words read correctly per minute on their Fluency Progress Chart in *First Stop.*

217d Working Together • Unit 2 • Week 1

Name _____

Read the Sentences

1. His family dwells on that farm in the north land.

2. I heard a large spotted cat roar in its cage.

3. Pull on this cord hard and then stop.

4. Listen as Kate informs us which chore we must do.

5. Will did not break his arm, but it is sore.

6. Barb helped Chan in his garden not once, but twice.

Reproducible Page. See also Assessment Handbook. © Pearson Education, Inc.

MONITOR PROGRESS	• Fluency • *r*-Controlled *ar, or, ore, oar* • High-frequency words

Tara and Tiree • **217e**

In Reading Street

Assessment On Day 5 assessments monitor progress in the target phonics skill, the week's high-frequency words, and the week's target comprehension skill. Students read aloud from reproducible pages while the teacher monitors progress in decoding, fluency, and comprehension. If children have difficulty reading the on-level fluency passage, the teacher provides additional opportunities for them to read text at their independent levels.

Because Research Says

Providing ongoing assessment of student reading progress may be one of the most valuable things teachers can do. The most valuable way to monitor student progress in fluency is to take timed measures of the number of words they read correctly in one minute. —(Vaughn and Linan-Thompson, 2004)

Pages 217f–217g are based on the same research as pages 217d–217e and 191c. Pages 217h–217i are based on the same research as pages 191d and 207d. Pages 217j–217k are based on the same research as page 207f.

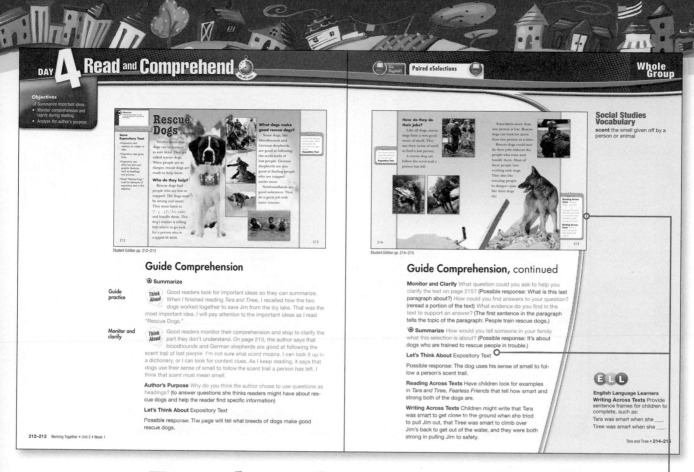

Read and Comprehend

Let's Think About It!

All of the second selections (except for 21st Century Skills lessons) and the first spread of each unit's Poetry Collection are annotated with thought-provoking Let's Think About It! questions. Main selection questions allow students to access the text by providing practice with the ten target strategies. Second selection questions guide students in identifying the elements of genre. Poetry Collection questions allow students to fully appreciate the poems by identifying the elements of poetry. All of these questions guide students in becoming strategic readers.

Research Says

"True comprehension goes beyond literal understanding and involves the reader's interaction with text. If students are to become thoughtful, insightful readers, they must merge their thinking with the text and extend their thinking beyond a superficial understanding." —(Harvey, Stephanie and Anne Goudvis. *Strategies That Work: Teaching Comprehension for Understanding and Engagement*, 2nd ed. Stenhouse Publishers, 2007.)

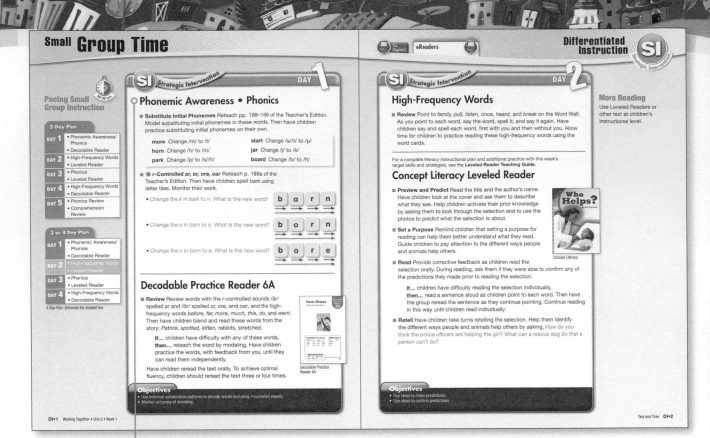

Pacing Small Group Instruction · 20–30 min.

5 Day Plan

DAY 1	• Phonemic Awareness/ Phonics • Decodable Reader
DAY 2	• High-Frequency Words • Leveled Reader
DAY 3	• Phonics • Leveled Reader
DAY 4	• High-Frequency Words • Decodable Reader
DAY 5	• Phonics Review • Comprehension Review

3 or 4 Day Plan

DAY 1	• Phonemic Awareness/ Phonics • Decodable Reader
DAY 2	• High-Frequency Words • Leveled Reader
DAY 3	• Phonics • Leveled Reader
DAY 4	• High-Frequency Words • Decodable Reader

3 Day Plan: Eliminate the shaded box

SI Strategic Intervention — DAY 1

Phonemic Awareness • Phonics

■ **Substitute Initial Phonemes** Reteach pp. 188–189 of the Teacher's Edition. Model substituting initial phonemes in these words. Then have children practice substituting initial phonemes on their own.

more Change /m/ to /t/	start Change /s//t/ to /p/
horn Change /h/ to /m/	jar Change /j/ to /k/
park Change /p/ to /s//h/	board Change /b/ to /h/

■ **r-Controlled *ar, or, ore, oar*** Reteach p. 189a of the Teacher's Edition. Then have children spell *bark* using letter tiles. Monitor their work.

• Change the *k* in *bark* to *n*. What is the new word? — b a r n

• Change the *a* in *barn* to *o*. What is the new word? — b o r n

• Change the *n* in *born* to *e*. What is the new word? — b o r e

Decodable Practice Reader 6A

■ **Review** Review words with the *r*-controlled sounds /är/ spelled *ar* and /ôr/ spelled *or, ore,* and *oar,* and the high-frequency words *before, far, more, much, this, do,* and *went.* Then have children blend and read these words from the story: *Patrick, spotted, kitten, rabbits, stretched.*

If... children have difficulty with any of these words,
then... reteach the word by modeling. Have children practice the words, with feedback from you, until they can read them independently.

Have children reread the text orally. To achieve optimal fluency, children should reread the text three or four times.

Farm Chores — Decodable Practice Reader 6A

Objectives
• Use common syllabication patterns to decode words including *r*-controlled vowels.
• Monitor accuracy of decoding.

DI•1 Working Together • Unit 2 • Week 1

SI Strategic Intervention — DAY 2

High-Frequency Words

■ **Review** Point to *family, pull, listen, once, heard,* and *break* on the Word Wall. As you point to each word, say the word, spell it, and say it again. Have children say and spell each word, first with you and then without you. Allow time for children to practice reading these high-frequency words using the word cards.

*For a complete literacy instructional plan and additional practice with this week's target skills and strategies, see the **Leveled Reader Teaching Guide.***

Concept Literacy Leveled Reader

■ **Preview and Predict** Read the title and the author's name. Have children look at the cover and ask them to describe what they see. Help children activate their prior knowledge by asking them to look through the selection and to use the photos to predict what the selection is about.

■ **Set a Purpose** Remind children that setting a purpose for reading can help them better understand what they read. Guide children to pay attention to the different ways people and animals help others.

■ **Read** Provide corrective feedback as children read the selection orally. During reading, ask them if they were able to confirm any of the predictions they made prior to reading the selection.

If... children have difficulty reading the selection individually,
then... read a sentence aloud as children point to each word. Then have the group reread the sentence as they continue pointing. Continue reading in this way until children read individually.

■ **Retell** Have children take turns retelling the selection. Help them identify the different ways people and animals help others by asking, How do you think the police officers are helping the girl? What can a rescue dog do that a person can't do?

Who Helps? — Concept Literacy

Objectives
• Use ideas to make predictions.
• Use ideas to confirm predictions.

Tara and Tiree DI•2

More Reading
Use Leveled Readers or other text at children's instructional level.

DIFFERENTIATED INSTRUCTION

In Reading Street

Strategic Intervention

Instruction Daily Small Group Time lessons provide struggling readers with more intensive instruction, more scaffolding, more practice with critical skills, and more opportunities to respond.

Because Research Says

▶ A combination of explicit and systematic instruction with carefully scaffolded instruction that provides modeling and feedback is associated with improved academic outcomes for students with reading and learning disabilities. —(Vaughn and Linan-Thompson, 2003)

Pages DI•3–DI•5 are based on the same research as pages DI•1–DI•2. Page DI•6 is based on the same research as pages DI•7–DI•8.

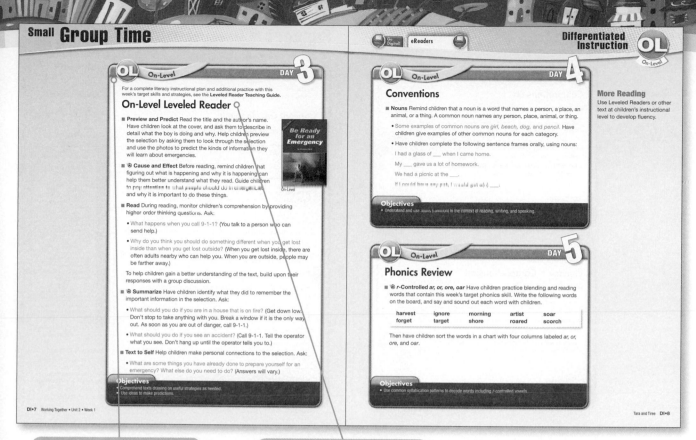

OL On-Level — DAY 3

For a complete literacy instructional plan and additional practice with this week's target skills and strategies, see the **Leveled Reader Teaching Guide.**

On-Level Leveled Reader

■ **Preview and Predict** Read the title and the author's name. Have children look at the cover, and ask them to describe in detail what the boy is doing and why. Help children preview the selection by asking them to look through the selection and use the photos to predict the kinds of information they will learn about emergencies.

■ ⊛ **Cause and Effect** Before reading, remind children that figuring out what is happening and why it is happening can help them better understand what they read. Guide children to pay attention to what people should do in emergencies and why it is important to do these things.

■ **Read** During reading, monitor children's comprehension by providing higher order thinking questions. Ask:

• What happens when you call 9-1-1? (You talk to a person who can send help.)

• Why do you think you should do something different when you get lost inside than when you get lost outside? (When you get lost inside, there are often adults nearby who can help you. When you are outside, people may be farther away.)

To help children gain a better understanding of the text, build upon their responses with a group discussion.

■ ⊛ **Summarize** Have children identify what they did to remember the important information in the selection. Ask:

• What should you do if you are in a house that is on fire? (Get down low. Don't stop to take anything with you. Break a window if it is the only way out. As soon as you are out of danger, call 9-1-1.)

• What should you do if you see an accident? (Call 9-1-1. Tell the operator what you see. Don't hang up until the operator tells you to.)

■ **Text to Self** Help children make personal connections to the selection. Ask:

• What are some things you have already done to prepare yourself for an emergency? What else do you need to do? (Answers will vary.)

Objectives
• Comprehend texts drawing on useful strategies as needed.
• Use ideas to make predictions.

Be Ready for an Emergency — On-Level

DI•7 Working Together • Unit 2 • Week 1

OL On-Level — DAY 4

Conventions

■ **Nouns** Remind children that a noun is a word that names a person, a place, an animal, or a thing. A common noun names any person, place, animal, or thing.

• Some examples of common nouns are *girl, beach, dog,* and *pencil.* Have children give examples of other common nouns for each category.

• Have children complete the following sentence frames orally, using nouns:

I had a glass of ___ when I came home.

My ___ gave us a lot of homework.

We had a picnic at the ___.

If I could have any pet, I would get a(n) ___.

Objectives
• Understand and use nouns (common) in the context of reading, writing, and speaking.

More Reading
Use Leveled Readers or other text at children's instructional level to develop fluency.

OL On-Level — DAY 5

Phonics Review

■ ⊛ *r-Controlled ar, or, ore, oar* Have children practice blending and reading words that contain this week's target phonics skill. Write the following words on the board, and say and sound out each word with children.

harvest	ignore	morning	artist	soar
forget	target	shore	roared	scorch

Then have children sort the words in a chart with four columns labeled *ar, or, ore,* and *oar.*

Objectives
• Use common syllabication patterns to decode words including *r*-controlled vowels.

Tara and Tiree DI•8

DIFFERENTIATED INSTRUCTION

In Reading Street

On-Level Instruction Daily Small Group Time lessons focus on appropriate instructional strategies for children reading at grade level.

Because Research Says

Smaller group ratios increase the likelihood of academic success through student-teacher interactions, individualization of instruction, student on-task behavior, and teacher monitoring of student progress and feedback. —(Vaughn, et al., 2003)

DIFFERENTIATED INSTRUCTION

In Reading Street

Leveled Readers Instructional-level fiction and nonfiction books are provided for readers at the Strategic Intervention, On-Level, and Advanced levels. These books relate to weekly concepts and offer children opportunities to read texts and practice targeted skills and strategies in small groups at their individual instructional levels. Teachers also use progress monitoring to move children along a continuum to independent reading.

Because Research Says

One of the five components of the model of explicit comprehension instruction best supported by research is guided practice with gradual release of responsibility. —(Duke and Pearson, 2002)

Pages DI•9–DI•10 are based on the same research as page DI•11.

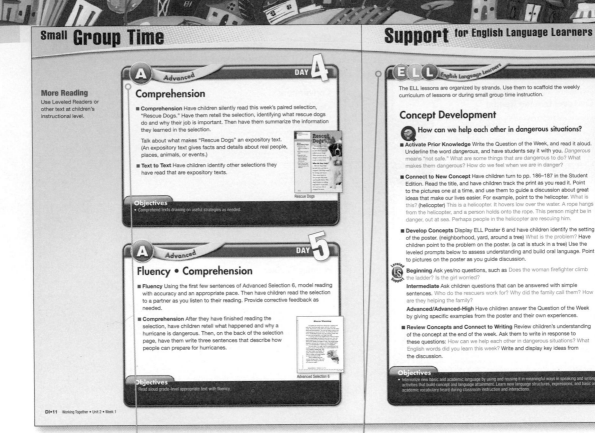

DIFFERENTIATED INSTRUCTION

In Reading Street

Advanced Instruction Daily Small Group Time lessons for children reading above grade level enhance the skills taught in the core lesson, provide exposure to more challenging reading and vocabulary, and incorporate independent investigative work. Activities provide advanced readers additional opportunities to engage in critical and creative thinking, and to focus on problem-solving skills.

Because Research Says

In general, grouping academically talented students together for instruction has been found to produce positive achievement outcomes when the curriculum provided to students in different groups is appropriately differentiated. In other words, it is the instruction that occurs within groups that makes grouping an appropriate instructional strategy. —(Reis, et al., 2003)

ENGLISH LANGUAGE LEARNERS

In Reading Street

ELL Instruction English learners receive extra support to allow them to successfully participate in and progress through the daily lessons of the basic program with their peers.

Because Research Says

Given the diversity in our society, it is imperative to recognize that young children may differ considerably in their inventory of skills and abilities, and these differences should not be treated as reflecting deficiencies in ability. —(Wong Fillmore and Snow, 2002)

ENGLISH LANGUAGE LEARNERS

In Reading Street

In the Comfort Zone Complex academic English instruction is made more accessible when English learners are comfortable in the classroom. Lessons for English language learners provide many strategies for increasing children's comfort level, including the use of visual supports in dramatizing, making personal and cultural connections, and total physical response.

Because Research Says

In second language acquisition, affective variables, such as motivation, self-confidence, and anxiety, play a role. Learners with high motivation and confidence and low anxiety are better equipped for success in the second language. A natural approach is to lower an affective barrier. —(Krashen and Terrell, 1983)

Pages DI•13–DI•18 are based on the same research as page DI•12.

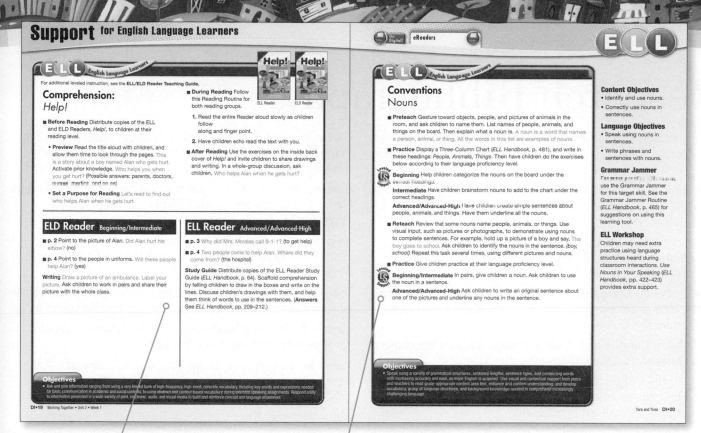

Comprehension:
Help!

- **Before Reading** Distribute copies of the ELL and ELD Readers, *Help!*, to children at their reading level.
  - **Preview** Read the title aloud with children, and allow them time to look through the pages. This is a story about a boy named Alan who gets hurt. Activate prior knowledge. Who helps you when you get hurt? (Possible answers: parents, doctors, nurses, medics, and so on)
  - **Set a Purpose for Reading** Let's read to find out who helps Alan when he gets hurt.

- **During Reading** Follow this Reading Routine for both reading groups.
  1. Read the entire Reader aloud slowly as children follow along and finger point.
  2. Have children echo read the text with you.

- **After Reading** Use the exercises on the inside back cover of *Help!* and invite children to share drawings and writing. In a whole-group discussion, ask children, Who helps Alan when he gets hurt?

ELD Reader Beginning/Intermediate

- **p. 2** Point to the picture of Alan. Did Alan hurt his elbow? (no)
- **p. 4** Point to the people in uniforms. Will these people help Alan? (yes)

Writing Draw a picture of an ambulance. Label your picture. Ask children to work in pairs and share their picture with the whole class.

ELL Reader Advanced/Advanced-High

- **p. 3** Why did Mrs. Morales call 9-1-1? (to get help)
- **p. 4** Two people come to help Alan. Where did they come from? (the hospital)

Study Guide Distribute copies of the ELL Reader Study Guide (*ELL Handbook*, p. 64). Scaffold comprehension by telling children to draw in the boxes and write on the lines. Discuss children's drawings with them, and help them think of words to use in the sentences. (**Answers** See *ELL Handbook*, pp. 209–212.)

Objectives
- Ask and give information ranging from using a very limited bank of high-frequency, high-need, concrete vocabulary, including key words and expressions needed for basic communication in academic and social contexts, to using abstract and content-based vocabulary during extended speaking assignments. Respond orally to information presented in a wide variety of print, electronic, audio, and visual media to build and reinforce concept and language attainment.

DI•19 Working Together • Unit 2 • Week 1

---

eReaders

Conventions
Nouns

- **Preteach** Gesture toward objects, people, and pictures of animals in the room, and ask children to name them. List names of people, animals, and things on the board. Then explain what a noun is. A noun is a word that names a person, animal, or thing. All the words in this list are examples of nouns.

- **Practice** Display a Three-Column Chart (*ELL Handbook*, p. 481), and write in these headings: *People, Animals, Things*. Then have children do the exercises below according to their language proficiency level.
  - **Beginning** Help children categorize the nouns on the board under the correct headings.
  - **Intermediate** Have children brainstorm nouns to add to the chart under the correct headings.
  - **Advanced/Advanced-High** Have children create simple sentences about people, animals, and things. Have them underline all the nouns.

- **Reteach** Review that some nouns name people, animals, or things. Use visual input, such as pictures or photographs, to demonstrate using nouns to complete sentences. For example, hold up a picture of a boy and say, The boy goes to school. Ask children to identify the nouns in the sentence. (boy, school) Repeat this task several times, using different pictures and nouns.

- **Practice** Give children practice at their language proficiency level.
  - **Beginning/Intermediate** In pairs, give children a noun. Ask children to use the noun in a sentence.
  - **Advanced/Advanced-High** Ask children to write an original sentence about one of the pictures and underline any nouns in the sentence.

Objectives
- Speak using a variety of grammatical structures, sentence lengths, sentence types, and connecting words with increasing accuracy and ease, as more English is acquired. Use visual and contextual support from peers and teachers to read grade-appropriate content area text, enhance and confirm understanding, and develop vocabulary, grasp of language structures, and background knowledge needed to comprehend increasingly challenging language.

Content Objectives
- Identify and use nouns.
- Correctly use nouns in sentences.

Language Objectives
- Speak using nouns in sentences.
- Write phrases and sentences with nouns.

Grammar Jammer
For more practice with nouns, use the Grammar Jammer for this target skill. See the Grammar Jammer Routine (*ELL Handbook*, p. 465) for suggestions on using this learning tool.

ELL Workshop
Children may need extra practice using language structures heard during classroom interactions. *Use Nouns in Your Speaking* (*ELL Handbook*, pp. 422–423) provides extra support.

Tara and Tiree DI•20

In Reading Street

ELL and ELD Readers Prompts and questions designed for English language learners help teachers guide children as they read and comprehend text. The prompts allow children at different English language levels to answer by pointing, with yes/no or single words, or with longer statements as they interact with text and pictures.

Because Research Says

Beginning and intermediate English language learners often do not understand what their classroom teachers say or read aloud, or what they read on their own in English. These students benefit when teachers shelter, or make comprehensible, their literacy instruction through a variety of sheltered techniques, including activities that integrate reading, writing, listening, and speaking.
—(García, 2010)

In Reading Street

ELL Leveled Support Teachers use a variety of instructional activities to support English language learners at different levels of proficiency. Different techniques can be chosen as the teacher observes which children need more support or more challenging language activities. At the beginning level, techniques include gesturing and having children draw. For more advanced levels, children are encouraged to speak in more complex sentences and use a wider range of vocabulary.

Because Research Says

Often beginning and intermediate English language learners may not understand what their classroom teachers say or read aloud in English. When it becomes clear from students' actions and responses that they understand what is being said, teachers can vary their strategies. —(García, 2010)

Page DI•21 is based on the same research as pages DI•19–DI•20.

Research Bibliography

Anderson, Jeff. *Mechanically Inclined: Building Grammar, Usage, and Style into Writer's Workshop.* Stenhouse Publishers, 2005.

Anderson, R., E. Hiebert, J. Scott, and I. Wilkinson. "The Report of the Commission on Reading." *Becoming a Nation of Readers.* The National Institute of Education, 1985.

Armbruster, B. B., F. Lehr and J. Osborn. *Put Reading First: The Research Building Blocks for Teaching Children to Read.* Partnership for Reading, 2001.

Beck, Isabel L., Margaret G. McKeown, Rebecca L. Hamilton, and Linda Kucan. *Bringing Words to Life: Robust Vocabulary Instruction.* The Guilford Press, 2002.

Blachowicz, Camille and Peter J. Fisher. *Teaching Vocabulary in All Classrooms,* 2nd ed. Merrill Prentice Hall, 2002.

Block, Cathy Collins and Michael Pressley. "Best Practices in Comprehension Instruction." *Best Practices in Literary Instruction.* The Guilford Press, 2003.

Coyne, Michael D., Deborah C. Simmons, and Edward J. Kame'enui. "Vocabulary Instruction for Young Children at Risk of Experiencing Reading Difficulties." *Vocabulary Instruction: Research to Practice.* The Guilford Press, 2004.

Cummins, Jim. "The Three Pillars of English Language Learning." *Pearson Scott Foresman EL Handbook Teacher's Manual,* 2010.

Duke, Nell K. and P. David Pearson. "Effective Practices for Developing Reading Comprehension." *What Research Has to Say About Reading Instruction,* 3rd ed. International Reading Association, 2002.

Duke, Nell K., V. Susan Bennett-Armistead, Ebony M. Roberts. "Bridging the Gap Between Learning to Read and Reading to Learn." *Literacy and Young Children: Research-Based Practices.* The Guilford Press, 2003.

Ehri, Linnea C. and Simone R. Nunes. "The Role of Phonemic Awareness in Learning to Read." *What Research Has to Say About Reading Instruction,* 3rd ed. International Reading Association, 2002.

Ehri, Linnea C., M. R., and S. A. Stahl. "Fluency: A Review of Developmental and Remedial Practices." *Journal of Educational Psychology,* vol. 95, 2003.

Ehri, Linnea C. "Grapheme-Phoneme Knowledge Is Essential for Learning to Read Words in English." *Word Recognition in Beginning Literacy.* Lawrence Erlbaum Associates, 1992.

Foorman, B. R., and J. Torgesen. "Critical Elements of Classroom and Small-Group Instruction Promote Reading Success in All Children." *Learning Disabilities Research and Practice,* vol. 16, November 2001.

Galda, Lee, and Richard Beach. "Response to Literature as a Cultural Activity." *Theoretical Models and Processes of Reading,* 5th ed. International Reading Association, 2004.

García, Georgia Earnest. "English Learners and Literacy: Best Practices." *Pearson Scott Foresman EL Handbook Teacher's Manual,* 2010.

Gaskins, Irene W. "A Multidimensional Approach to Beginning Literacy." *Literacy and Young Children: Research-Based Practices.* The Guilford Press, 2003.

Ivey, Gay. "Building Comprehension When They're Still Learning to Read the Words." *Comprehension Instruction: Research-Based Best Practices.* The Guilford Press, 2002.

Juel, Connie. "Impact of Early School Experiences," *Handbook of Early Literacy Research,* 2nd ed. The Guilford Press, 2005.

Kaplan, S. "Reading Strategies for Gifted Readers." *Teaching for High Potential,* vol. 1, no. 2, 1999.

Kuhn, M. R., and S. A. Stahl. "Fluency: A Review of Developmental and Remedial Practices." *Journal of Educational Psychology,* vol. 95, 2003.

Kuhn, Melanie. "How Can I Help Them Pull It All Together? A Guide to Fluent Reading Instruction." *Literacy and Young Children: Research-Based Practices.* The Guilford Press, 2003.

Krashen, Stephen D., and Tracy D. Terrell. *The Natural Approach: Language Acquisition in the Classroom.* Alemany Press, 1983.

Leu, D. J. Jr., C. K. Kinzer, J. Coiro, and D. Cammack. "Toward a Theory of New Literacies Emerging from the Internet and Other Information and Communication Technologies." *Theoretical Models and Processes of Reading,* 5th ed. International Reading Association, 2004.

Leu, Donald and Charles Kinzer. "The Convergence of Literary Instruction with Networked Technologies for Information and Communication." *Reading Research Quarterly,* vol. 35, no. 1, January/February/March 2000.

Leu, Donald. "The New Literacies: Research on Reading Instruction With the Internet." *What Research Has to Say About Reading Instruction,* 3rd ed., International Reading Association, 2002.

McKee, Judith and Donna Ogle. *Integrating Instruction, Literacy and Science.* The Guilford Press, 2005.

Morrow, Lesley Mandel and Linda Gambrell. "Literature-Based Instruction in the Early Years." *Handbook of Early Literacy Research.* The Guilford Press, 2002.

Morrow, L. M., "Story Retelling: A Discussion Strategy to Develop and Assess Comprehension." *Lively Discussions! Fostering Engaged Reading.* International Reading Association, 1996.

National Reading Panel. *Teaching Children to Read.* National Institute of Child Health and Human Development. 1999.

National Writing Project and Carl Nagin. *Because Writing Matters.* Jossey-Bass, 2003.

Noguchi, Rei R. *The English Record.* Winter, 2002.

Ogle, D. and C. L. Blachowicz. "Beyond Literature Circles: Helping Students Comprehend Informational Texts." *Comprehension Instruction: Research-Based Best Practices.* The Guilford Press, 2002.

Paratore, Jeanne and Rachel McCormack. *Teaching Literacy in Second Grade.* The Guilford Press, 2005.

Pearson, P. D., L. R. Roehler, J. A. Dole, and G. G. Duffy. "Developing Expertise in Reading Comprehension." *What Research Says About Reading Instruction,* 2nd ed. International Reading Association, 1992.

Pearson, P. David and Nell K. Duke. "Comprehension Instruction in the Primary Grades." *Comprehension Instruction: Research-Based Best Practices.* The Guilford Press, 2002.

Pressley, M., and C. C. Block. "Summing Up: What Comprehension Instruction Could Be." *Comprehension Instruction: Research-Based Best Practices.* The Guilford Press, 2002.

Pressley, M. "Metacognition and Self-Regulated Comprehension." *What Research Has to Say About Reading Instruction,* 3rd ed. International Reading Association, 2002.

Reis, Sally M., E. Jean Gubbins, Christine Briggs, Fredric J. Schreiber, Susannah Richards, Joan Jacobs, Rebecca D. Eckert, Joseph S. Renzulli, and Margaret Alexander. *Reading Instruction for Talented Readers: Case Studies Documenting Few Opportunities for Continuous Progress* (RM03184). The National Research Center on the Gifted and Talented, University of Connecticut, 2003.

Reis, Sally M., and Joseph S. Renzulli. "Developing Challenging Programs for Gifted Readers." *The Reading Instruction Journal,* vol. 32, 1989.

Samuels, S. J. "Reading Fluency: Its Development and Assessment." *What Research Has to Say About Reading Instruction,* 3rd ed. International Reading Association, 2002.

Seefeldt, Carol and Barbara A. Wasik. *Early Education: Three-, Four-, and Five-Year Olds Go to School,* 2nd ed. Pearson Merrill Prentice Hall, 2006.

Smith, Sylvia B., Deborah C. Simmons, and Edward J. Kame'enui. "Phonological Awareness: Instructional and Curricular Basics and Implications." *What Reading Research Tells Us About Children With Diverse Learning Needs: Bases and Basics.* Lawrence Erlbaum Associates, 1998.

Snow, Catherine E., M. Susan Burns, and Peg Griffin, eds. *Preventing Reading Difficulties in Young Children.* National Research Council, 1998.

Spandel, Vicki. "Assessing With Heart." National Staff Development Council, vol. 27, no. 3. Summer 2006.

_____. *Creating Writers Through 6-Trait Writing Assessment and Instruction.* 2nd ed. Merrill Prentice Hall, 2002.

_____. *Creating Writers Through 6-Trait Writing Assessment and Instruction.* 3rd ed. Addison Wesley Longman, 2001.

_____. *Creating Writers Through 6-Trait Writing Assessment and Instruction.* 4th ed. Allyn and Bacon, 2004.

Stahl, Steven A. and Katherine A. Dougherty Stahl. "Word Wizards All! Teaching Word Meanings in Preschool and Primary Education." *Vocabulary Instruction: Research to Practice.* The Guilford Press, 2004.

Tatum, Alfred. *Teaching Reading to Black Adolescent Males.* Stenhouse Publishers, 2005.

Taylor, Barbara M., P. David Pearson, Debra S. Peterson, and Michael C. Rodriguez. "The CIERA School Change Framework: An Evidence-Based Approach to Professional Development and School Reading Improvement." *Reading Research Quarterly,* vol. 40, no. 1, January/February/March 2005.

VanTassel-Baska, J. "Effective Curriculum and Instructional Models for Talented Students." *Gifted Child Quarterly,* vol. 30, 1996.

Vaughn, Sharon and Sylvia Linan-Thompson. *Research-Based Methods of Reading Instruction.* Association for Supervision and Curriculum Development, 2004.

_____. "Group Size and Time Allotted to Intervention: Effects for Students with Reading Difficulties." *Preventing and Remediating Reading Difficulties: Bringing Science to Scale.* Baltimore York Press, 2003.

Vaughn, Sharon, Sylvia Linan-Thompson, Kamiar Kouzekanani, Diane Pedrotty, Shirley Dickson, and Shelly Blozis. "Reading Instruction Grouping for Students with Reading Difficulties." *Remedial and Special Education,* vol. 24, no. 5, September/October 2003.

Weaver, Constance. *Grammar for Teachers: Perspectives and Definitions.* NCTE, 1979.

Wiggins, Grant and Jay McTighe. *Understanding by Design.* Pearson Education, Inc., 2006.

Wilkinson, L. C. and E. R. Silliman. "Classroom Language and Literacy Learning." *Handbook of Reading Research,* vol. III. Lawrence Erlbaum Associates, 2000.

Wong Fillmore, Lily and Catherine E. Snow. "What Teachers Need to Know About Language." *What Teachers Need to Know About Language.* The Center for Applied Linguistics and Delta Systems Co., Inc., 2002.

Wong Fillmore, Lily. "Preparing English Language Learners for Assessment." *Pearson Scott Foresman EL Handbook Teacher's Manual,* 2010.

Wray, David and Maureen Lewis. "But Bonsai Tress Don't Grow in Baskets: Young Children's Talk During Authentic Inquiry." *Lively Discussions! Fostering Engaged Reading.* International Reading Association, 1996.

Zevenenbergen, Andrea and Grover Whitehurst. *On Reading Books to Children: Parents and Teacher.* Lawrence Erlbaum Associates, 2003.

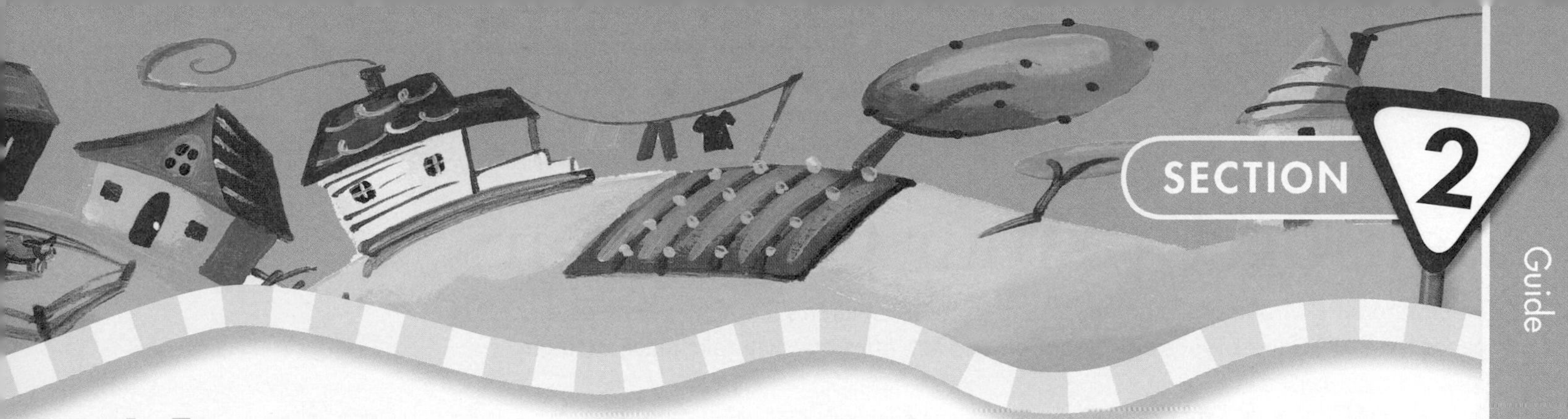

Guide to
Reading Street

Section 2 is your easy guide to *Reading Street*. You'll find out how to set up your classroom and manage it effectively. Stop here when you need suggestions and background information for teaching these critical elements of literacy:

- Phonics

- Phonemic Awareness

- Word Structure

- Fluency

- Vocabulary

- Comprehension

- Writing

The section ends with a visit with the distinguished authors whose research is the foundation of *Scott Foresman Reading Street* so they can answer some of your questions.

Setting Up Your Classroom

The classroom environment is an important factor in children's learning. Create separate spaces for the different types of instruction and activities that will take place each day.

How Should I Organize My Classroom?

Whole-Group Instruction

Bring the whole group together in an open area from which all children can easily see the chalkboard, chart, or instructional materials. In many classrooms children will be seated at desks that may be arranged in groups. During the day children can also use their own desks for independent work.

Differentiated Instruction for Small Group Time

Meet with a small group of children at a table near convenient storage space for the leveled materials you need. Your position at the table should allow you to monitor the other practice stations while you conduct the small-group lesson. The Word Wall should be visible from both large- and small-group areas.

Practice Stations

These practice stations should be inviting areas where children can work independently, in pairs, or in small groups. Set up a variety of stations in your classroom. The *Scott Foresman Reading Street Practice Stations Kit* helps simplify the task of managing practice stations by providing ideas for setting up your stations, weekly activities, and suggested routines for each station. You will find weekly activities for vocabulary, writing, phonics, spelling, comprehension, fluency, and technology in your *Scott Foresman Reading Street Teacher's Edition.*

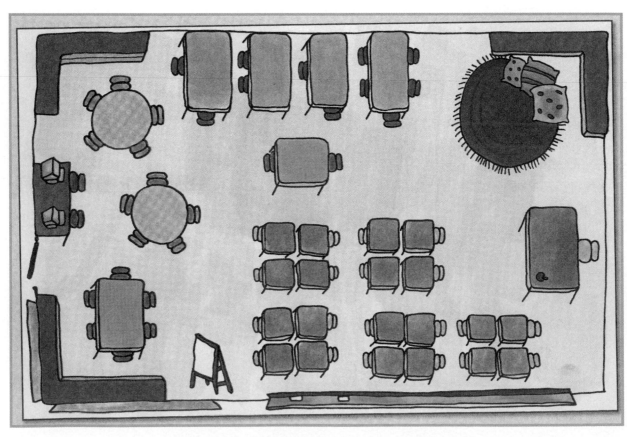

Effective Classroom Management

How Can I Teach Effectively?

Fast-Paced, High-Density Instruction Children should be on-task most of the time. Planning is a key to keeping children actively engaged in learning.

Explicit, Systematic Instruction Throughout *Reading Street*, you'll find routines that contain the language and steps you need to make instruction explicit. You'll also have built-in supports for incorporating these practices throughout each day.

- Connect to what children already know; encourage children to activate and build on their prior knowledge.
- Introduce a small amount of new information at a time.
- Always model a new skill before asking children to use it.
- Provide ample practice.
- Monitor children's progress regularly and provide corrective feedback.
- Use visuals and graphic organizers to clarify instruction.
- Provide a cumulative and spiraled review of previously learned skills.

Scaffold Children's Learning *Reading Street* instruction incorporates the additional steps needed in instruction to help children bridge gaps in learning. Model a new skill and then guide children with prompts. Use "Think Alouds" to model skills and strategies.

Differentiate Instruction Group children according to their instructional levels. With children's abilities in mind, you can go on to plan either additional intensive instruction and practice or more challenging work.

Establish Routines Children work best when they know what they're supposed to do. As children move routinely from one task to another, you will be able to devote more attention to small-group instruction.

Create High Expectations Convey your confidence in each child. Send the message that you expect all children can and will read and learn.

Reinforce Achievement Use praise and recognition when children meet individual and group goals.

Encourage Self-Regulation Praise children often for making their own good decisions.

Spiral Review: In addition to teaching new skills each week, you review both new skills and those you taught before. The spiral review is systematic, so you spend the right amount of time reviewing each skill.

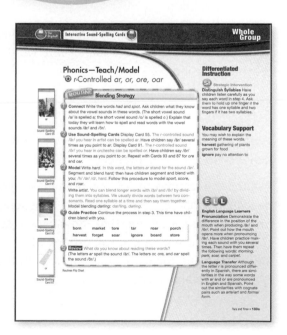

Phonics

Sounds and Symbols

Beginning readers are a step ahead when they learn phonics in *Scott Foresman Reading Street*. During this phonics instruction, children learn to relate the **sounds** of spoken English to the **symbols** of the written language. This instruction is effective because it is explicit and systematic:

Explicit >> You directly model, teach, practice, and review the skills.

Systematic >> You use a defined sequence of skills that includes a spiral review of skills you previously taught.

Blending Sounds to Decode

Your phonics instruction begins with introducing letter-sounds in isolation. You quickly move children from recognizing sounds to blending sounds to decoding words. It's an exciting moment for children when they "crack the code" and read words with meanings they understand!

At each step, you use teaching routines to make instruction explicit. Children learn to blend the sounds into words when you use this teaching routine.

Expecting Symbols to Make Sense

What is a new word? Is the new word a word you know? Does it make sense in the sentence?

Ask these questions to help children make sense of written symbols they decode. As children respond to your questions, they reevaluate and adapt until they are successful. That "on my own" success encourages children to ask *themselves* the same questions when they read independently. You're teaching them an important lesson: they can expect written symbols to make sense.

Teaching Routine

Sound-by-Sound Blending

1. **Display** Write the word *sat* or spell it with letter cards.
2. **Segment** Put your hand under *s* and say /s/. Move your hand to *a* and say /a/. Move to *t* and say /t/.
3. **Blend** Then move your hand below the word *sat* from left to right and blend the sounds sequentially, with no pause between letter-sounds, /sat/.
4. **Read** Then pronounce the word normally.
5. **Repeat** Have children repeat the blending process for *sat,* first with you, and then as a group.

Segmenting Sounds to Write

Your phonics instruction naturally moves from listening and decoding to using letter sounds in order to write words. To "write for sounds," children perform the complex mental process of thinking about sounds, their sequence in a word, and the letters that stand for those sounds. For children to succeed, this instruction needs to be explicit.

Teaching Routine

Segmenting

1. **Say** Pronounce each word and each sound slowly and distinctly.

2. **Listen** Have children listen for each sound in order.

3. **Write** Have children write what they hear, sound by sound.

How Blending Instruction Builds

Children move beyond sound-by-sound blending throughout Grade 2. As they learn to look at longer word parts and syllable patterns, they decode more efficiently. With this defined sequence and the teaching routines, you can implement the explicit instruction that beginning readers need.

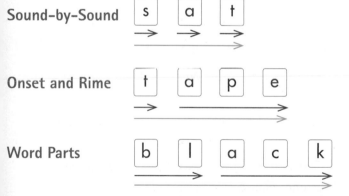

Sound–by–Sound   s   a   t

Onset and Rime   t   a   p   e

Word Parts   b   l   a   c   k

Robust and Engaging Practice

Effective phonics instruction is supported by a variety of substantial practice opportunities. With *Scott Foresman Reading Street*, you guide children to use engaging activities for blending, building, and sorting words according to sounds and spellings. Children also practice with the *Phonics Songs and Rhymes Charts.* Practice is even more rewarding as they read Decodable Readers each week. Children quickly use what they learn to read real stories on their own!

The Maple Tree
Written by Kara Linden

Decodable Practice Reader 16C

Final Syllable -*le*

maple	simple	stumble
table	bottle	bubbles
able	puddle	giggle

High-Frequency Words

seen	tree	find
show	turn	want

11

Phonemic Awareness

The Sounds of Language

phonological awareness >> an awareness of the sounds that make up spoken language

phonemic awareness >> one kind of phonological awareness, which includes the ability to hear individual sounds in words and to identify and manipulate those sounds

To learn to read, children must understand that spoken language is made up of a series of sounds. This knowledge is **phonological awareness.** Phonological awareness skills can be sequenced into several levels of development. Phonemic awareness is the most complex of these levels. It is one of the strongest predictors of a child's future reading ability.

How Can I Help Children Develop Phonemic Awareness?

Phonemic awareness must be taught explicitly and systematically. *Reading Street* includes daily phonemic awareness instruction in the first half of second grade to ensure that children have moved through the different levels. Research shows that phonemic awareness instruction is most effective when it leads immediately to connecting the sound to the letter. That immediate connection is a hallmark of instruction in *Reading Street*.

What Do Children Do at Different Levels?

1st Level of Phonological Awareness

Words How many words do you hear in the sentence?

Rhymes Do *cat* and *bat* rhyme? What else rhymes with *cat* and *bat*?

Syllables How many syllables do you hear in *dinosaur*?

2nd Level of Phonological Awareness

Identify Initial Sounds Do *bear* and *boat* begin with the same sound?

Compare Sounds in Words Which words have the same sounds at the beginning—*bear, boat, tiger*?

Onset and Rime What word am I trying to say: /m/ -*ouse*?

3rd Level of Phonological Awareness

Isolate Phonemes What sound do you hear at the beginning of *dog*?

Identify Phonemes What sound is the same in *bear, ball,* and *bat*?

Categorize Phonemes Which word doesn't belong: *mouse, moose,* or *cat*?

Blend Phonemes What word is /k/ /a/ /t/?

Segment Phonemes How many sounds do you hear in *hippo*?

Delete Phonemes What word is *snail* without the /s/?

Add Phonemes What word do you make when you add /t/ to *rain*?

Substitute Phonemes What word do you make when you change /n/ to /p/ in *can*?

How Can I Help Children Move from Level to Level?

In the Grade 2 program every **phonemic awareness** lesson is tied to the phonics lesson that follows it. For example, if the day's phonics instruction is short *a*, the phonemic awareness lesson that precedes it focuses on blending or segmenting short *a* words. Children benefit most from phonemic awareness instruction that connects sounds to letters. This connection is a built-in feature in *Reading Street*.

The early levels of **phonological awareness** include:

- segmenting words into syllables
- identifying words that begin with the same sound
- blending onset and rime into a word and segmenting words into onset and rime
- progress monitoring opportunities

When children move on from review and begin Unit 1, they focus on **phonemic awareness.** At this level children develop the skills they need to benefit from phonics instruction. They learn to

- isolate individual sounds at the beginning, middle, or end of words
- blend individual sounds to make words
- segment a spoken word into its individual sounds
- add, delete, and substitute sounds in spoken words

Routines in *Reading Street* provide each step of instruction you need to support children working at the phonemic awareness level. You help children to

- blend individual sounds to form words. For example, if you say /b/ /a/ /th/, they say *bath*.
- segment spoken words into individual sounds. For example, if you say *me*, they say /m/ /ē/.
- add or delete sounds from spoken words. For example, *Say* late *without the /l/. Say* ear *with /f/ at the beginning.*
- change a sound in a spoken word to make a new word. For example, *Change the first sound in* ham *to /j/. Change the last sound in* ham *to /d/.*

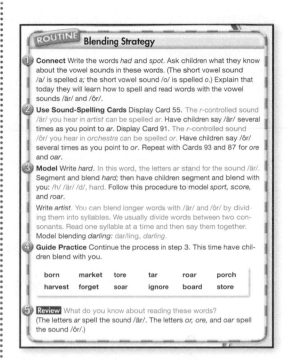

ROUTINE Blending Strategy

1. **Connect** Write the words *had* and *spot*. Ask children what they know about the vowel sounds in these words. (The short vowel sound /a/ is spelled *a*; the short vowel sound /o/ is spelled *o*.) Explain that today they will learn how to spell and read words with the vowel sounds /är/ and /ôr/.

2. **Use Sound-Spelling Cards** Display Card 55. The *r*-controlled sound /är/ you hear in *artist* can be spelled *ar*. Have children say /är/ several times as you point to *ar*. Display Card 91. The *r*-controlled sound /ôr/ you hear in *orchestra* can be spelled *or*. Have children say /ôr/ several times as you point to *or*. Repeat with Cards 93 and 87 for *ore* and *oar*.

3. **Model** Write *hard*. In this word, the letters *ar* stand for the sound /är/. Segment and blend *hard*; then have children segment and blend with you: /h/ /är/ /d/, hard. Follow this procedure to model *sport*, *score*, and *roar*.

    Write *artist*. You can blend longer words with /är/ and /ôr/ by dividing them into syllables. We usually divide words between two consonants. Read one syllable at a time and then say them together. Model blending *darling*: dar/ling, *darling*.

4. **Guide Practice** Continue the process in step 3. This time have children blend with you.

born	market	tore	tar	roar	porch
harvest	forget	soar	ignore	board	store

5. **Review** What do you know about reading these words? (The letters *ar* spell the sound /är/. The letters *or*, *ore*, and *oar* spell the sound /ôr/.)

Word Structure

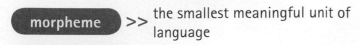 **morpheme** >> the smallest meaningful unit of language

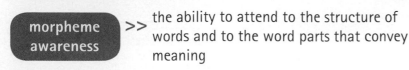 **morpheme awareness** >> the ability to attend to the structure of words and to the word parts that convey meaning

Along with an awareness of letter-sound relationships, children must develop an awareness of morphemes. **Morphemes** are the smallest meaningful units of language and include word parts such as base words, prefixes, and suffixes. A morpheme may be the whole word or a part of a word. A word may be made up of one or more morphemes. *Friend* consists of one morpheme; *friendly,* two; *unfriendly,* three; *unfriendliest,* four.

Children who learn to examine these important word parts gain a powerful strategy for identifying unfamiliar words as they read, for expanding their vocabularies, and for spelling.

How Does Word Structure Aid Decoding?

For morphemes to be useful to children, they must be taught explicitly, sequentially, and systematically. Instruction in Grade 2 includes inflected endings, such as *-s, -es, -ed, -ing*; compound words; the most common suffixes and prefixes; and spelling changes. Instructional routines for blending the syllables in multisyllabic words are provided in word structure lessons throughout *Scott Foresman Reading Street.*

Read Multisyllabic Words

How Does Word Structure Give Clues to Meaning?

Since morphemes are meaningful units, instruction must include the meaning conveyed by each word part. For example, children should understand that *-s* or *-es* may convey "more than one," *-ed* signals an action that happened in the past, and *un-* means "not" or "the opposite of." Teaching meaning-related words together will help children determine the meaning of new words and allow them to read with greater comprehension.

> **Teaching Routine**
>
> ## Word Parts Strategy
>
> - **Examine** a word for its word parts.
> - **Take off** first any prefixes and then any endings or suffixes.
> - **Determine** if the base word is known or can be decoded.
> - **Add back** the prefixes, endings, and suffixes and pronounce the word in sequence, part by part.

loud
loudly
louder
loudest

Fluency

What Is Fluency?

Fluency is the ability to read quickly and accurately. Fluency develops over time and with considerable practice. Fluent readers decode words automatically. This freedom from decoding allows them to concentrate on understanding their reading.

How Do I Help Children Become Fluent Readers?

You can develop children's fluency in two ways. First, **model fluent reading** to demonstrate the ways good readers read with accuracy, appropriate pace, attention to punctuation, and expression.

Second, have children engage in **repeated oral reading** as you monitor them and provide guidance and feedback. *Reading Street* provides explicit instruction for each of these key fluency skills.

In *Reading Street* you'll find a variety of methods to practice fluency. The lessons in the Teacher's Editions will help you establish fluency routines for oral rereading, paired reading, echo reading, choral reading, and Reader's Theater. Children can practice with you or an aide, other children, or even by themselves.

What Should Children Read to Develop Fluency?

Have children reread a variety of short texts that are relatively easy. The texts should be at their independent reading level, that is, readers should have a 95% success rate (misreading only about 1 in 20 words). When instructing children, you may use an instructional level text—a challenging but manageable text—with which children will have a 90% success rate (misreading only about 1 in 10 words). Text that is too difficult does not allow children to develop fluency or to experience success. *Reading Street* offers many materials that can be used for fluency practice: Student Editions, Decodable Practice Readers, Leveled Readers, and Audio CDs.

How Do I Monitor Progress in Fluency?

To assess children's fluency formally, take timed samples of their oral reading, measure words read correctly per minute, and set goals for progress. *Reading Street* provides weekly opportunities for fluency assessment, including benchmark goals for words correct per minute and a Fluency Assessment Plan that identifies which children to assess each week.

Fluency Is Important

A **fluent reader** reads accurately and quickly with expressiveness, stress, and intonation. This reader can also interpret text. **Fluent readers** can comprehend and decode at the same time. Without fluency, children are unable to comprehend what they have read.

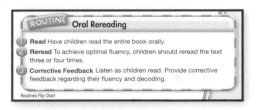

ROUTINE   Oral Rereading

1. **Read** Have children read the entire book orally.
2. **Reread** To achieve optimal fluency, children should reread the text three or four times.
3. **Corrective Feedback** Listen as children read. Provide corrective feedback regarding their fluency and decoding.

Routines Flip Chart

Decodable Practice Readers

- Practice phonics skills
- Blending practice
- Reread for fluency

"Children must have at least a basic vocabulary, a reasonable range of knowledge about the world around them, and the ability to talk about their knowledge." Anderson, R., E. Hiebert, J. Scott, and I. Wilkinson

Vocabulary

Vocabulary knowledge has been strongly correlated with reading comprehension in many studies. Research shows that oral vocabulary and reading vocabulary can be learned both directly and indirectly. Vocabulary is learned indirectly when children hear books read aloud, when they take part in conversations, and when they read. Direct instruction involves systematic teaching of specific words. Studies show that direct instruction in vocabulary leads to gains in reading comprehension.

How Do I Help Children Increase Their Oral Vocabulary?

In *Reading Street*, oral language is developed both directly and indirectly. A set of conceptually related "Amazing Words" is identified each week. These concept words are reviewed throughout the week, allowing children to encounter and use them frequently. An Oral Vocabulary Routine that includes multiple examples of each word's use is provided for direct instruction of these words.

In addition, daily Anchored Talk provides opportunities for children to use and apply oral vocabulary in focused discussions.

How Do I Help Children Increase Their Reading Vocabulary?

- Teach important selection words prior to reading and link them to children's reading. Encourage children to use the new vocabulary when they talk and write about the selection.

- Use graphic organizers to build concepts and vocabulary. Semantic webs are powerful ways to learn new words.

- Teach word learning strategies so children will become independent word learners. Instruct them in how to use dictionaries and other reference sources; how to use word parts, such as prefixes and suffixes, to determine word meanings; and how to use context to figure out meanings of unfamiliar words.

- Provide ongoing opportunities for children to read a wide variety of texts. The more children read, the more vocabulary they will learn.

Vocabulary Support
You may wish to explain the meaning of these words.
harvest gathering of plants grown for food
ignore pay no attention to

Comprehension

Why is comprehension important? It's the ultimate goal of your reading instruction. **Comprehension** is the process of making meaning from text. It involves not just reading words accurately, but drawing on prior knowledge, making inferences, making connections, and using strategies to make sense of text. In second grade, **comprehension skills and strategies** should be taught through both listening and reading.

Why Is Listening Comprehension Important?

Research has shown that instruction in listening comprehension transfers to reading comprehension. Even before children are able to read complex literature on their own, you can develop their higher-level thinking skills by using read-alouds and shared reading. *Scott Foresman Reading Street* has theme-related read-alouds and shared readings built into the program. All second-grade comprehension skills are introduced with text that is read aloud. Use this text to model the how good readers use comprehension skills and strategies.

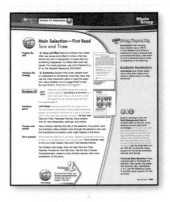

How Can I Help Children Develop Reading Comprehension?

Teachers who provide explicit comprehension instruction will see growth in children's progress and will increase children's enjoyment of reading. Effective instructional practices include

- **Explicit Teaching** Children must be taught what the skill or strategy is as well as when and how to use it.

- **Teacher Modeling** In *Scott Foresman Reading Street*, this is accomplished in think-alouds that appear in comprehension skill and strategy lessons.

- **Guided Practice** Guided comprehension practice appears in *Scott Foresman Reading Street* both during whole-group and small-group instruction.

- **Frequent Application of the Skill or Strategy** When reading occurs in small groups, teachers can guide children's application of skills and strategies and provide feedback to individuals.

- **Monitoring Progress** In second grade, this assessment can be done by having children retell stories or summarize the main ideas of expository text. Scoring rubrics for assessing retellings are provided with every selection in *Scott Foresman Reading Street*. A Retelling Plan suggests which children to assess each week.

Writing

Why Is Writing Instruction Valuable?

Writing and reading are closely connected. Teachers who spend time on focused writing instruction in second grade know that it plays a central role in early reading development.

How Can I Help Children Become Writers?

Just as with reading fluency, children need explicit and systematic instruction as well as considerable practice to become fluent writers. In *Reading Street* you will find daily writing instruction, and culminating unit activities that take children through the writing process.

As you guide children through the steps of these teaching methods, your role gradually decreases as children apply writing skills and strategies.

Weekly writing instruction features **mini-lessons** to help children learn about the key features of the product or form that is the weekly writing focus and the organizational patterns of that type of writing. Mini-lessons also focus on the writing traits and on writer's craft skills. Children learn through direct instruction and teacher-modeling. They then apply what they have learned in their own writing.

Helping children become fluent writers is an important part of the writing instruction in *Reading Street*. And the more children write, the better writers they become. A daily writing routine, **Quick Write for Fluency,** engages children in a short writing activity every day.

It is also important for children to learn the process of writing. Starting in Unit 1, there is a **writing process** lesson at the end of each unit. These lessons are carefully focused on teaching the process of writing: prewrite and plan, draft, revise, edit, and publish and present.

It's also important to prepare children for the future. In the middle of each unit, at the end of the first Teacher's Edition volume, you'll find a **21st Century Writing** project. These projects focus on new literacies and are dependent on the use of technology.

Help children generate ideas

Sharing the Writing

Think Aloud To plan a paragraph, the first thing we will do is choose a topic. Let's make a chart of rescue workers and the jobs they do. Display a T-chart. I'll start with *firefighters*.

Guide children in identifying rescue workers and the jobs they do. Possible ideas are shown. Record the responses, and keep the chart so that children can refer to it as they plan and draft their paragraphs.

Rescue Worker	Job
firefighters	save people and pets from fires save pets from dangerous places
animal rescue workers	help animals that are mistreated
police officers	rescue people in a car crash
ambulance drivers	help sick or injured people

Have each child choose a rescue worker for a narrative nonfiction paragraph. Circulate to guide them. Tell them to select a topic that is interesting to them.

How Do I Monitor Progress in Writing?

A rubric is often the best way to assess children's writing. A rubric is a guide for assessing a writing assignment. It describes the qualities of a good, average, and poor product along a scaled continuum. *Scott Foresman Reading Street* provides weekly rubrics that cover these writing traits: focus/ideas, word choice, organization, voice sentences, and rules of grammar and punctuation.

How Can I Help Children Develop Good Writing Traits?

Each week, you'll focus on a writing trait in *Scott Foresman Reading Street.* Your weekly instruction, which includes introducing the trait and providing modeling, strategies, and practice, is connected to the writing that children do during the Unit Writing Workshop.

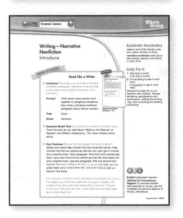

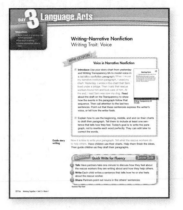

The Traits of Good Writing
Teach these writing traits to help children improve their writing:

1. **Focus** the writing on your main **ideas**.
2. **Organize** your ideas in the right order so your **paragraphs** make sense.
3. Show your **voice** in your writing. It's how you feel about your ideas.
4. **Choose words** that make your writing interesting.
5. Write so that your **sentences** make sense.
6. Use **conventions**, or correct rules of writing words and sentences.

The *Reading Street* Authors answer the most Frequently Asked Questions

Here's "the scoop" on *Reading Street!*

1. **What's the underlying "story" of *Reading Street?***
Reading Street provides explicit, systematic, high-quality instruction focusing on the five critical elements of reading identified by research: phonemic awareness, phonics, fluency, vocabulary, and text comprehension, as well as an emphasis on concept and oral language development.

2. **How is *Reading Street* different from other basal programs?**
Reading Street is built around the "Understanding by Design" model of instruction. Each unit focuses on a "big question" that connects reading, vocabulary, and writing for a full six weeks. Children expand their higher order thinking skills and conceptual understanding by exploring different aspects of the "big question" and a series of related sub-questions each week, creating a culture of engaging inquiry around ideas and texts.

3. **Is there a Spanish program? Are the same resources available in Spanish?**
Calle de la Lectura is *Reading Street's* fully aligned Spanish literacy system. It provides parallel Spanish instruction, as well as integrated language and concept development.

4. **How are the Student and Teacher's editions organized?**
Student Editions include six units of integrated reading, writing, skill, and vocabulary development organized under a unit concept. Weekly paired texts further develop each concept and are aligned to either Science or Social Studies.

Our Teacher's Editions have a unique delivery system of 12 slim, manageable volumes, allowing for greater pacing flexibility while keeping the integrity of our validated scope and sequence. Teachers will find opportunities to customize grade level lesson plans to serve all learners for both reading and language arts instruction.

5. **Is *Reading Street* for all students? What about below and above level learners, English Language Learners, and other learners?**
One of the key goals of *Reading Street* is to support and meet the individualized needs of all learners. Focused differentiated group work provides targeted and explicit instruction that helps all learners participate alongside their peers.

6. **Why is there a student book at Kindergarten?**
Young children respond to lively, interactive print materials as they are building a sense of themselves as readers and learners. *My Skills Buddy*, designed to be a companion to the classroom content, serves as a handbook children can visit to apply and practice newly acquired skills.

7. **How does *Reading Street* help teachers assess students?**
Reading Street's assessment plan helps teachers assess their students both formally and informally. Daily Success Predictors help teachers monitor priority skills by assessing predictors of reading success. Weekly Assessment Checkpoints provide a more formal way of identifying students' understanding of key concepts and skills.

8. **Are there digital resources that go with this program (or an online version)?**
Reading Street provides a robust digital path that aligns with each week of instruction. Digital components such as animations, songs, videos, and interactive games support instruction and make the content relevant, motivating, and accessible to all learners.

9. **What other products and support materials come with the program?**
Reading Street provides a wide array of text products, digital products, and interactive products that support the varying modalities and levels of all children.

Assessment on Reading Street

Assessment is not a destination when you teach. It's integrated all along the way so you can keep your second graders on the path to reading success.

With *Scott Foresman Reading Street*, you have assessment planning and tools at your fingertips. The **Section 3** overview shows how each type of assessment is ready for you to use when you need it. You'll see at a glance how you can make decisions about the focus, pacing, and grouping for your instruction throughout your lesson and week and at other key times through the year.

You'll also learn more about the assessment tools. They provide the data-driven instruction you need for your second graders on *Reading Street*.

When you continue the assessment process throughout the year, you effectively build on the knowledge these children had when they entered second grade. Then they're well on their way to becoming even more sophisticated readers.

Assessment and Grouping

What Makes Grouping and Assessment Effective?

At the beginning of the year, you want know your second graders' interests, learning styles, and academic needs. When you use the right assessments at the right times, you get to know children quickly. The next step, determining your groups for effective instruction, becomes easier. All along the way, you monitor children's progress and use that information to regroup them.

When and How Is It Best to Assess?

In order to know your second graders, you need critical information all through the year. This data comes through a 4-step process:

1. Diagnose and Differentiate
2. Monitor Progress
3. Assess and Regroup
4. Summative Assessment

1 Diagnose and Differentiate

At the beginning of the year, it is important to diagnose children's instructional needs. Use the Baseline Group Test or another initial placement test such as the DIBELS. Then you can plan your groups.

Why Is Diagnosing a Critical Step?

Diagnosis gives you a picture of where each child is at that moment. When you diagnose early, you have data to identify who is at risk of failing and needs extra support. It also helps you determine which children have not mastered the previous year's standards. You also find out who is performing on level or above level.

How Do I Provide Differentiated Instruction for Different Abilities?

After you diagnose, you can turn to *Scott Foresman Reading Street* for lessons and pacing designed for three levels.

If children assess at the **SI** level, use the regular instruction and the daily **Strategic Intervention** small group lessons.

If children assess at the **OL** level, use the regular instruction and the daily **On Level** small group lessons.

If children assess at the **A** level, use the regular instruction and the daily **Advanced** small group lessons.

The lessons focus on target strategies and skills as they help you offer intensive, explicit, and advanced instructional approaches. When it's time for children to read, you can match them to a wide array of books at their instructional and independent reading levels. With leveled books, children are continually challenged and engaged.

For more support for struggling readers, you can also use the Strategic Intervention lessons in the Teacher's Edition and the Reading Street Intervention Kit for children who need intensive intervention.

2 Monitor Progress

Each week you can assess at the lesson level by taking time to monitor targeted skills and strategy instruction. Using a variety of these "during-the-lesson" and weekly assessments, you are consistently aware of how children change and develop throughout the year. You are equipped with performance data so you can meet individual needs.

Scott Foresman Reading Street offers tools that allow you to pause for assessment at different critical points of instruction.

During lesson instruction, pause for spiral review and *if...,* *then...* suggestions. They help you quickly track children's understanding of key instruction. You can use Don't Wait Until Friday checklists to assess children's progress for word reading, retelling, fluency, and oral vocabulary. At various points during instruction, you can use Reader's and Writer's Notebook activities as assessment tools. When you determine that children are ready for comprehension and fluency assessment as they read new texts, assign Fresh Reads.

When you teach the weekly skills and strategies, you don't want to wait until the weekly tests on Friday, or even later, to find if your teaching has been effective for all children. An effective practice is to monitor children's progress at key times during the week. These informal assessments are guides that help you identify children who need extra support as well as those who will benefit from challenge activities.

③ Assess and Regroup

A clearer picture of each second grader is coming into focus as a result of your assessment throughout the weekly lessons. The initial groups you formed were based on data from diagnosis at the beginning of the year. As children change and develop throughout second grade, you will need to regroup them for differentiated instruction.

When Is It Best to Regroup? Regrouping is a part of the assessment process, so you rely on assessments to help you determine new groups. Recommendations in *Scott Foresman Reading Street* guide teachers to begin by recording the results of the Weekly Assessments. Then they use the data from retelling, phonics, and fluency to track progress. *Reading Street's* Unit Benchmark Test results are important to include. This summative assessment reveals how children are achieving mastery of the unit skills.

Other assessments, such as DIBELS, may recommend regrouping at other times during the year.

These assessments keep the goal of mastery reachable for all children because you quickly identify children in need of additional practice or reteaching. Responsive individual or group instruction will return children to on-level learning. Begin to think about regrouping as you near the end of the second unit of instruction, and then regroup for subsequent units.

④ Summative Assessment

At fixed times, you need to check children's progress toward skills and standards. These assessments show the effectiveness of your instruction.

The Unit Benchmark Tests measure children's mastery of target skills taught throughout the unit.

The End-of-Year test measures children's mastery of target skills taught throughout the six units of the program.

Grouping Throughout the Year	
Initial Grouping	Diagnose using the Baseline Group Test. Use the same groups for Units 1 and 2.
Regroup	for Unit 3
Regroup	for Unit 4
Regroup	for Unit 5
Regroup	for Unit 6

Teacher Form
Narrative Retelling Chart

Unit _____ Selection Title _____   Name _____   Date _____

Retelling Criteria/Teacher Prompt	Teacher-Aided Response	Student-Generated Response	Rubric Score (Circle one.)			
Connections Does this story remind you of anything else?			4	3	2	1
Author's Purpose Why do you think the author wrote this story? What was the author trying to tell us?			4	3	2	1
Characters What can you tell me about _____ (use character's name)?			4	3	2	1
Setting Where and when did the story happen?			4	3	2	1
Plot What happened in the story?			4	3	2	1

Summative Retelling Score   4   3   2   1

Comments _____

See also *Assessment Handbook* | © Pearson Education, Inc.

Teacher Form

Expository Summarizing Chart

Unit _____ Selection Title _____ Name _____ Date _____

Summarizing Criteria/Teacher Prompt	Teacher-Aided Response	Student-Generated Response	Rubric Score (Circle one.)			
Connections Did this selection make you think about something else you have read? What did you learn about as you read this selection?			4	3	2	1
Author's Purpose Why do you think the author wrote this selection?			4	3	2	1
Topic What was the selection mostly about?			4	3	2	1
Important Ideas What is important for me to know about _____ (topic)?			4	3	2	1
Conclusions What did you learn from reading this selection?			4	3	2	1

Summative Retelling Score 4 3 2 1

Comments _____

Monitoring Fluency
How to Measure Words Correct Per Minute—WCPM

Ongoing assessment of student reading fluency is one of the most valuable measures we have of childrens' reading skills. One of the most effective ways to assess fluency is taking timed samples of children's oral reading and measuring the number of words correct per minute (WCPM).

Choose A Text Start by choosing the appropriate week's fluency passage from the Teacher's Edition. Make a copy of the text for yourself and have one for the child.

Timed reading of the text Tell the child: *As you read this aloud, I want you to do your best reading and to read as quickly as you can. That doesn't mean it's a race. Just do your best, fast reading. When I say* begin, *start reading.* As the child reads, follow along in your copy. Mark words that are read incorrectly.

<u>Incorrect</u>	<u>Correct</u>
• omissions	• self-corrections within 3 seconds
• substitutions	• repeated words
• mispronunciations	
• reversals	

After one minute At the end of one minute, draw a line after the last word that was read. Have the child finish reading but don't count any words beyond one minute. Arrive at the words correct per minute—WCPM—by counting the total number of words that the child read correctly in one minute.

FLUENCY GOALS	
Grade 2 End-of-Year Goal = 90 WCPM	
Target goals by unit	
Unit 1 50 to 60 WCPM	**Unit 4** 74 to 84 WCPM
Unit 2 58 to 68 WCPM	**Unit 5** 82 to 92 WCPM
Unit 3 66 to 76 WCPM	**Unit 6** 90 to 100 WCPM

More frequent monitoring You may want to monitor some children more frequently because they are falling far below grade-level benchmarks or they have a result that doesn't seem to align with their previous performance. Follow the same steps above, but choose 2 or 3 additional texts at their independent reading level.

Fluency Progress Chart Copy the chart on the next page. Use it to record each child's progress across the year.

See also *Assessment Handbook* | © Pearson Education, Inc.

Fluency Progress Chart, Grade 2

Name _____

WCPM

| | 125 | 120 | 115 | 110 | 105 | 100 | 95 | 90 | 85 | 80 | 75 | 70 | 65 | 60 | 55 | 50 | 45 | 40 | 35 | 30 |

| 1 | 2 | 3 | 4 | 5 | 6 | 7 | 8 | 9 | 10 | 11 | 12 | 13 | 14 | 15 | 16 | 17 | 18 | 19 | 20 | 21 | 22 | 23 | 24 | 25 | 26 | 27 | 28 | 29 | 30 | 31 | 32 | 33 | 34 | 35 | 36 |

Timed Reading/Week

Name _____

Sentence Reading Chart

USE WITH GRADE 2 UNIT 1

	Phonics		High-Frequency		Reteach	Reassess: Words Correct
	Total Words	Words Correct	Total Words	Words Correct	✔	
Week 1 *The Twin Club*						
Short Vowels and Consonants	56					
High-Frequency Words				6		
Week 2 *Exploring Space with an Astronaut*						
Long Vowels (vowel_e)	21					
High-Frequency Words				7		
Week 3 *Henry and Mudge and the Starry Night*						
Consonant Blends	14					
High-Frequency Words				7		
Week 4 *A Walk in the Desert*						
Inflected Endings -s, -ed, -ing	12					
High-Frequency Words				6		
Week 5 *The Strongest One*						
Consonant Digraphs	21					
High-Frequency Words				7		
Unit Scores	124		33			

- **RECORD SCORES** Use this chart to record scores for the Day 5 Sentence Reading Assessment.

- **RETEACH PHONICS SKILLS** If the child is unable to read all the tested phonics words, then reteach the phonics skills using the Reteach lessons in *First Stop*.

- **PRACTICE HIGH-FREQUENCY WORDS** If the child is unable to read all the tested high-frequency words, then provide additional practice for the week's words.

- **REASSESS** Use two different sentences for reassessment.

See also Assessment Handbook | © Pearson Education, Inc.

Name _____

Sentence Reading Chart

	Phonics		High-Frequency		Reteach	Reassess:
	Total Words	Words Correct	Total Words	Words Correct	✔	Words Correct
Week 1 *Tara and Tiree, Fearless Friends*						
r-Controlled *ar, or, ore, oar*	12					
High-Frequency Words			6			
Week 2 *Abraham Lincoln*						
Contractions *n't, 's, 'll, 'm*	14					
High-Frequency Words			7			
Week 3 *Scarcity*						
r-Controlled *er, ir, ur*	12					
High-Frequency Words			6			
Week 4 *The Bremen Town Musicians*						
Plurals *-s, -es, -ies*	14					
High-Frequency Words			7			
Week 5 *One Good Turn Deserves Another*						
Long *a: a, ai, ay*	14					
High-Frequency Words			7			
Unit Scores	66		33			

- **RECORD SCORES** Use this chart to record scores for the Day 5 Sentence Reading Assessment.

- **RETEACH PHONICS SKILLS** If the child is unable to read all the tested phonics words, then reteach the phonics skills using the Reteach lessons in *First Stop*.

- **PRACTICE HIGH-FREQUENCY WORDS** If the child is unable to read all the tested high-frequency words, then provide additional practice for the week's words.

- **REASSESS** Use two different sentences for reassessment.

Sentence Reading Chart

USE WITH GRADE 2 UNIT 3

	Phonics		High-Frequency		Reteach	Reassess: Words Correct
	Total Words	Words Correct	Total Words	Words Correct	✔	
Week 1 *Pearl and Wagner: Two Good Friends*						
Long *e: e, ee, ea, y*	21					
High-Frequency Words			7			
Week 2 *Dear Juno*						
Long *o: o, oa, ow*	21					
High-Frequency Words			7			
Week 3 *Anansi Goes Fishing*						
Compound Words	14					
High-Frequency Words			7			
Week 4 *Rosa and Blanca*						
Long *i: i, ie, igh, y*	14					
High-Frequency Words			7			
Week 5 *A Weed Is a Flower*						
Comparative Endings *-er, -est*	14					
High-Frequency Words			7			
Unit Scores	84		35			

See also Assessment Handbook | © Pearson Education, Inc.

- **RECORD SCORES** Use this chart to record scores for the Day 5 Sentence Reading Assessment.

- **RETEACH PHONICS SKILLS** If the child is unable to read all the tested phonics words, then reteach the phonics skills using the Reteach lessons in *First Stop*.

- **PRACTICE HIGH-FREQUENCY WORDS** If the child is unable to read all the tested high-frequency words, then provide additional practice for the week's words.

- **REASSESS** Use two different sentences for reassessment.

Sentence Reading Chart

USE WITH GRADE 2 UNIT 4

	Phonics		Reteach	Reassess: Words Correct
	Total Words	Words Correct	✔	
Week 1 *A Froggy Fable*				
Syllables C + *le*	12			
Week 2 *Life Cycle of a Pumpkin*				
Vowels *oo, u*	12			
Week 3 *Soil*				
Diphthongs /ou/*ou, ow*, /oi/*oi, oy*	18			
Week 4 *The Night the Moon Fell*				
Syllable Patterns	18			
Week 5 *The First Tortilla*				
Vowels *oo, ue, ew, ui*	19			
Unit Scores	79			

See also *Assessment Handbook* | © Pearson Education, Inc.

- **RECORD SCORES** Use this chart to record scores for the Day 5 Sentence Reading Assessment.

- **RETEACH PHONICS SKILLS** If the child is unable to read all the tested phonics words, then reteach the phonics skills using the Reteach lessons in *First Stop*.

- **REASSESS** Use two different sentences for reassessment.

Name _____

Sentence Reading Chart

USE WITH GRADE 2 UNIT 5

| | Phonics | | Reteach | Reassess: |
	Total Words	Words Correct	✔	Words Correct
Week 1 *Firefighter!*				
Suffixes *-ly, -ful, -er, -or, -ish*	18			
Week 2 *Carl the Complainer*				
Prefixes *un-, re-, pre-, dis-*	12			
Week 3 *Bad Dog, Dodger!*				
Silent Consonants *kn, wr, gn, mb*	12			
Week 4 *Horace and Morris but mostly Dolores*				
ph, gh, ck, ng	12			
Week 5 *The Signmaker's Assistant*				
Vowels *aw, au, augh, al*	12			
Unit Scores	66			

- **RECORD SCORES** Use this chart to record scores for the Day 5 Sentence Reading Assessment.

- **RETEACH PHONICS SKILLS** If the child is unable to read all the tested phonics words, then reteach the phonics skills using the Reteach lessons in *First Stop*.

- **REASSESS** Use two different sentences for reassessment.

See also Assessment Handbook | © Pearson Education, Inc.

Sentence Reading Chart

USE WITH GRADE 2 UNIT 6

	Phonics		Reteach	Reassess: Words Correct
	Total Words	Words Correct	✔	
Week 1 *Just Like Josh Gibson*				
Inflected Endings	12			
Week 2 *Red, White and Blue: The Story of the American Flag*				
Abbreviations	12			
Week 3 *A Birthday Basket for Tía*				
Syllables *-tion, -ture, -ion*	12			
Week 4 *Cowboys*				
Suffixes *-ness, -less, -able, -ible*	12			
Week 5 *Grace For President*				
Prefixes *mis-, micro-, mid-, non-*	12			
Unit Scores	60			

- **RECORD SCORES** Use this chart to record scores for the Day 5 Sentence Reading Assessment.

- **RETEACH PHONICS SKILLS** If the child is unable to read all the tested phonics words, then reteach the phonics skills using the Reteach lessons in *First Stop*.

- **REASSESS** Use two different sentences for reassessment.

Unit 1
Assess and Regroup

FYI In Grade 2 there are opportunities for regrouping every five weeks—at the end of Units 2, 3, 4, and 5. These options offer sensitivity to each child's progress, although some teachers may prefer to regroup less frequently.

Regroup at the End of Unit 2
Regrouping is not recommended at this time. Record children's Unit 1 scores to inform regrouping decisions at the end of Unit 2. At that time, consider children's scores for
- Unit 1 Sentence Reading (Day 5 Assessments)
- Fluency (WCPM)
- Unit 1 Benchmark Test

Group Time

On-Level

Children's performance is On-Level if they
- score 80% or better on their cumulative Unit Scores for Sentence Reading for phonics and high-frequency words
- meet the current benchmark for fluency (50–60 WCPM), reading On-Level text such as Student Edition selections
- score 66% or better on the Unit 1 Benchmark Test
- are capable of working in the On-Level group based on teacher judgment

Strategic Intervention

Children's performance is Below Level if they
- score 60% or lower on their cumulative Unit Scores for Sentence Reading for phonics and high-frequency words, regardless of their fluency scores
- do not meet the current benchmark for fluency (50–60 WCPM)
- score below 80% on their cumulative Unit Scores for Sentence Reading for phonics and high-frequency words AND have fluency scores below the current benchmark of 50–60 WCPM
- score below 66% on the Unit 1 Benchmark Test
- are struggling to keep up with the On-Level group based on teacher judgment

Advanced

Children's performance is Advanced if they
- score 100% on their cumulative Unit Scores for Sentence Reading for phonics and high-frequency words
- score 91% or better on the Unit 1 Benchmark Test
- read above grade-level material (50–60 WCPM) with speed, accuracy, and expression. You may try them out on one of the Advanced Selections.
- use expansive vocabulary and ease of language in retelling
- are capable of handling the problem solving and the investigative work of the Advanced group based on teacher judgment

Questions to Consider

- What types of test questions did the child miss? Are they specific to a particular skill or strategy?
- Does the child have adequate background knowledge to understand the test passages or selections for retelling?

- Has the child's performance met expectations for daily lessons and assessments with little or no reteaching?
- Is the child performing more like children in another group?
- Does the child read for enjoyment, different purposes, and with varied interests?

Benchmark Fluency Scores
Mid-Year Goal: 50–60 WCPM
End-of-Year Goal: 90 WCPM

Unit 2
Assess and Regroup

FYI In Grade 2 there are opportunities for regrouping every five weeks—at the end of Units 2, 3, 4, and 5. These options offer sensitivity to each child's progress, although some teachers may prefer to regroup less frequently.

Regroup for Unit 3

To make regrouping decisions at the end of Unit 2, consider children's end-of-unit scores for

- Units 1 and 2 Sentence Reading (Day 5 Assessments)
- Fluency (WCPM)
- Units 1 and 2 Benchmark Tests

Group Time

On-Level

To continue On-Level or to move into the On-Level group, children should

- score 80% or better on their cumulative Units 1 and 2 Scores for Sentence Reading for phonics and high-frequency words
- meet the current benchmark for fluency (58–68 WCPM), reading On-Level text such as Student Edition selections
- score 66% or better on the Units 1 and 2 Benchmark Tests
- be capable of working in the On-Level group based on teacher judgment

Strategic Intervention

Children would benefit from Strategic Intervention if they

- score 60% or lower on their cumulative Units 1 and 2 Scores for Sentence Reading for phonics and high-frequency words, regardless of their fluency scores
- do not meet the current benchmark for fluency (58–68 WCPM)
- score below 80% on their cumulative Units 1 and 2 Scores for Sentence Reading for phonics and high-frequency words AND have fluency scores below the current benchmark of 58–68 WCPM
- score below 66% on the Units 1 and 2 Benchmark Tests
- are struggling to keep up with the On-Level group based on teacher judgment

Advanced

To move to the Advanced group, children should

- score 100% on their cumulative Units 1 and 2 Scores for Sentence Reading for phonics and high-frequency words
- score 91% or better on the Units 1 and 2 Benchmark Tests
- read above grade-level material (58–68 WCPM) with speed, accuracy, and expression. You may try them out on one of the Advanced Selections.
- use expansive vocabulary and ease of language in retelling
- be capable of handling the problem solving and the investigative work of the Advanced group based on teacher judgment

Questions to Consider

- What types of test questions did the child miss? Are they specific to a particular skill or strategy?
- Does the child have adequate background knowledge to understand the test passages or selections for retelling?

- Has the child's performance met expectations for daily lessons and assessments with little or no reteaching?
- Is the child performing more like children in another group?
- Does the child read for enjoyment, different purposes, and with varied interests?

Benchmark Fluency Scores
Mid-Year Goal: 58–68 WCPM
End-of-Year Goal: 90 WCPM

Unit 3
Assess and Regroup

FYI In Grade 2 there are opportunities for regrouping every five weeks—at the end of Units 2, 3, 4, and 5. These options offer sensitivity to each child's progress although some teachers may prefer to regroup less frequently.

Regroup for Unit 4
To make regrouping decisions at the end of Unit 3, consider children's end-of-unit scores for
- Unit 3 Sentence Reading (Day 5 Assessments)
- Fluency (WCPM)
- Unit 3 Benchmark Test

Group Time

On-Level	Strategic Intervention	Advanced
To continue On-Level or to move into the On-Level group, children should - score 80% or better on their cumulative Unit Scores for Sentence Reading for phonics and high-frequency words - meet the current benchmark for fluency (66–76 WCPM), reading On-Level text such as Student Edition selections - score 66% or better on the Unit 3 Benchmark Test - be capable of working in the On-Level group based on teacher judgment	Children would benefit from Strategic Intervention if they - score 60% or lower on their cumulative Unit Scores for Sentence Reading for phonics and high-frequency words, regardless of their fluency scores - do not meet the current benchmark for fluency (66–76 WCPM) - score below 80% on their cumulative Unit Scores for Sentence Reading for phonics and high-frequency words AND have fluency scores below the current benchmark of 66–76 WCPM - score below 66% on the Unit 3 Benchmark Test - are struggling to keep up with the On-Level group based on teacher judgment	To move to the Advanced group, children should - score 100% on their cumulative Unit Scores for Sentence Reading for phonics and high-frequency words - score 91% or better on the Unit 3 Benchmark Test - read above grade-level material (66–76 WCPM) with speed, accuracy, and expression. You may try them out on one of the Advanced Selections. - use expansive vocabulary and ease of language in retelling - be capable of handling the problem solving and the investigative work of the Advanced group based on teacher judgment

Questions to Consider
- What types of test questions did the child miss? Are they specific to a particular skill or strategy?
- Does the child have adequate background knowledge to understand the test passages or selections for retelling?

- Has the child's performance met expectations for daily lessons and assessments with little or no reteaching?
- Is the child performing more like children in another group?
- Does the child read for enjoyment, different purposes, and with varied interests?

Benchmark Fluency Scores
Mid-Year Goal: 66–76 WCPM
End-of-Year Goal: 90 WCPM

Unit 4
Assess and Regroup

FYI In Grade 2 there are opportunities for regrouping every five weeks—at the end of Units 2, 3, 4, and 5. These options offer sensitivity to each child's progress although some teachers may prefer to regroup less frequently.

Regroup for Unit 5

To make regrouping decisions at the end of Unit 4, consider children's end-of-unit scores for

- Unit 4 Sentence Reading (Day 5 Assessments)
- Fluency (WCPM)
- Unit 4 Benchmark Test

Group Time

On-Level	Strategic Intervention	Advanced
To continue On-Level or to move into the On-Level group, children should	Children would benefit from Strategic Intervention if they	To move to the Advanced group, children should
• score 80% or better on their cumulative Unit Scores for Sentence Reading for phonics and high-frequency words	• score 60% or lower on their cumulative Unit Scores for Sentence Reading for phonics and high-frequency words, regardless of their fluency scores	• score 100% on their cumulative Unit Scores for Sentence Reading for phonics and high-frequency words
• meet the current benchmark for fluency (74–84 WCPM), reading On-Level text such as Student Edition selections	• do not meet the current benchmark for fluency (74–84 WCPM)	• score 91% or better on the Unit 4 Benchmark Test
• score 66% or better on the Unit 4 Benchmark Test	• score below 66% on their cumulative Unit Scores for Sentence Reading for phonics and high-frequency words AND have fluency scores below the current benchmark of 74–84 WCPM	• read above grade-level material (74–84 WCPM) with speed, accuracy, and expression. You may try them out on one of the Advanced Selections.
• be capable of working in the On-Level group based on teacher judgment	• score below 60% on the Unit 4 Benchmark Test	• use expansive vocabulary and ease of language in retelling.
	• are struggling to keep up with the On-Level group based on teacher judgment	• be capable of handling the problem solving and the investigative work of the Advanced group based on teacher judgment

Questions to Consider

- What types of test questions did the child miss? Are they specific to a particular skill or strategy?
- Does the child have adequate background knowledge to understand the test passages or selections for retelling?
- Has the child's performance met expectations for daily lessons and assessments with little or no reteaching?
- Is the child performing more like children in another group?
- Does the child read for enjoyment, different purposes, and with varied interests?

Benchmark Fluency Scores
Mid-Year Goal: 74–84 WCPM
End-of-Year Goal: 90 WCPM

Unit 5
Assess and Regroup

FYI In Grade 2 there are opportunities for regrouping every five weeks—at the end of Units 2, 3, 4, and 5. These options offer sensitivity to each child's progress, although some teachers may prefer to regroup less frequently.

Regroup for Unit 6
To make regrouping decisions at the end of Unit 5, consider children's end-of-unit scores for
- Unit 5 Sentence Reading (Day 5 Assessments)
- Fluency (WCPM)
- Unit 5 Benchmark Test

Group Time

On-Level	Strategic Intervention	Advanced
To continue On-Level or to move into the On-Level group, children should • score 80% or better on their cumulative Unit Scores for Sentence Reading for phonics and lesson vocabulary • meet the current benchmark for fluency (82–92 WCPM), reading On-Level text such as Student Edition selections • score 66% or better on the Unit 5 Benchmark Test • be capable of working in the On-Level group based on teacher judgment	Children would benefit from Strategic Intervention if they • score 60% or lower on their cumulative Unit Scores for Sentence Reading for phonics and lesson vocabulary, regardless of their fluency scores • do not meet the current benchmark for fluency (82–92 WCPM) • score below 80% on their cumulative Unit Scores for Sentence Reading for phonics and lesson vocabulary AND have fluency scores below the current benchmark of 82–92 WCPM • score below 66% on the Unit 5 Benchmark Test • are struggling to keep up with the On-Level group based on teacher judgment	To move to the Advanced group, children should • score 100% on their cumulative Unit Scores for Sentence Reading for phonics and lesson vocabulary • score 91% or better on the Unit 5 Benchmark Test • read above grade-level material (82–92 WCPM) with speed, accuracy, and expression. You may try them out on one of the Advanced Selections. • use expansive vocabulary and ease of language in retelling • be capable of handling the problem solving and the investigative work of the Advanced group based on teacher judgment

Questions to Consider
- What types of test questions did the child miss? Are they specific to a particular skill or strategy?
- Does the child have adequate background knowledge to understand the test passages or selections for retelling?
- Has the child's performance met expectations for daily lessons and assessments with little or no reteaching?
- Is the child performing more like children in another group?
- Does the child read for enjoyment, different purposes, and with varied interests?

Benchmark Fluency Scores
Mid-Year Goal: 82–92 WCPM
End-of-Year Goal: 90 WCPM

Unit 6
Assess and Regroup

FYI In Grade 2 there are opportunities for regrouping every five weeks—at the end of Units 2, 3, 4, and 5. These options offer sensitivity to each child's progress although some teachers may prefer to regroup less frequently.

End-of-Year Performance

There is no need to regroup at the end of Unit 6. To assess children's end-of-year performance, consider their scores for

- Unit 6 Sentence Reading (Day 5 Assessments)
- Fluency (wcpm)
- Unit 6 Benchmark Test

Group Time

On-Level	Strategic Intervention	Advanced
Children's performance is On-Level if they	Children's performance is below level if they	Children's performance is advanced if they
• score 80% or better on their cumulative Unit Scores for Sentence Reading for phonics and lesson vocabulary	• score 60% or lower on their cumulative Unit Scores for Sentence Reading for phonics and lesson vocabulary, regardless of their fluency scores	• score 100% on their cumulative Unit Scores for Sentence Reading for phonics and lesson vocabulary
• meet the current benchmark for fluency (90–100 wcpm), reading On-Level text such as Student Edition selections	• do not meet the current benchmark for fluency (90–100 wcpm)	• score 91% or better on the Unit 6 Benchmark Test
• score 66% or better on the Unit 6 Benchmark Test	• score below 80% on their cumulative Unit Scores for Sentence Reading for phonics and lesson vocabulary AND have fluency scores below the current benchmark of 90–100 wcpm	• read above grade-level material (90–100 wcpm) with speed, accuracy, and expression. You may try them out on one of the Advanced Selections.
• are capable of working in the On-Level group based on teacher judgment	• score below 66% on the Unit 6 Benchmark Test	• use expansive vocabulary and ease of language in retelling
	• are struggling to keep up with the On-Level group based on teacher judgment	• are capable of handling the problem solving and the investigative work of the Advanced group based on teacher judgment

Questions to Consider

- What types of test questions did the child miss? Are they specific to a particular skill or strategy?
- Does the child have adequate background knowledge to understand the test passages or selections for retelling?

- Has the child's performance met expectations for daily lessons and assessments with little or no reteaching?
- Is the child performing more like children in another group?
- Does the child read for enjoyment, different purposes, and with varied interests?

Benchmark Fluency Scores
Mid-Year Goal: 90–100 wcpm
End-of-Year Goal: 90 wcpm

Writing
on Reading Street

Children in second grade are learning to communicate now—in a century that continually sends messages in new ways.

Section 4 provides ways that you can help children write their messages in a variety of forms and for purposes that reflect the world they'll grow into.

You'll discover effective ways to lead Writer's Workshops and to conference with them about their writing. You'll also find how to evaluate children's writing using the Writing Rubrics and Anchor Papers. Customized Writing approaches are infused throughout *Scott Foresman Reading Street.*

When children delight in stories and gain a sense of wonder from nonfiction, they want to communicate these reactions. You can help them write about it as you guide them on the bridge from reading to writing.

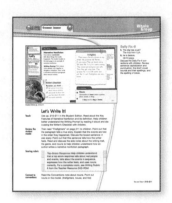

Writing on *Reading Street*

Writing instruction on *Reading Street* emphasizes the reciprocal nature of reading and writing. Writing instruction integrates the skills and knowledge that children learn and practice as they read and helps children apply those skills and that knowledge in their writing. The instruction is also designed to give the teacher as much support as possible for teaching writing.

Read Like a Writer

Mentor Text The wonderful literature in the Student Editions and the Big Books are used as mentor text in the writing instruction. Not only do children examine the literature for the key features of the genre, but they also look at how the authors choose words and construct sentences. Mentor text is a cornerstone of the writing instruction on *Reading Street*.

Interact with Text In addition to examining mentor text, children also interact with model text. These models exemplify the features of good writing. Children might be asked to find and circle the time and order words in a piece of model text. Or they might be asked to highlight the main idea and number the supporting details. This interaction with text gives children a hands-on learning experience.

Weekly Writing

Writing Forms and Patterns In their weekly writing, children focus on a different product each week. Instruction focuses on the organizational patterns of that product or writing form. For example:
Writing Product/Form: Instructions
Organizational Pattern: Sequence

Mini-Lessons Daily 5- to 10-minute mini-lessons help children learn about the craft of writing and writing traits. Each weekly lesson focuses on one writing trait and one or two aspects of the writer's craft.

Writing Process

Six writing process lessons provide structure to help children learn the process of writing. These lessons are designed for flexible use by the teacher. For example, if a teacher likes to organize writing time as a Writing Workshop, the writing process lessons will work with the Writing Workshop approach. Also, 1-week and 2-week pacing plans allow teachers to customize the lessons to fit the needs of their own classrooms.

21st Century Writing Projects

Structured as collaborative writing process lessons, children write, process, and organize information using the Internet and other electronic resources. The 21st Century Writing Projects

- integrate traditional literacies and new literacies.
- foster authentic communication.
- focus critical thinking on real-life applications.
- encourage creativity and innovation.

There are six 21st Century Writing Projects in second grade. The second-grade projects are:

- Keyboarding—children do small writing projects while learning to use the keyboard and the mouse.
- Electronic Pen Pals—children exchange e-mails with an older grade in their school.
- Story Starter—from a story starter, children use a word processing program to create a class story.
- E-Newsletter—children create a class newsletter using one of a variety of electronic platforms.
- Community Interview—children interview school workers and others in their community and compile these into a presentation.
- Blogging—children create a class blog about traditions.

Internet Guy
Don Leu

New Literacies

New literacies are especially important to the effective use of content area information on the Internet. They allow us to identify important questions, navigate complex information networks to locate appropriate information, critically evaluate that information, synthesize it to address those questions, and then communicate the answers to others. These five functions help define the new literacies that your students need to be successful with the Internet and other information and communication technologies.

Teacher Conferencing

Conferencing with children is an important part of writing instruction. The writing conference gives you the opportunity to assess how each child's writing is progressing. This program encourages teachers to conference with children on a regular basis. We do understand that conferencing is difficult to manage when you have a whole classroom full of children.

Managing Writing Conferences It is certainly beneficial to conference with every child every week, but that's not very realistic, is it? These tips can help manage writing conferences in your classroom.

- **Individual Conferences** Limit the time of each writing conference to three to five minutes and keep it positive. Try to meet with a few children every day. Ask questions that prompt children to talk to you about their writing. For example:
    Tell me about what you have written.
    What part is your favorite?
    What do you need help with?
    What else can you say about this part?
    I really liked the part where you . . .

- **Fishbowl Conference** When you can't confer with every child, a "fishbowl conference" with one willing child can allow others to observe, listen, and explore how to appropriately respond to others' writing. It's important to focus on what the child is doing well and how a draft might be revised and improved.

Write Guy
Jeff Anderson

Conferencing Is Listening

Conferring about children's writing is more about teachers *listening* than teachers speaking. What is the child thinking or trying to say? What help does he or she need? We can ask questions to keep kids speaking. "What do you want your reader to know? Wow, how did you think of this vivid phrase?"

Peer Conferencing

Peer conferencing is an important part of the writing process. It gets children actively involved in their own writing and the writing of others. Although second graders may not be ready to conference right at the beginning of the year, we encourage weekly peer conferencing as soon as they are ready. Remember that it is very important to take time to teach children how to respond to their peer's writing.

- The Fishbowl Conference, where you as the teacher model a conference with a child, is a good way to model a meaningful conversation about writing.

- To get Peer Conferences started, have the children pair up and exchange papers. Have Child 1 read Child 2's paper aloud. Then have Child 1 respond.

- When Child 1 is responding to Child 2's writing, Child 1 should focus on two things:
  Compliments—What did you really like about what your friend wrote? Why did you like it?
  Questions—What would you like to ask the writer?

- Give Child 2 a chance to respond to any questions asked by Child 1 and to ask additional questions to clarify or focus the comments on the writing.

- Then switch.

Remember that peer conferencing is difficult for children. They may not feel confident in their ability to respond to their peers. They may not be able to accept feedback from their peers gracefully. That's why it is really important that you teach and model for children how to conference on writing.

Write Guy
Jeff Anderson

The Sunny Side

I like to look for what's *right* in children's writing rather than focusing on things that need to be edited or fixed. It's important that as we teach children how to peer conference, we also encourage them to focus on the positive. Most children don't write flawlessly—who does? However, they will learn what they are doing well if we point it out.

Evaluating Writing

Reading Street provides tools to help as you evaluate children's writing. A well-done evaluation of a child's writing:

- provides feedback to children about the strengths of what they have written.
- provides guidance on areas for improvement.
- puts primary emphasis on the content and structure of the writing, while not ignoring conventions and mechanics.

Writing Rubrics

Each writing lesson includes a top-score rubric to help you evaluate children's writing based on writing traits. There are full rubrics available also. The rubrics are intended to help you discern the differences between different levels of writing.

Writing Rubrics and Anchor Papers

This product provides four student models for each of the writing process lessons in second grade. Models are written by real second-grade children. Each writing model is evaluated using the writing rubric from the lesson. Narrative is provided to explain how the score was decided for each anchor paper.

In addition, this product includes additional writing rubrics, so if you use a 6-point, 5-point, or 3-point evaluation system, we have rubrics for you to use to evaluate all student writing.

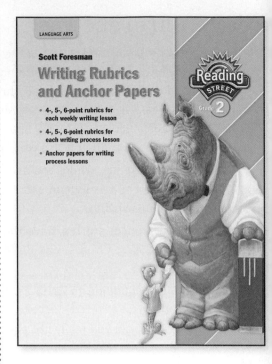

LANGUAGE ARTS

Scott Foresman

Writing Rubrics and Anchor Papers

Reading STREET
Grade 2

- 4-, 5-, 6-point rubrics for each weekly writing lesson
- 4-, 5-, 6-point rubrics for each writing process lesson
- Anchor papers for writing process lessons

Differentiate Instruction
on Reading Street

Some children won't get near a swimming pool without a flotation device. Others dive right in, but need coaching to learn good swimming technique. At school, children need different kinds of support as well.

Section 5 explains the multiple options for differentiating instruction in *Scott Foresman Reading Street*.

- Strategic Intervention

- On-Level

- Advanced

- English Language Learners

Academic success depends on learning to read well. In turn, learning to read well depends on rich language knowledge. In this section, you'll see how the program's plans for small groups are carefully designed so that all children reach high and experience an increasingly rich language environment.

Differentiated Instruction for Group Time

How Can I Use Flexible Groups for Instruction?

The Baseline Group Test, published by Scott Foresman, will help identify children's needs at the beginning of the year. Throughout the year, use the results of regular progress monitoring to make regrouping decisions.

Reading Street provides weekly plans and daily lessons for these types of small group instruction: Strategic Intervention, On-level, Advanced, and English Language Learners. Keep flexible groups small with no more than five children per group.

SI Strategic Intervention

OL On-Level

A Advanced

ELL English Language Learners

Reading Street follows the Response to Intervention model (RTI) to help you reach your goal of meeting the instructional needs of all children. It offers a process that monitors children's progress throughout the year so you can support on-level and advanced children and identify struggling readers early. More support is in the Response to Intervention Kit, which addresses the five core areas of reading instruction: phonemic awareness, phonics, fluency, vocabulary, and comprehension. As you work with struggling readers in small groups, you can use the kit for additional teacher modeling, more scaffolding, and multiple opportunities for practice. You have the strategies and tools you need to prevent these children from falling behind.

How Do I Use Practice Stations to Manage Small Groups?

During group time, children will need independent literacy activities to complete while you meet with small groups. Paired reading for fluency practice, journal writing, and activities at practice stations are all good activities for this time. The weekly Differentiated Instruction pages in each Teacher's Edition tell you where to find instruction for each group and provides *If . . . Then . . .* activities to support individual children.

Spend time at the beginning of the year coaching children on how to take responsibility for completing their independent work. Establish expectations, routines, and rules. Discuss rules with children and post them. Make sure children know what to do if they run out of materials or finish early. Support them in solving problems that may arise during this time.

The Scott Foresman Reading Street Practice Stations Kit contains grade level Practice Stations Flipcharts and a Management Handbook that includes lesson-specific reproducible work plans for children.

The Practice Stations Kit provides suggestions for six practice stations each week. The station activities support the week's skills and expand the week's concepts. Informal, ongoing assessments are an important means of guiding classroom instruction, and station activities provide excellent opportunities for ongoing assessments. Rubrics, portfolios, and other informal observation ideas are included in the Practice Stations Kit.

Differentiated Instruction for Strategic Intervention

Identifying your second graders who need intervention is essential. Reading accomplishments in second grade set the stage for much of the learning that follows. Observe children who are at risk of problems in learning to read and plan early for intervention. These children will exhibit one or more of these characteristics:

- **Lack of phonemic awareness.** Phonemic awareness in children entering second grade is a strong predictor of later reading ability. It has been found that deficits in phonological abilities are the basis of some reading disabilities. Explicit, intense phonological training should be part of any preventive or remedial program for children who are at-risk for reading problems.

- **Difficulties in mapping speech to print.** Children may struggle when applying sound-spelling meanings to printed words. Providing children with intensive, systematic, explicit instruction in word analysis along with additional practice and teacher feedback are essential components of *Reading Street*.

- **Lack of fluency in reading connected text.** Poor decoding skills lead to an inability to read accurately, fluently, and with expression. Repeated reading and other methods for improving fluency are especially important for struggling readers.

How Can I Help Children with a Very Low Reading Ability?

Some children come to second grade reading at a lower level than other children in the Strategic Intervention group. To provide them additional support in skills and concepts, the Small Group Instruction lessons for Strategic Intervention include the Concept Literacy Leveled Readers. Each book is written at a lower level than the Below-Level Reader for the week. The books align with the weekly concepts in each unit and provide struggling readers with a way to practice independent reading as they build understanding and develop concept knowledge. The Concept Literacy Readers play a role in the instruction for the Strategic Intervention group, but they can be used for independent reading practice for any struggling reader.

As necessary, use a variety of approaches and equipment aids in your classroom. They'll allow all children to succeed using *Reading Street*.

What Is Strategic Intervention?

Scott Foresman Reading Street integrates into the core program daily extra support strategies for strategic intervention—the differentiated instruction that children who are struggling need. You have comprehensive guidance and effective, efficient, and explicit instruction for readers who struggle. This extra support includes

- materials to reinforce and extend the daily lessons.
- instructional opportunities to increase background knowledge and reteach prerequisite skills.
- preteaching and reteaching of lesson skills.
- additional practice in key skills and strategies taught in the lesson.
- additional opportunities for vocabulary and concept development.
- more frequent opportunities to read and respond with teacher feedback.
- additional opportunities for checking understanding.

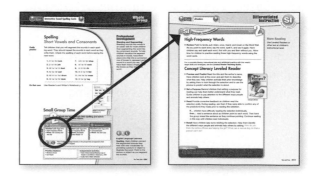

Differentiated Instruction for Advanced Learners

How Do Advanced Learners Differ from Other Learners?

Research suggests that advanced learners learn faster, identify and solve problems more easily, and understand and make connections among abstract concepts. Advanced readers show these characteristics:

- They enjoy reading. They read for knowledge and seek depth and complexity in their reading. They tend to prefer nonfiction and pursue interest-based reading opportunities.

- They read early and above-level. These learners read at least one-and-a-half to two grade levels above their chronological grade placement.

- They have advanced processing skills in reading. They retain large amounts of information and analyze and synthesize ideas quickly.

- They have advanced language skills. They enjoy the subtleties of language and use an expansive vocabulary.

Reading Street integrates daily instruction for advanced learners into the core program. The Advanced lessons include these strategies to meet advanced learners' needs:

- acceleration of the curriculum to provide more advanced work

- replacement of regular reading material with more advanced selections

- creative or critical thinking activities and advanced inquiry projects

- opportunities for independent study

- recommendations for advanced trade books on the week's theme

- interest-based reading opportunities

- small group instruction

All children should have opportunities to participate in appropriately challenging learning experiences. Advanced lessons will ensure that all learners make continuous progress in reading.

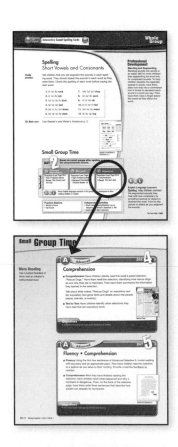

Differentiated Instruction for English Language Learners

How Do English Language Learners Differ from Other Learners?

Academic success depends on learning to read well. Learning to read well depends on rich language knowledge—which presents unique challenges for English language learners and others who have not acquired academic English.

A lack of reading and language skills should not be taken as a sign that children have a language or reading deficit, but rather that their language experiences haven't included sufficient academic instruction. In order for English language learners to participate fully in reading/language arts instruction and thrive as readers and writers, these language needs must be provided for.

How Do I Meet the Needs of English Language Learners?

Daily support for English language learners can be found in the Differentiated Instruction feature in the *Reading Street* Teacher's Edition, as well as daily lessons for your ELL group. They offer pacing suggestions for the week and scaffolded instruction for the week's target skills and strategies.

English language learner support is designed to enable you to "front-load," or preteach, the core instruction. It is also beneficial to children as reteaching. Activities address various levels of proficiency of English language learners, writing, science and history-social science, vocabulary, and transfer skills.

Support for English Language Learners on *Reading Street* includes

ELL Posters

- Large-format posters that support tested vocabulary and weekly concepts
- Daily structured talk for practice of speaking and listening skills

ELL/ELD Readers

- Weekly accessible readers specifically developed to support English language learners
- Readers that reinforce the weekly concept and vocabulary while building language and fluency

ELL Handbook

- Additional materials including grammar and phonics lessons, transference notes, reproducible pages for additional practice, language activities, and articles by notable experts in the English language learner community

Differentiated Instruction for On-Level Learners

The main instruction in *Reading Street* is designed for children who need instruction right at the second-grade level. While your small groups for Strategic Intervention, Advanced, and English Language Learners are engaged at their levels, your on-level children will benefit from small-group instruction that expands their knowledge of skills and strategies and provides on-level reading opportunities.

Reading Street integrates daily instruction for on-level children into the core program. On-level children are ready to expand what they learned in whole group lesson. The On-Level lessons provide multiple opportunities for children to talk and explore concepts in more depth.

- They expand their background knowledge of literature selections.
- They expand their understanding of the weekly concept by connecting it to a weekly question.
- They expand comprehension through focused activities.
- They expand their knowledge of vocabulary and word structure.

The On-Level daily lessons also offer

- opportunities for in-depth review of skills and strategies.
- on-level readers with practice for skills and strategies.
- multiple opportunities for retelling and fluency practice.
- writing response activities that extend reading skills and strategies.

Use the on-level lessons and choose from 5-Day and 3- or

4-Day pacing plans as a guide to ensure success.

How Do I Support Children with Different Needs in the Groups?

To form groups, it's necessary to give them labels. But never lose awareness that each child within a group is an individual with unique abilities and challenges. Small group time presents teachers the opportunity to become aware of children's needs and how best to support those needs. You can gain insight into children with special needs who may be in an advanced, on-level, or strategic intervention group. For these children, you can also use *Reading Street* materials to help them express their abilities and demonstrate their competence. These and many other activities can be used for children with different special needs:

Dyslexia—Guide the child's hand in forming letters or writing legibly.

Hearing Impairment—Pair children with others who can repeat explicit instructions.

Physical Disabilities—Suggest procedural or equipment modifications, such as modified computers, keyboards, scanners, and spell checkers.

English Language Learners
on Reading Street

Like countless classrooms across the United States, your second grade classroom may welcome increasing numbers of English language learners. ELLs are the fastest growing K–12 student population in the United States.

Section 6 starts you off with the overview of why it's important to support instruction for ELLs and how to use the wide array of English language learning resources in *Scott Foresman Reading Street*.

Then, you'll share the expertise of renowned ELL researchers as you read their findings and practical tips for language instruction, best practices in the classroom, and assessment.

Using these proven instructional approaches, you'll help ELLs excel.

Essentials of ELL Instruction in Scott Foresman Reading Street

Identify and Communicate Content Objectives and Language Objectives

Frontload the Lesson

Provide Comprehensible Input

Enable Language Production

Assess for Content and Language Understanding

Overview of English Language Learners

You may have noticed children from diverse language backgrounds communicating in English at recess and in other social situations. They seem to be fluent English speakers, but it's possible they're still beginners at academic English—the English they use for learning purposes. Research proves that it takes at least five years of exposure to academic English to catch up with native-speaker proficiency in school.

How Do English Language Learners Differ from Other Learners?

ELLs face challenges because they have not acquired academic English. Children's reading and language skills may seem deficient because their language experiences have lacked academic instruction. ELLs need targeted instruction to participate fully in reading/language arts lessons with their peers. Helping ELLs achieve academically is critically important because they must meet the same state and federal grade-level standards as other children. Their academic success depends on learning to read well, and this depends on rich language knowledge.

> **Academic Language** is the language of classroom talk. It's used for academic purposes, not social or personal ones.

Essentials of ELL Instruction

These five essential practices take into account language and academic needs of English language learners. They are incorporated into *Scott Foresman Reading Street* as common-sense, everyday strategies that help you build an effective learning relationship between you and your ELL children.

Identify and Communicate Content Objectives and Language Objectives

English language learners need instruction for the same grade-level skills and strategies as children whose first language is English. Deliver your instruction with clear, simple language. Provide extra support for academic vocabulary. Provide direct instruction for the academic language that children need to use to complete classroom tasks successfully.

> **ELL** **Preteach Concepts** Use the Day 1 instruction on ELL Poster 6 to assess and build background knowledge, develop concepts, and build oral vocabulary.

Frontload the Lesson

When new information arrives as a blur to ELL children, they are lost at beginning of a lesson. Taking time to frontload, or preteach, lesson elements will bring them into mainstream instruction. Activating prior knowledge, building background, previewing, and setting a purpose for reading are frontloading methods that remove learning obstacles. Asking children to make personal connections helps them see relationships and gives you insight into their experiences and backgrounds.

Provide Comprehensible Input

The instruction and content you present to ELL children may be unclear because of language barriers. Using visual supports, multimedia, examples of real items, and demonstrations are a few ways to provide comprehensible instruction. Communicating through non-linguistic methods such as gestures, props, and dramatization can be an effective approach. Hands-on activities and multiple exposures to new concepts can lessen confusion.

Enable Language Production

The listening, speaking, reading, and writing ELLs do for school is different from the language they use in everyday conversation. In school, ELLs need ample opportunities to demonstrate their use of English. Two critical methods for enabling children's English language production are direct instruction and modeling the use of a skill in a comprehensible way. Create scaffolds so that children can read and hear English language patterns and build on them to express their own thoughts. Paraphrasing, restatements, cloze sentences, writing prompts, and templated forms for note-taking are other useful supports. Responding to children's strengths and needs by modifying instruction gives them opportunities to express themselves in an academic setting and gain proficiency in English.

Assess for Content and Language Understanding Since ELLs are required to achieve the same high standards as mainstream children, you need assessment tools that help you plan how to support ELLs' strengths and address their challenges. Keep in mind that children are at different stages for learning English language and literacy skills. Asking these questions frequently and using assessments will help you determine how to modify your instruction for different proficiency levels.

- Where are ELL children in their **acquisition of English** language proficiency?
- Where are they in their **acquisition of literacy** skills?

Just as for all children, you will rely on diagnostic, formative, and summative assessments for ELLs. Consistently integrate informal assessment into your lessons to target specific problem areas for learning, adapt your instruction, and intervene earlier rather than later.

You can modify both formal and informal assessments so that ELLs show their proficiency in literacy skills with a minimal amount of negative impact. These modifications include time extensions, use of bilingual dictionaries and glossaries, repeated readings of listening passages, use of dual-language assessments, and allowing written responses in the first language.

To meet ELLs at their own level of English acquisition, teachers use instructional supports and tools. Through scaffolding and modifying instruction you can lead ELLs to achieve the same instructional goals that mainstream children do. The ELL strategies and supports in *Scott Foresman Reading Street* have the five essential principles of ELL as their foundation. Use them throughout your instruction to modify or scaffold core instruction. With ELL Leveled Support activities, you meet children where they are—from beginning to advanced levels of English proficiency.

Tips for Providing Comprehensible Input

- Face children when speaking.
- Use vocabulary-rich visuals such as ELL Posters.
- Use teaching techniques that involve the senses.
- Use ELL Readers and other materials with ELL supports.

The features provide on-the-spot information for vocabulary, writing, and language transfer information.

Other English language learner resources include:

Student Edition The second-grade student edition builds every child's reading and language skills.

Teacher's Edition The teacher's edition has ELL instructional strategies built into the lesson plans. The ELL weekly lessons have pacing plans to help you carefully integrate instruction. The lessons guide you in using sheltered techniques and routines for teaching academic vocabulary, listening comprehension, phonics, vocabulary, comprehension, and writing.

ELL Readers ELL readers develop English learners' vocabulary and comprehension skills.

ELL Posters ELL posters contain high-quality illustrations and five days of activities supporting key oral vocabulary, selection vocabulary, and lesson concepts.

English Language Support These supports are all provided as reproducible masters: English Language Support resource books with comprehension skill practice, selection vocabulary word cards, multilingual summaries of Student Edition literature, study guides for ELL Readers, and multilingual vocabulary charts. The English selection summaries and vocabulary charts are accompanied by translations in Spanish and in several other languages.

Ten Important Sentences The Ten Important Sentences reproducibles help children focus on comprehension while they expand their English proficiency.

ELL Handbook The ELL Handbook supports teachers' professional development and children's transition to advanced levels of proficiency.

The Three Pillars of English Language Learning

Dr. Jim Cummins, the University of Toronto

In order to understand how English learners develop second-language literacy and reading comprehension, we must distinguish between three different aspects of language proficiency:

Conversational fluency This dimension of proficiency represents the ability to carry on a conversation in face-to-face situations. Most native speakers of English have developed conversational fluency by age 5. This fluency involves use of high-frequency words and simple grammatical constructions. English learners generally develop fluency in conversational English within a year or two of intensive exposure to the language in school or in their neighborhood environments.

Discrete language skills These skills reflect specific phonological, literacy, and grammatical knowledge that students can acquire in two ways—through direct instruction and through immersion in a literacy-rich and language-rich environment in home or in school. The discrete language skills acquired early include:

- knowledge of the letters of the alphabet
- knowledge of the sounds represented by individual letters and combinations of letters
- the ability to decode written words

Children can learn these specific language skills concurrently with their development of basic English vocabulary and conversational fluency.

Academic language proficiency This dimension of proficiency includes knowledge of the less frequent vocabulary of English as well as the ability to interpret and produce increasingly complex written language. As students progress through the grades, they encounter:

- far more low-frequency words, primarily from Greek and Latin sources
- complex syntax (for example, sentences in passive voice)
- abstract expressions

Acquiring academic language is challenging. Schools spend at least 12 years trying to teach all students the complex language associated with academic success. It is hardly surprising that research has repeatedly shown that English language learners, on average, require *at least* 5 years of exposure to academic English to catch up to native-speaker norms.

Effective instruction for English language learners is built on three fundamental pillars.

English Learners

Activate Prior Knowledge/ Build Background	Access Content	Extend Language

Activate Prior Knowledge/ Build Background

No learner is a blank slate. Each person's prior experience provides the foundation for interpreting new information. In reading, we construct meaning by bringing our prior knowledge of language and of the world to the text. The more we already know about the topic in the text, the more of the text we can understand. Our prior knowledge enables us to make inferences about the meaning of words and expressions that we may not have come across before. Furthermore, the more of the text we understand, the more new knowledge we can acquire. This expands our knowledge base (what cognitive psychologists call *schemata*, or underlying patterns of concepts). Such comprehension, in turn, enables us to understand even more concepts and vocabulary.

It is important to *activate* students' prior knowledge because students may not realize what they know about a particular topic or issue. Their knowledge may not facilitate learning unless that knowledge is brought to consciousness.

Teachers can use a variety of strategies to activate students' prior knowledge:	
Brainstorming/Discussion	Visual stimuli
Direct experience	Student writing
Dramatization	Drawing

When students don't already have knowledge about a topic, it is important to help them acquire that knowledge. For example, in order to comprehend texts such as *The Midnight Ride of Paul Revere*, students need to have background knowledge about the origin of the United States.

Access Content

How can teachers make complex academic English comprehensible for students who are still in the process of learning English?

We can *scaffold* students' learning by modifying the input itself. Here are a variety of ways of modifying the presentation of academic content to students so that they can more effectively gain access to the meaning.

Using Visuals
Visuals enable students to "see" the basic concepts we are trying to teach much more effectively than if we rely only on words. Among the visuals we can use are:

- *pictures/diagrams*
- *vocabulary cards*
- *real objects*
- *graphic organizers*
- *maps*

Dramatization/Acting Out
For beginning English learners, Total Physical Response, in which they follow commands such as "Turn around," can be highly effective. The meanings of words can be demonstrated through *gestures* and *pantomime*.

Language Clarification
This category of teaching methods includes language-oriented activities that clarify the meaning of new words and concepts. *Use of dictionaries*, either bilingual or English-only, is still the most direct method of getting access to meaning.

Making Personal and Cultural Connections
We should constantly search for ways to link academic content with what students already know or what is familiar to them from their family or cultural experiences. This not only validates children's sense of identity, but it also makes the learning more meaningful.

Extend Language

A systematic exploration of language is essential if students are to develop a curiosity about language and deepen their understanding of how words work. Students should become *language detectives* who investigate the mysteries of language and how it has been used throughout history to shape and change society.

Students also can explore the building blocks of language. A large percentage of the less frequently heard academic vocabulary of English derives from Latin and Greek roots. Word formation follows predictable patterns. These patterns are very similar in English and Spanish.

When students know rules or conventions of how words are formed, it gives them an edge in extending vocabulary. It helps them figure out the meanings of words and how to form different parts of speech from words. The exploration of language can focus on meaning, form, or use:

Focus on meaning Categories that can be explored within a focus on meaning include:

- *home language equivalents or cognates*
- *synonyms, antonyms, and homonyms*
- *meanings of prefixes, roots, and suffixes*

Focus on form Categories that can be explored within a focus on form include:

- *word families*
- *grammatical patterns*
- *words with same prefixes, roots, or suffixes*

Focus on use Categories that can be explored within a focus on use include:

- *general uses*
- *idioms*
- *metaphorical use*
- *proverbs*
- *advertisements*
- *puns and jokes*

The Three Pillars

- Activate Prior Knowledge/ Build Background
- Access Content
- Extend Language

The Three Pillars establish a solid structure for the effective instruction of English language learners.

English Learners and Literacy: Best Practices

Dr. Georgia Earnest García, the University of Illinois at Urbana-Champaign

Like other children, English language learners come to school with much oral language knowledge and experience. Their knowledge and experience in languages other than English provide skills and world knowledge that teachers can build on.

Making literacy instruction comprehensible to English language learners is essential. Many of the teaching strategies developed for children who are proficient in English can be adapted for English learners, and many strategies from an English as a Second Language curriculum are also useful in "mainstream" reading education.

Building on Children's Knowledge

It is vital to learn about each student's literacy development and proficiency in the home language. School personnel should ask parents:

- How many years of school instruction has the child received in the home language?
- Can the child read and write in that language?
- Can the child read in any other language?

Students can transfer aspects of home-language literacy to their English literacy development, such as phonological awareness and reading (or listening) comprehension strategies. If they already know key concepts and vocabulary in their home languages, then they can transfer that knowledge to English. For the vocabulary concepts they already know in their home languages, they only need to learn the English labels. Not all English learners automatically transfer what they have learned in the home language to their reading in English. Teachers can help facilitate relevant transfer by explicitly asking English learners to think about what they have learned about a topic in the home language.

A teacher need not speak each student's home language to encourage English language learners to work together and benefit from one another's knowledge. Students can communicate in their home languages and English, building the content knowledge, confidence, and English skills that they need to participate fully in learning. Devising activities in which students who share home languages can work together also allows a school to pool resources, such as bilingual dictionaries and other books, as well as home-language tutors or aides.

Sheltering Instruction in English

Often, beginning and intermediate English language learners may not understand what their classroom teachers say or read aloud in English. These students benefit when teachers shelter, or make comprehensible, their literacy instruction.

Sheltered techniques include using:

- consistent, simplified, clearly enunciated, and slower-paced oral language to explain literacy concepts or activities
- gestures, photos, illustrations, drawings, real objects, dramatization, and/or physical action to illustrate important concepts and vocabulary
- activities that integrate reading, writing, listening, and speaking, so students see, hear, read, and write new vocabulary, sentence structures, and content

When it is clear from students' actions and responses that they understand what is being said, teachers can vary their strategies. As students' comprehension expands, teachers can gradually curtail their use of adapted oral language and of gestures, illustrations, and dramatizations.

Adapting Literacy Activities

Teachers can use many instructional activities developed for native English speakers with English language learners. For example, teacher read-alouds, shared reading, and paired reading can allow an English learner to follow the text during a reading. Such techniques greatly improve students' learning skills and comprehension.

Similarly, interactive journal writing, in which the teacher and student take turns writing entries, allows students to explore topics and ask questions. It also allows teachers to engage in ongoing authentic assessment of student proficiency and to pinpoint areas of misunderstanding.

Small group instruction and discussion also are helpful. Beginning English language learners benefit from the repeated readings of predictable texts with illustrations, especially when the teacher has provided a brief preview of each text to introduce the topic of the story and preview new vocabulary.

Repeated reading aloud of such predictable, patterned, illustrated texts provides English language learners with multiple opportunities to match the text they read with the words they hear. When students participate in shared reading and echo the spoken text or read the words aloud chorally, anxiety about pronunciation or decoding errors is reduced. When teachers choose texts that are culturally familiar and ask English language learners personal questions related to the text, the result is a lower-risk learning environment and an increased opportunity for students to make accurate inferences.

Examples of Teaching Strategies

Before students read content material, provide them with hands-on or visual experience directly related to the content. Then, have them use a graphic organizer to map what they have learned or seen about the topic. Let pairs or small groups of students brainstorm for words that are related to the concept. Then introduce other related words, including vocabulary from the reading. Illustrate new concepts or vocabulary with drawings, photographs, or artifacts that represent the concepts. The hands-on experience and graphic

organizer that precede the reading help introduce students to new concepts. Students will thus be familiar with the selection's subject before they begin to read.

Semantic Mapping Working with graphic organizers can help teach vocabulary and concepts in subject areas.

For example, before a reading on the subject of baby animals, have students help you to complete a semantic map showing pictures of animals and the names of baby animals. Ask them to volunteer the names for animal babies in their home language and transcribe their responses. Then, show students examples of the different forms of writing. Ask students to meet in small groups to identify the examples. They may do this in English or their home language. If they use the home language, the teacher needs to write the English labels on the board for each form of writing. Then, students need to enter the words for the different forms of writing, with drawings or home language equivalents, into a vocabulary notebook.

Summarizing After reading, students can dictate what they remember from their reading to the teacher. Students can then illustrate their summaries, and label the illustrations with vocabulary from the reading.

Preparing English Language Learners for Assessment

Dr. Lily Wong Fillmore, the University of California, Berkeley

Under federal and state law, all students—including English learners—must be assessed annually on their progress toward mastery of academic standards in reading, math, and science. Many questions arise when such assessments are used with ELLs, because their test scores are never easy to interpret when they are assessed in English. The most critical question is this: What do test scores mean when they are based on instruction and assessments given in a language students have not yet mastered? Although difficult to interpret, these assessments are required of all students, so we must consider how to help ELLs perform as well as possible.

Addressed in this essay

- What can teachers do to fast-track their ELL students' mastery of the language and content needed to perform as well as possible in required assessments?
- What language and literacy skills are needed?
- What learning strategies can teachers promote to facilitate language and literacy development?

Three types of assessments are vital to reading instruction for all students, including ELLs.

1. Ongoing informal assessments

The assessments that provide teachers the most useful and important information about English learners are those used as part of the instructional process. How well do children understand the materials they are working with, and what needs adjustment or modification in instruction? These are built into these instructional materials and help teachers keep an ongoing record of student progress over time. Such assessments do not need to

be elaborate. Asking children what they think is happening in a text can reveal how well they comprehend what they are reading. Asking children what they think words or phrases mean can show whether they are trying to make sense of text. These types of questions are highly useful to teachers since they allow them to monitor participation levels and help them discover who understands the materials and who needs more attention and support.

2. Diagnostic assessments

A second type of assessment that some ELLs may require is diagnostic, and it is needed when individuals are not making the progress expected of them. The school must determine where student problems lie (e.g., skill development, perception or awareness of English sounds, vocabulary, or grammar) before teachers can provide the corrective help needed.

3. Standardized assessments

The type of assessments that cause teachers of ELLs the greatest concern are the standards-based tests of English Language Arts and content area tests (especially in Math). These state tests are required of all students and are recognized as "high stakes" tests for students and for schools. They are often used to evaluate the effectiveness of a curriculum, the teacher, or the instructional approach used.

What's involved in reading?

Reading skills are built on several types of knowledge: linguistic, symbolic, experiential, and strategic. Each is crucial and is linked with the others. *Language is fundamental*; it is the medium through which meaning—information, story, knowledge, poetry, and thought—is communicated from writer to reader. Unlike speech, what is communicated by written language is indirect and *encoded in symbols* that must be deciphered before access to meaning is possible.

But reading goes beyond mere decoding. Texts call for readers to apply what they know about how language is used to convey thought and ideas to interpret what they are reading. Having *experienced reading as a sense-making activity*, readers will seek meaning as they learn to read. This calls for *special strategies:* they look for meaning if they assume it is to be found in texts. If they do not know the language in which the texts are written, they will recognize that learning the code is the key to unlocking meaning. They will pay attention to the language, and ask: What is this saying? What does this mean? How does this relate to what I already know about the way the language works?

English learners have an easier time learning to read in English if they have already learned to read in their first language. Without question, a language barrier makes learning to read a more difficult task. But if students have already learned to read in their primary language, they know what is involved, what to expect, and thus, they are in a better position to deal with learning to read in the new language in order to access meaning.

Can children learn to read in a language before they are fully proficient in that language?

Can they in fact learn the language through reading? *Yes, but only with ample instructional assistance that supports the development of both.* Ideally, reading instruction in English comes after ELLs have gained some familiarity with the sounds and patterns of spoken English. Children need to hear the sounds of the new language before they can connect symbols to those sounds. For example, in order for children to gain confidence relating the many vowel sounds of English to the 5 vowel symbols used to "spell them" they need help hearing them and differentiating them in words.

Similarly, many ELLs need help dealing with the ways consonants pile up at the beginning and at the ends of syllables and words in English, which may be quite different than the way consonants are used in their primary language. Most crucially, ELLs need help in connecting the words they are learning to decode from the text to their referents. Using pictures, demonstrations, diagrams, gestures, and enactments, teachers can help ELLs see how the words, phrases, and sentences in the reading selections have meaning that can be accessed through the language they are learning.

Helping ELLs become successful readers

The most important way to help ELLs perform well in mandated reading assessments is by giving them the instructional support they need to become successful readers. This involves help in:

- Learning English
- Discovering the purpose of reading
- Becoming active learners
- Gaining access to academic language

Learning English

The more proficient children are in the language they are reading, the more readily they learn to read. For ELLs, support for learning English is support for learning to read. The most effective kind of help comes in content-focused language instruction, where learners are engaged in grade-level-appropriate instructional activities and their participation is scaffolded and supported as needed.

The most effective activities provide ELLs ample opportunity to hear English and to use it productively in meaningful communication. Teachers play a vital role in creating a supportive classroom environment. ELLs must be able to participate to the extent possible (again, with as much support as needed) in discussions with classmates who are more proficient in English. Peers can offer practice and support, but only teachers can ensure that ELLs get access to the kind of language needed for literacy development.

Purpose of reading

The greatest dangers ELLs face in learning to read in English before they are proficient in that language is that the effort involved in decoding takes precedence in their minds over all else. Connections between words and referents, between words and structures, and between text and meaning are overlooked when children focus on sounding out, figuring out symbols, and figuring out sounds. This is especially likely to happen when there is too little emphasis placed on reading as a sense-making activity in instructional programs. If meaning—no matter how difficult it is to come by—is not constantly emphasized in reading instruction, children end up believing that decoding is reading, and that there is nothing missing when they read without understanding. Decoding

becomes an end in itself, and the real purpose of reading is lost. Unfortunately, this is the outcome for many ELLs, who even after having learned English do not perform well in reading assessments.

Literacy in English begins as deciphering for ELLs—they must first figure out how the code in which the text is written works. It is not until the reader engages in an interpretive process in which the thoughts, information,  concepts, situations, and relations encoded in the texts are manifested as meanings that there is real reading. This is true for both ELLs and for native English speakers. ELLs, however, will need a lot of guidance and instructional support from teachers to do that. Once children have gained enough familiarity with English to participate even at a rudimentary level in discussions about reading selections and content, they begin to learn that the materials they are reading have something to say to them and that hearing what they have to say is the real purpose of learning to read.

Active readers

Helping children become active learners of English and users of the literacy skills they are acquiring is a key to their becoming successful students and performing well in the assessments they have to take. This is accomplished by encouraging children to take an active role in instructional activities, asking questions, seeking answers, and trying to make sense of what they are studying in school.

Both teachers and students can have many preconceived ideas about the roles they play as teachers and learners. Children sometimes come to school believing that learning is something that will be done to them, rather than something they must take an active role in doing. In their view, the role of the teacher is active and the role they play as learners is passive. When teachers share that belief, there is little likelihood of active or independent learning. Instruction is most effective when teachers are knowledgeable about the subject matter they are teaching and they create a classroom environment in which learners can take an active role in discovering how things work, what things mean, and how to get and make sense of information.

Academic English

Teachers are aware that the language used in written texts is sufficiently different from everyday spoken language to constitute a barrier to children who are not already familiar with it. Academic English is not just another name for "standard English." It is, instead, the special forms of standard English used in academic discourse and in written texts. It makes use of grammatical constructions, words, and rhetorical conventions that are not often used in everyday spoken language.

Paradoxically, academic language is both a prerequisite for full literacy and the outcome of it. Some children arrive at school with a running start in acquiring it. Children who come from homes where family members engage in frequent discussions of books and ideas are already familiar with it, and thus have an advantage learning to read.

It should be noted that the language used at home does *not* have to be English for children to benefit from such experiences. Teachers can provide their students, irrespective of background, experiences with academic language by reading to them and discussing readings, instructional activities, and experiences. By drawing children into instructional conversations focused on the language they encounter in their school texts and other materials, teachers get children to notice language itself and to figure out how it works.

Supporting language and literacy development for ELLs

Teachers support language development by engaging children as active participants in making sense of the texts they are working on. They do it by drawing the English learners into discussions relating to the texts. Even relative newcomers are able to participate in these discussions as long as ample scaffolding is provided:

It says here, "Her teacher picked up the paper and studied it carefully."

Hector, what does the text tell us Vashti's teacher did first?

Yes, she picked up the paper first.

Take a look at the picture. Marta, can you show us, which part of the sentence tells us what the teacher is doing?

Can you tell us what she is doing?

Yes! She is studying the paper carefully.

Teachers draw attention to words, phrases, and sentences, asking: "Let's see if we can figure out what that means!" By relating language to meaning, they help students gain access to meaning by demonstrating, referring to illustrations and diagrams, and by paraphrasing in simpler language.

Instructional conversations about the texts they are reading are as essential for newcomers as they are for ELLs who have already gained some proficiency in English. It is vital to their literacy development to realize that what they are "reading" can be understood, even if its meaning is not immediately available to them as it would be to readers who are fully proficient in English. Without such help, ELLs sometimes come to believe that decoding without access to meaning is an empty exercise one does in school, and except for that, it has little relevance to their lives.

Teachers can help students discover how the language works and how to extract meaning from texts by considering how the language they encounter can convey information, ideas, stories, feelings, and images. This cannot wait until the learners are fully proficient in the language they are reading. It can enhance language development if done from the start, as soon as ELLs are introduced to English reading.

Strategies for supporting language and literacy development and preparing ELLs for assessment

The most effective support comes in the form of instructional conversations in which ELLs are drawn into discussions of reading selections and content. By hearing their teachers and other classmates discuss the materials they are reading, they gradually learn how the language works in texts and in conversation.

- Draw attention to the language used in reading selections and other text materials—words, phrases, and sentences— and relate them to meaning that is discussed and commented on, both locally and globally, to help ELLs learn how to get at meaning in texts.

- Provide students ample opportunity to use the language of texts in speaking (during discussions of the reading selections, for example) and in writing (in response to writing prompts).

- Teach English learners to be strategic readers by guiding them to assume that the text should make sense and that meaning can be accessed by figuring out what the words, phrases, and sentences mean.

- Teach students to ask questions about meaning as it unfolds in the text. Help them recognize that some parts of texts provide background knowledge while other parts reveal new information.

- Teach children how to relate new information presented in a text to what is already known. Train students to make inferences about meaning based on the words and phrases used in a text.

- Expect ELLs to make progress, and then ensure it by providing ample grade level discussion of content. At the same time, recognize that it takes time to learn English, and that learners may differ in the amount and kind of help they need in order to make progress.

- Recognize that the most crucial kind of preparation for assessment is in helping children develop the **language and literacy skills** that are essential to successful performance in tests and for academic progress itself.

- Call children's attention to words, phrases, and constructions that often figure in text items. For example, words such as *both, not,* and *best* may not seem to be noteworthy, but their uses in test questions prove otherwise. ELLs need help in seeing how such words frame and constrain the ideas expressed in sentences in which they appear.

- Teach children the logic of test questions. Use released test items or models of test items (both of which are likely to be available online from your state department of education or district web sites). Show children, for example, that the question, "Which of the following is NOT a sentence?" entails that all of the listed options except one *are* sentences.

- Teach children to read carefully. Children who are fully proficient in English may occasionally benefit from test-taking strategies such as reading the test question and answer options first and then skimming the test passage to find information that will aid in the selection of the

correct answer to the question. This tactic does not serve English learners well. They need to read and understand the passage carefully, and then consider how to answer the questions asked.

- Teach children when the text calls for activation of prior knowledge. All children have such knowledge, but English learners need help in deciding where it is called for and how they should bring what they already know to interpret the texts they are reading.

- Expand children's horizons by reading them texts that may be too difficult to handle on their own. Help them make sense of such materials by commenting on meaning, drawing attention to how language is used in them, and engaging children in discussions about aspects of the texts.

The texts that are read to children, and the ones they read themselves, provide reliable access to the academic language they need for literacy and for assessment, provided teachers call their attention to language, and help children see how it works. Teachers do this by identifying interesting (not just new) phrases and commenting on them, inviting children to try using the phrases, and providing scaffolds as needed; they model the uses of language from texts in subsequent instructional activities; they encourage children to remember and keep records of words they learn from texts; they remind them when words and phrases encountered earlier show up again in different contexts.

The Concept of Transfer

Dr. Elena Izquierdo, the University of Texas at El Paso

Research continues to support the critical role of the child's first language (L1) in literacy development and its effect on literacy in (L2) English. Strong (L1) literacy skills facilitate the *transfer* into English literacy, and students ultimately progress rapidly into learning in English. In reality, the concept of transfer refers to the child's facility in appropriating knowledge from one language to the other. *Children do not know they know, but they know.* They are constantly and indirectly, unconsciously and automatically, constructing the knowledge that is inherent in the contexts for which each of these languages can function. The effective transfer of skills transpires as students develop their metalinguistic and metacognitive skills and as they engage in a contrastive analysis of the two languages (Cummins, 2007).

Matters of transfer occur within essentials of language that are (1) *common* to L1 and L2; (2) *similar*, but not exact in both languages; and (3) *specific* to each language and not applicable to the other language. In essence, children develop a special awareness of language and its function; learn that some sounds are the same in both languages; and also learn that there are certain boundaries for specific sounds depending on the language.

Children who have developed an awareness for phonemes, phonics, vocabulary building, and reading comprehension skills, can transfer these skills to English. They develop an enhanced awareness of the relationship between their L1 and English, which leads them to successfully appropriate strategies of transfer in similar types of word recognition processing; searching for cognates; making reference to prior knowledge, inferencing, questioning, and monitoring. Facilitating these cognitive skills in children will support their success in English literacy and their learning in English.

Introduction to Linguistics
How People Speak

All languages have both consonants and vowels. Consonants are made with some obstruction of the vocal tract, either a complete stoppage of air or enough constriction to create friction. Vowels are produced with the vocal tract more open, with no constriction that might cause friction.

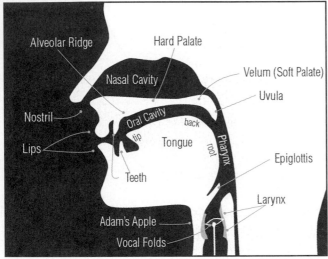

Figure 1: The human vocal tract makes the sounds of speech.

Place of Articulation Terms

Alveolar: tongue tip and ridge behind teeth

Bilabial: using both lips

Glottal: produced at the larynx

Interdental: tongue tip between upper and lower teeth

Labio–dental: upper teeth and lower lip

Labio–velar: rounding of lips; tongue body raised toward velum

Palatal: body of tongue and high part of palate

Palato–alveolar: tongue tip and palate behind alveolar ridge

Velar: body of tongue and velum (soft palate)

Manner of Articulation This is the type or degree of constriction that occurs in an articulation. For example, the /t/ sound completely stops the airflow with the tongue tip at the alveolar ridge, but /s/ allows air to pass noisily through a small opening.

Manner of Articulation Terms

Affricate: complete constriction followed by slow separation of the articulators resulting in friction

Approximant: close constriction, but not enough for friction

Fricative: narrow constriction; turbulent airflow causing friction

Glottal: produced at the larynx

Lateral: air passes over sides of tongue

Nasal: lowered velum to let air escape through the nose

Stop: complete constriction, closure so that air cannot escape through the oral cavity

Tap: brief contact between tongue tip and alveolar ridge

Consonants

Every consonant can be described by noting three characteristics: voicing, place of articulation, and manner of articulation.

Voicing Many sounds of language, including all vowels, employ vibration of the vocal folds in the larynx. This creates more resonance and energy for the sound. All speech sounds are characterized as either voiced (with vocal fold vibration) or voiceless (with no vocal fold vibration). Feeling the vibration around the Adam's apple can help you understand this difference. If you say "sssss" and then "zzzzz," you can feel the distinction: /s/ is voiceless and /z/ is voiced.

Place of Articulation This is the location in the vocal tract where the air stream may be constricted. The /s/ sound, for example, is made with the tongue tip close to the alveolar ridge (see Figure 1).

Vowels

Vowels are open, sonorous sounds. Each vowel can be uniquely described by noting the position of the tongue, the tension of the vocal tract, and the position of the lips. Vowels are described by *height,* where the tongue is relative to the roof of the mouth. They can be high, mid, or low. Tongue backness tells if the tongue articulation is in the front or back of the mouth. Tense vowels are more common around the world. In English, they are longer and include an expansion of the throat at the pharynx. Lax vowels are shorter with a more neutral pharynx. An example is the tense long *e* as in *meet* versus the lax short *i* as in *mitt.* The lips either can be in a spread or neutral position, or they can be rounded and protrude slightly.

Speaking English

English is the third most widely spoken native language in the world, after Mandarin and Spanish. There are about 330 million native speakers of English and 600 million who speak it as a foreign language.

English Consonant Sounds

The following chart gives the International Phonetic Alphabet (IPA) symbol for each English consonant along with its voicing, place, and manner of articulation. This information can be used to understand and help identify problems that non-native speakers may encounter when learning to speak English.

Consonants of English		
IPA	Articulation	Example
p	voiceless bilabial stop	pit
b	voiced bilabial stop	bit
m	voiced bilabial nasal stop	man
w	voiced labio-velar approximant	win
f	voiceless labio-dental fricative	fun
v	voiced labio-dental fricative	very
θ	voiceless interdental fricative	thing
ð	voiced interdental fricative	there
t	voiceless alveolar stop	time
d	voiced alveolar stop	dime
n	voiced alveolar nasal stop	name
s	voiceless alveolar fricative	soy
z	voiced alveolar fricative	zeal
ɾ	voiced alveolar tap	butter
l	voiced alveolar lateral approximant	loop
ɹ	voiced alveolar central approximant	red
ʃ	voiceless palato-alveolar fricative	shallow
ʒ	voiced palato-alveolar fricative	vision
ʧ	voiceless palato-alveolar affricate	chirp
ʤ	voiced palato-alveolar affricate	joy
j	voiced palatal approximant	you
k	voiceless velar stop	kite
g	voiced velar stop	goat
ŋ	voiced velar nasal stop	king
h	voiceless glottal fricative	hope

English Vowel Sounds

Most languages in the world have around five vowel sounds. English has 13 common vowel sounds, which means that many students of English must learn more vowel distinctions than there are in their native language. The lax vowels are most difficult. Some vowels are diphthongs, meaning the tongue is in one position at the beginning of the sound, and it moves to another position by the end of it.

Vowels of English		
IPA	Sound	Example
i	ē	beat
ɪ	ĭ	bit
e	ā	bait
ɛ	ĕ	bet
æ	ă	bat
u	ōō	boot
ʊ	ŏŏ	could
o	ō	boat
ɔ	aw	law
ɑ	ŏ	hot
ə	ə	about
ʌ	ŭ	cut
ɝ	er	bird
ɑ ʊ	ow	house
ɔ ɪ	oy	boy
ɑ ɪ	ī	bite

Figure 2 is a schematic of the mouth. The left is the front of the mouth; the right is the back. The top is the roof of the mouth and the bottom is the floor. Placement of the vowel shows where the tongue reaches its maximum in the English articulation.

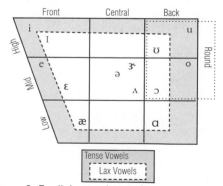

Figure 2: English vowel sounds

Introduction to Linguistics
Transference

Pronunciation

All languages build on the same fundamentals. All languages contrast voiced and voiceless sound, and have stops and fricatives. Many languages use the same places of articulation for consonants as well. The majority of sounds will easily transfer from another language to English.

However, there will always be some sounds that are not found in a person's native language that can pose a challenge to the English language learner. English has a few relatively rare sounds, such as the interdental sounds spelled with *th*, /ɵ/ and /ð/. The /r/ sound in English is also a very rare type of sound. Most other languages use a tap or trill articulation for an /r/ sound.

In some languages, the /l/ and /r/ sounds belong to one psychological category. This means that they count as the same sound in that language. In this case, it is not the articulation that is difficult, but the perception of the difference and consistent use of one versus the other in any word context. This type of psychological category is called a *phoneme*, and multiple speech sounds all can be categorized as the same phoneme in that language.

This is true for English as well, where, for example, the alveolar lateral /l/ as in *lob* and the velarized lateral /ł/ as in *ball* are both counted as the same sound—an l—to native speakers of English. It is important to keep in mind that both the phonetic articulation of a sound and its psychological, phonemic category factor into the learning of a new language.

Grammar

Pronouncing English is not the only stumbling block for English learners. The grammar and usage, or syntax, of English may present distinctions that are unique to the language. For example, English syntax requires adjectives to precede the nouns they modify, as in *the tall girl*. In other languages, such as Spanish, Hmong, and Vietnamese, adjectives follow nouns, as in *la chica alta* (literally *the girl tall* in Spanish). This may cause word-order problems, particularly for less advanced English learners.

Other syntactic differences are less obvious and may cause problems even for advanced learners. For example, many East Asian languages (such as Mandarin, Cantonese, and Korean) do not mark agreement between subject and verb. Speakers of these languages may therefore leave out agreement markers such as the *-s* in *The girl like cats*.

The use of articles varies across languages. For instance, Spanish uses the definite article more often than English, while Mandarin and Cantonese do not have articles. A Spanish-speaking English learner might say *The girl likes the cats* instead of *The girl likes cats*, and a Mandarin or Cantonese speaker might say *Girl like cat*.

Plural marking is another potential trouble spot: Vietnamese, Filipino, Cantonese, and Mandarin do not add plural markers to nouns. Learners speaking these languages may have difficulty with English plurals, saying *cat* instead of *cats*.

> **Grammar Hot Spots**
> Look for Grammar Hot Spots on the following pages for tips on the most common syntax errors by speakers of languages other than English.

Common First Languages

In the Common First Languages section, you will find details of some common non-English languages spoken in the United States. They are:

- Spanish
- Vietnamese
- Cantonese
- Hmong
- Filipino
- Korean
- Mandarin

You can use the fundamentals of speech articulation already covered to help you understand where the languages differ from English. Differences in the spoken language and in the writing systems are explored as well. These sections pinpoint common trouble spots specific to learners of English.

> **Culture Clues**
> Look to Culture Clues for insights into the cultural differences of each language learner as well as ideas for ways to embrace students' diversity.

Linguistic Contrastive Analysis

The Linguistic Contrastive Analysis Charts provide a quick reference for comparing English sounds with those of other languages. The charts allow you to check at a glance which sounds have equivalents in other languages. For those sounds that don't have equivalents, you can find the closest sound used as a substitute and suggestions for helping someone gain a native English articulation.

In these charts, the sounds are notated using the International Phonetic Alphabet (IPA). This is the most widely recognized and used standard for representing speech sounds in any language. A guiding principle of the IPA across all languages is that each sound is uniquely represented by one symbol, and each symbol represents only one sound.

The chart has columns for each native language with rows corresponding to each English phoneme. Each cell in the chart gives an example word using that sound in the native language, a definition in parenthesis, and transference tips below. If there is no sound equivalent to English, a common substitution used by speakers of that language may be provided.

> **Transference Tips**
> Transference Tips give you ideas of how the sound will be produced by the learner. Cells in bold note where the English learner will have particular difficulty with the English sound.

Common First Languages
Spanish

Background Spanish is the second most widely spoken language in the world. There are more than 400 million native Spanish speakers in 20-plus countries on three continents. Spanish vocabulary and pronunciation differ from country to country. While most dialect differences in English are in vowel sounds, Spanish dialects differ in their consonants.

Spoken Spanish sounds are similar to those found in English, so there is a strong foundation for the native Spanish speaker learning English. However, there are three key differences between English and Spanish consonants:

> **Culture Clues**
>
> The Spanish language covers many countries, dialects, and cultures. Always encourage students to share special things about their culture, such as foods, festivals, or social customs.

1. Most of the alveolar sounds in English, such as /t/, /d/, and /n/ are produced farther forward in the mouth in Spanish. Instead of the tongue touching the alveolar ridge as in English, in Spanish it touches the back of the teeth.

2. Another difference is that the /r/ sound in English is not found in Spanish. There are two /r/ sounds in Spanish. One is the tap /ɾ/, which occurs in English as the quick sound in the middle of the name *Betty*. Psychologically, this tap sound is a kind of /t/ or /d/ sound in English, while in Spanish it is perceived as an /r/. The other /r/ sound in Spanish is a trill, or series of tongue taps on the alveolar ridge. This does not occur in English.

3. The third key difference between English and Spanish can be found in the English production of the voiceless stops /p/, /t/, and /k/. In English these sounds are aspirated, with an extra puff of air at the end, when the sound occurs at the beginning of a word or stressed syllable. So, /p/ is aspirated in *pit*. Learners can add a puff of air to such sounds to sound more like native English speakers.

There are five vowels in Spanish, which are a subset of the English vowels. Spanish vowels include tense vowel sounds /a/ /e/ /i/ /o/ /u/. Lax vowel sounds in English are the problematic ones for native Spanish speakers.

Written Like English, written Spanish uses the Roman alphabet, so both writing systems are similar. There are a few orthographic differences to note, however:

- The letter *h* in Spanish is silent, but the sound /h/ is written as *j* or *g*.

- A single letter *r* in Spanish represents a tap, while the double *rr* represents a trill.

- Accents are used to show the stress on a syllable when the stress is different from the usual rules. In some cases, words change meaning according to the accents. For example, *el* means *the* while *él* means *he*.

Written Spanish vowels are pronounced like the symbols in the IPA. So, the Spanish "i" is pronounced with the long ē as in the word *beat*. The IPA and Spanish symbol for this letter is the same: i.

> **Grammar Hot Spots**
>
> - Double negatives are part of standard grammar in Spanish. Stress the single negative construction in English.
> - English prepositions are a common stumbling block for Spanish speakers.

Vietnamese

Background Approximately eighty million people in Vietnam speak Vietnamese. The northern dialect is the standard, though central and southern dialects also exist. Most Vietnamese speakers in the United States are from southern Vietnam and speak the southern dialect.

Spoken Vietnamese is a tonal language, so each syllable is pronounced with a distinctive tone that affects meaning. Vietnamese has a complex vowel system of 12 vowels and 26 diphthongs. Its consonants are simpler, but Vietnamese syllable structure allows few possibilities for final consonants.

> **Culture Clues**
>
> In traditional Vietnamese education, there is a strict division between the roles of student and teacher. Students may be confused if asked to direct a part of their own study, so encourage group work.

Students may need help noticing and learning to reproduce final consonant sounds in English words and syllables. Vietnamese syllable structure allows for limited combinations of initial consonants. Students also may need help with the more complex initial consonant clusters of English words and syllables.

Written Since the 1600s, Vietnamese has used a Romanized alphabet. Many characters written in Vietnamese have sounds different from their English counterparts, such as *d, x, ch, nh, kh, g, tr, r,* and *e*.

> **Grammar Hot Spots**
>
> - Like English, Vietnamese uses Subject-Verb-Object (SVO) syntax, or word order.
> - Vietnamese does not use affixes; instead, syntax expresses number, case, and tense.

Cantonese

Background Cantonese is one of the seven major Chinese languages, not all of which are mutually intelligible. Cantonese is mostly spoken in China's southern provinces, Hong Kong, and Macau by about 66 million people. It is a tonal language, and the same sequence of letters can have different meanings depending on their pitch.

Spoken Cantonese has six stops, aspirated and non-aspirated /p/, /t/, /k/; three fricatives /f/, /s/, /h/, and two affricates /ts/, /tsʰ/. Some sounds which do not exist in Cantonese can be difficult for the English language learner. The /v/ often gets pronounced as /f/ or /w/; the /z/ is often said as /s/; the sounds spelled with *th* are often said as /t/, /d/, or /f/. Cantonese speakers have difficulty distinguishing between /l/ and /r/, since /r/ is not present in their language. They tend to produce an /l/-like sound for both English sounds in words such as *ride* and *lied*.

Cantonese has 11 vowels and 10 diphthongs. One of the major problems for Cantonese speakers is distinguishing between English tense and lax vowels, because the distribution of Cantonese short and long vowels is determined by the sound context.

Syllables in Cantonese don't have consonant clusters. English consonant clusters are often deleted or broken up by vowel insertion (e.g., *list* becomes *lis*). This may be especially problematic when producing English past tense (e.g., *baked*).

Written Cantonese is written with standard Chinese characters known as *Hànzi* where each character represents a syllable and has a meaning. Additional Cantonese-specific characters were also added. Cantonese speakers may have difficulty with sound-letter correspondences in English.

> **Grammar Hot Spots**
>
> - English articles and prepositions are difficult for Cantonese speakers. *In, on,* and *at,* for instance, can be translated as the same pronoun in Cantonese.
> - Plurals, tenses, and gerund endings are difficult for Cantonese speakers to transfer to English.

Common First Languages

Hmong

Background Hmong is a group of approximately 18 languages within the Hmong-Mien family. There are roughly four million speakers of Hmong, including 200,000 in the United States. They are mainly from two groups with mutually intelligible dialects—Hmong Daw and Mong Leng.

Spoken Hmong vowels are few and simple, but its consonants are complex and differ from those of English. Notable features of Hmong phonology absent from English include consonantal pre-nasalization (the /m/n/ŋ/ sound before a consonant) and the contrast between nasalized and non-nasalized vowels. Hmong is tonal. Each syllable is pronounced with a distinctive pitch.

> **Culture Clues**
>
> In traditional Hmong culture, learning takes place through hands-on experience. Students may find it difficult to adjust to the use of graphics or print media. Competition, personal achievement, and self-directed instruction may be unfamiliar concepts, so students may prefer group work.

Written The Romanized Popular Alphabet (RPA), developed in the 1950s, is the usual way of transcribing Hmong. Syllable-final consonants are absent in pronunciation but are used to represent orthographically the tonal value of a given syllable. Students may need particular help in identifying and learning to reproduce the final consonant sounds of English words and syllables.

> **Grammar Hot Spots**
>
> - Like English, Hmong is an SVO language. Personal pronouns are marked for number, including inflection for singular, dual, and plural, though they are not marked for case.
> - Because Hmong and English prepositions often have different semantic qualities, students may need help mastering uses of English prepositions. For example, it is correct to say "think <u>about</u> [something]" rather than "think <u>on</u> [something]."

Filipino

Background Filipino and English are the official languages of the Philippines, where 175 languages are spoken. There are about 24 million native speakers of Filipino, and more than 50 million people speak Filipino as a second language. You may hear the terms Filipino and Tagalog being used interchangeably.

Spoken Filipino has many similar speech sounds to English. The notable exceptions are the lack of the consonant sounds /f/, /v/, and those spelled with *th*. Of these, the English /f/ and /v/ cause the most difficulty for learners. The distinction between long *e* (as in *beat*) and short *i* (as in *bit*) is also a trouble spot. Filipino does not allow consonant clusters at the end of syllables, so *detect* may be simplified to just one final consonant *(detec)*.

> **Culture Clues**
>
> Most people from the Philippines can speak Filipino, but for many it is not their first language. Ask Filipino students about other languages they speak. Because English is used alongside Filipino as the language of instruction in the Philippines, most Filipinos are familiar with English.

Written The Filipino alphabet has 28 letters and is based on the Spanish alphabet, so the English writing system poses little problem.

> **Grammar Hot Spots**
>
> - Filipino word order is Verb-Subject-Object (VSO), which does not transfer well to English.
> - Inflectional verb endings, such as *-s*, *-en*, *-ed*, and *-ing* do not exist in Filipino, so it is common to leave out the third person singular verb marker (*"He walk,"* not *"He walks"*).

Korean

Background Korean is spoken by 71 million people in North and South Korea. Standard Korean is based on the speech in and around Seoul.

Spoken Korean does not have corresponding sounds for English /f/, /v/, /θ/, /ð/, and /ʤ/. In word-initial position, all Korean stops are voiceless. Voiced stops /b/, /d/, and /g/ are only produced between two vowels. Korean speakers may have difficulty producing /s/, /ʃ/, and /z/ in some contexts, in addition to English /r/ and /l/ sounds (e.g., *rock* and *lock*). They may have problems in producing English consonant clusters (e.g., *str-, sk-*). These problems can often be eliminated by vowel insertion or consonant deletion. In addition, the distinction between English tense and lax vowels (e.g., /i/ as in *beat* vs. /ɪ/ as in *bit*) may be problematic for Korean speakers.

> **Culture Clues**
> Korean uses a complex system of honorifics, so it is unusual for Korean students to use the pronoun *you* or call their teachers by their first name.

Written Modern Korean uses the Korean alphabet *(Hangul)* or a mixed script of *Hangul* and Chinese. *Hangul* is an alphabetic script organized into syllabic blocks.

> **Grammar Hot Spots**
> - In contrast to English, Korean word order is Subject-Object-Verb (SOV). The verb always comes at the end of a sentence.
> - Korean syllable stress is different, so learners may have difficulties with the rhythm of English.

Mandarin

Background Chinese encompasses a wide range of dialects and is the native language of two-thirds of China. There are approximately 870 million Mandarin speakers worldwide. North Mandarin, as found in Beijing, is the basis of the modern standard language.

Spoken Mandarin Chinese and English differ substantially in their sound structure. Mandarin lacks voiced obstruent consonants (/b/, /d/, /g/, /ʤ/), causing difficulty for speakers in perceiving and producing English voiced consonants (e.g., *buy* may be pronounced and perceived as *pie*). The sounds spelled with th are not present in Mandarin, so they are often substituted with /s/ or /t/ causing, for example, *fourth* to be pronounced as *fours*. Mandarin Chinese has five vowels. Due to the relatively small vowel inventory and contextual effects on vowels in Mandarin, many English vowels and tense/lax distinctions present problems for speakers of Mandarin Chinese. Mandarin allows only a very simple syllable structure, causing problems in producing consonant clusters in English. Speakers may drop consonants or insert vowels between them (e.g., *film* may become /filəm/). The use of tones in Mandarin may result in the rising and falling of pitch when speaking English.

Written Chinese is written with characters known as Hànzi. Each character represents a syllable and also has a meaning. A Romanized alphabet called Pinyin marks pronunciation of characters. Chinese speakers may have problems mastering letter-sound correspondences in written English, especially for sounds that are not present in Mandarin.

> **Grammar Hot Spots**
> - The non-inflected nature of Chinese causes Mandarin speakers to have problems with plurals, past-tense markers, and gerund forms *(-s, -ed, -ing)*.
> - Mastering English tenses and passive is difficult. Students should be familiarized with correct lexical and syntactic features as well as appropriate situations for the use of various tenses and passives.

Linguistic Contrastive Analysis Char
The Consonants of English

IPA	ENGLISH	SPANISH	VIETNAMESE	CANTONESE
p	*p*it Aspirated at the start of a word or stressed syllable	*p*ato (duck) Never aspirated	*p*in (battery)	*p*ʰa *(to lie prone)* Always aspirated
b	*b*it	*b*arco (boat) Substitute voiced bilabial fricative /�/ in between vowels	*b*a (three) Implosive (air moves into the mouth during articulation)	**NO EQUIVALENT** Substitute /p/
m	*m*an	*m*undo (world)	*m*ot (one)	*m*a (mother)
w	*w*in	ag*u*a (water)	**NO EQUIVALENT** Substitute word-initial /u/	*w*a (frog)
f	*f*un	*f*lor (flower)	*ph*uˀoˀng (phoenix) Substitute sound made with both lips, rather than with the lower lip and the teeth like English /f/	*f*a (flower) Only occurs at the beginning of syllables
v	*v*ery	**NO EQUIVALENT** Learners can use correct sound	*V*iệt Nam (Vietnam)	**NO EQUIVALENT** Substitute /f/
θ	*th*ing Rare in other languages. When done correctly, the tongue will stick out between the teeth.	**NO EQUIVALENT** Learners can use correct sound	**NO EQUIVALENT** Substitute /tʰ/ or /f/	**NO EQUIVALENT** Substitute /tʰ/ or /f/
ð	*th*ere Rare in other languages. When done correctly, the tongue will stick out between the teeth.	ca*d*a (every) Sound exists in Spanish only between vowels; sometimes substitute voiceless θ.	**NO EQUIVALENT** Substitute /d/	**NO EQUIVALENT** Substitute /t/ or /f/
t	*t*ime Aspirated at the start of a word or stressed syllable English tongue-touch. Is a little farther back in the mouth than the other languages.	*t*ocar (touch) Never aspirated	*t*ám (eight) Distinguishes aspirated and non-aspirated	*t*ʰa (he/she) Distinguishes aspirated and non-aspirated
d	*d*ime English tongue-touch is a little farther back in the mouth than the other languages.	*d*os (two)	*Đ*ồng (Dong = unit of currency) Vietnamese /d/ is implosive (air moves into the mouth during articulation)	**NO EQUIVALENT** Substitute /t/
n	*n*ame English tongue-touch is a little farther back in the mouth than the other languages.	*n*ube (cloud)	*n*am (south)	*n*a (take)
s	*s*oy	*s*eco (dry)	*x*em (to see)	*s*a (sand) Substitute *sh*- sound before /u/ Difficult at ends of syllables and words
z	*z*eal	**NO EQUIVALENT** Learners can use correct sound	*r*òi (already) In northern dialect only Southern dialect, substitute /y/	**NO EQUIVALENT** Substitute /s/
ɾ	bu*tt*er Written 't' and 'd' are pronounced with a quick tongue-tip tap.	*r*ana (toad) Written as single *r* and thought of as an /r/ sound.	**NO EQUIVALENT** Substitute /t/	**NO EQUIVALENT** Substitute /t/
l	*l*oop English tongue-touch is a little farther back in the mouth than the other languages. At the ends of syllables, the /l/ bunches up the back of the tongue, becoming velarized /ɫ/ or dark-l as in the word *ball*.	*l*ibro (book)	cú *l*ao (island) /l/ does not occur at the ends of syllables	*l*au (angry) /l/ does not occur at the ends of syllables

HMONG	FILIPINO	KOREAN	MANDARIN
*p*eb (we/us/our) Distinguishes aspirated and non-aspirated	*p*aalam (goodbye) Never aspirated	*p*al (sucking)	*pʰei* (cape) Always aspirated
NO EQUIVALENT Substitute /p/	*b*aka (beef)	NO EQUIVALENT /b/ said between vowels Substitute /p/ elsewhere	NO EQUIVALENT
*m*us (to go)	*m*abuti (good)	*m*al (horse)	*m*ei (rose)
NO EQUIVALENT Substitute word-initial /*u*/	*w*alo (eight)	*g*we (box)	*w*en (mosquito)
*f*aib (to divide)	NO EQUIVALENT Substitute /p/	NO EQUIVALENT Substitute /p/	*f*a (issue)
*V*aj ('Vang' clan name)	NO EQUIVALENT Substitute /b/	NO EQUIVALENT Substitute /b/	NO EQUIVALENT Substitute /w/ or /f/
NO EQUIVALENT Substitute /tʰ/ or /f/	NO EQUIVALENT Learners can use correct sound, but sometimes mispronounce voiced /ð/.	NO EQUIVALENT Substitute /t/	NO EQUIVALENT Substitute /t/ or /s/
NO EQUIVALENT Substitute /d/	NO EQUIVALENT Learners can use correct sound	NO EQUIVALENT Substitute /d/	NO EQUIVALENT Substitute /t/ or /s/
*th*em (to pay) Distinguishes aspirated and non-aspirated	*t*akbo (run) Never aspirated	*t*al (daughter)	*t*a (wet) Distinguishes aspirated and non-aspirated
*d*ev (dog)	*d*erətso (straight)	NO EQUIVALENT Substitute /d/ when said between vowels and /t/ elsewhere.	NO EQUIVALENT Substitute /t/
*n*oj (to eat)	*n*aman (too)	*n*al (day)	*n*i (you) May be confused with /l/
*x*a (to send)	*s*ila (they)	*s*al (rice) Substitute *shi*– sound before /i/ and /z/ after a nasal consonant	*s*an (three)
NO EQUIVALENT Learners can use correct sound	NO EQUIVALENT Learners can use correct sound	NO EQUIVALENT Learners can use correct sound	NO EQUIVALENT Substitute /ts/ or /tsʰ/
NO EQUIVALENT Substitute /t/	rin/*d*in (too) Variant of the /d/ sound	Only occurs between two vowels Considered an /l/ sound	NO EQUIVALENT
*l*os (to come) /l/ does not occur at the ends of syllables	sa*l*amat (thank you)	ba*l*am (wind)	*l*an (blue) Can be confused and substituted with /r/

The Consonants of English *(continued)*

IPA	ENGLISH	SPANISH	VIETNAMESE	CANTONESE
ɹ	*red* Rare sound in the world Includes lip-rounding	**NO EQUIVALENT** Substitute /r/ sound such as the tap /ɾ/ or the trilled /r/	**NO EQUIVALENT** Substitute /l/	**NO EQUIVALENT** Substitute /l/
ʃ	*shallow* Often said with lip-rounding	**NO EQUIVALENT** Substitute /s/ or /tʃ/	*sieu thị* (supermarket) Southern dialect only	**NO EQUIVALENT** Substitute /s/
ʒ	*vision* Rare sound in English	**NO EQUIVALENT** Substitute /z/ or /dʒ/	**NO EQUIVALENT** Substitute /s/	**NO EQUIVALENT** Substitute /s/
tʃ	*chirp*	*chico* (boy)	*chính phủ* (government) Pronounced harder than English *ch*	**NO EQUIVALENT** Substitute /ts/
dʒ	*joy*	**NO EQUIVALENT** Sometimes substituted with /ʃ/ sound Some dialects have this sound for the *ll* spelling as in *llamar*	**NO EQUIVALENT** Substitute /c/, the equivalent sound, but voiceless	**NO EQUIVALENT** Substitute /ts/ Only occurs at beginnings of syllables
j	*you*	*cielo* (sky) Often substitute /dʒ/	*yeu* (to love)	*jau* (worry)
k	*kite* Aspirated at the start of a word or stressed syllable	*casa* (house) Never aspirated	*com* (rice) Never aspirated	*kʰa* (family) Distinguishes aspirated and non-aspirated
g	*goat*	*gato* (cat)	**NO EQUIVALENT** Substitute /k/	**NO EQUIVALENT** Substitute /k/
ŋ	*king*	*mango* (mango)	*Ngūyen* (proper last name)	*phaŋ* (to cook)
h	*hope*	*gente* (people) Sometimes substitute sound with friction higher in the vocal tract as velar /x/ or uvular /χ/	*hoa* (flower)	*ha* (shrimp)

HMONG	FILIPINO	KOREAN	MANDARIN
NO EQUIVALENT Substitute /l/	**NO EQUIVALENT** Substitute the tap /ɾ/	**NO EQUIVALENT** Substitute the tap or /l/ confused with /l/	*ran* (caterpillar) Tongue tip curled further backward than for English /r/
sau (to write)	*siya* (s/he)	Only occurs before /i/; Considered an /s/ sound	*shi* (wet)
zos village)	**NO EQUIVALENT** Learners can use correct sound	**NO EQUIVALENT**	**NO EQUIVALENT** Substitute palatal affricate /tɕ/
cheb (to sweep)	*tsa* (tea)	*cʰal* (kicking)	*cheng* (red)
NO EQUIVALENT Substitute *ch* sound	*Dios* (God)	**NO EQUIVALENT** Substitute *ch* sound	**NO EQUIVALENT** Substitute /ts/
Yaj (Yang, clan name)	*tayo* (we)	*je:zan* (budget)	*yan* (eye)
Koo (Kong, clan name) Distinguishes aspirated and non-aspirated	*kalian* (when) Never aspirated	*kal* (spreading)	*ke* (nest) Distinguishes aspirated and non-aspirated
NO EQUIVALENT Substitute /k/	*gulay* (vegetable)	**NO EQUIVALENT** Substitute /k/ Learners use correct sound between two vowels	**NO EQUIVALENT** Substitute /k/
gus (goose)	*angaw* (one million)	*baŋ* (room)	*tang* (gong) Sometimes add /k/ sound to the end
hais (to speak)	*hindi* (no)	*hal* (doing)	**NO EQUIVALENT** Substitute velar fricative /x/

Linguistic Contrastive Analysis Char
The Vowels of English

IPA	ENGLISH	SPANISH	VIETNAMESE	CANTONESE
i	*beat*	*hijo* (son)	*di* (to go)	*si* (silk)
ɪ	*bit* Rare in other languages Usually confused with /i/ (*meat* vs. *mit*)	NO EQUIVALENT Substitute /ē/	NO EQUIVALENT Substitute /ē/	*sik* (color) Only occurs before velars Substitute /ē/
e	*bait* End of vowel diphthongized—tongue moves up to /ē/ or short *e* position	*eco* (echo)	*kê* (millet)	*se* (to lend)
ɛ	*bet* Rare in other languages Learners may have difficulty distinguishing /ā/ and /e/ (short *e*): *pain* vs. *pen*	NO EQUIVALENT Substitute /ā/	NO EQUIVALENT Substitute /ā/	*seŋ* (sound) Only occurs before velars; difficult to distinguish from /ā/ in all positions
æ	*bat* Rare in other languages Learners may have trouble getting the tongue farther forward in the mouth	NO EQUIVALENT Substitute mid central /u/ (short *u*) or low front tense /o/ (short *o*)	*ghe* (boat)	NO EQUIVALENT Hard to distinguish between /æ/ and /ā/
u	*boot*	*uva* (grape)	*mua* (to buy)	*fu* (husband)
ʊ	*could* Rare in other languages Learners may have difficulty distinguishing the vowel sounds in *wooed* vs. *wood*	NO EQUIVALENT Substitute long *u*	NO EQUIVALENT Substitute long *u* (high back unrounded)	*suk* (uncle) Only occurs before velars Difficult to distinguish from long *u* in all positions
o	*boat* End of vowel diphthongized—tongue moves up to long *u* or ʊ position	*ojo* (eye)	*cô* (aunt)	*so* (comb)
ɔ	*law*	NO EQUIVALENT Substitute long *o* or short *o* Substituting long *o* will cause confusion (*low* vs. *law*); substituting short *o* will not	*cá* (fish)	*hok* (shell) Only occurs before velars Difficult to distinguish from long *o* in all positions
ɑ	*hot*	*mal* (bad)	*con* (child)	*sa* (sand)
ɑ ʊ	*house* Diphthong	*pauta*	*dao* (knife)	*sau* (basket)
ɔ ɪ	*boy* Diphthong	*hoy* (today)	*ròi* (already)	*soi* (grill)
ɑ ɪ	*bite* Diphthong	*baile* (dance)	*hai* (two)	*sai* (to waste)
ə	*about* Most common vowel in English; only in unstressed syllables Learners may have difficulty keeping it very short	NO EQUIVALENT Substitute short *u* or the full vowel from the word's spelling	*mua* (to buy)	NO EQUIVALENT
ʌ	*cut* Similar to schwa /ə/	NO EQUIVALENT Substitute short *o*	*giờ'* (time)	*san* (new)
ɝ	*bird* Difficult articulation, unusual in the world but common in American English Learners must bunch the tongue and constrict the throat	NO EQUIVALENT Substitute short *u* or /er/ with trill	NO EQUIVALENT Substitute /i/	*hæ* (boot)

HMONG	FILIPINO	KOREAN	MANDARIN
ib (one)	*ikaw* (you) This vowel is interchangeable with /ɪ/; hard for speakers to distinguish these	zɪːʃaŋ (market)	*ti* (ladder) Sometimes English /i/ can be produced shorter
NO EQUIVALENT Substitute /ē/	*li*mampu (fifty) This vowel is interchangeable with /ē/; hard for speakers to distinguish these	NO EQUIVALENT Substitute /ē/	NO EQUIVALENT
tes (hand)	*se*ro (zero)	*be*ːda (to cut)	*te* (nervous) Sometimes substitute English schwa /ə/
NO EQUIVALENT Substitute /ā/	*se*ro (zero) This vowel interchanges with /ā/ like *bait*; not difficult for speakers to learn	thɛːdo (attitude)	NO EQUIVALENT
NO EQUIVALENT Substitute short *e*	NO EQUIVALENT Substitute short *o* as in *hot*	NO EQUIVALENT	NO EQUIVALENT Substitute /ə/ or short *u*
kub (hot or gold)	*tu*nay (actual) This vowel interchanges with vowel in *could*; not difficult for speakers to learn	*zu*ːbag (watermelon)	*lu* (hut) Sometimes English long *u* can be produced shorter
NO EQUIVALENT Substitute a sound like long *e* (mid central with lips slightly rounded)	*gu*mawa (act) This vowel interchanges with long *u* like *boot*; not difficult for speakers to learn	NO EQUIVALENT	NO EQUIVALENT
NO EQUIVALENT	*ub*o (cough)	*bo*ːzu (salary)	*mo* (sword) This vowel is a little lower than English vowel
Yaj (Yang clan name)	NO EQUIVALENT Spoken as short *o*, as in *hot*	NO EQUIVALENT	NO EQUIVALENT Substitute long *o*
mov (cooked rice)	*ta*lim (blade)	*ma*ːl (speech)	*ta* (he/she) Sometimes substitute back long *o* or *u*
plaub (four)	*ikaw* (you)	NO EQUIVALENT	NO EQUIVALENT
NO EQUIVALENT	*apoy* (fire)	NO EQUIVALENT	NO EQUIVALENT
qaib (chicken)	*himatay* (faint)	NO EQUIVALENT	NO EQUIVALENT
NO EQUIVALENT	NO EQUIVALENT Spoken as short *o*, as in *hot*	NO EQUIVALENT Difficult sound for learners	NO EQUIVALENT
NO EQUIVALENT	NO EQUIVALENT Spoken as short *o*, as in *hot*	NO EQUIVALENT	NO EQUIVALENT
NO EQUIVALENT Substitute diphthong /əɨ/	NO EQUIVALENT Spoken as many different vowels (depending on English spelling) plus tongue tap /ɾ/	NO EQUIVALENT	NO EQUIVALENT

Comparative Oral Language Proficiency Chart

Levels of Proficiency	Level 1	Level II	Level III	Level IV	Level V
	Entering	Beginning	Developing	Expanding	Bridging
	Beginning	Early Intermediate	Intermediate	Early Advanced	Advanced
	Beginning	**Intermediate**	**Intermediate**	**Advanced**	**Advanced High**
Characteristics of the English Language Learner	• Minimal comprehension • May be very shy • No verbal production • Non-English speaker • Silent period (10 hours to 3 months) • Uses gestures and actions to communicate	• Limited comprehension • Gives one- or two-word responses • May use two- or three-word phrases • Stage may last 6 months to 2 years	• Comprehension increases • Errors still occur in speech • Simple sentences • Stage may last 2 to 4 years	• Good comprehension • Sentences become more complex • Engages in conversation • Errors in speech are more complex	• Few errors in speech • Orally proficient • Near-native vocabulary • Lacks writing skill • Uses complex sentences
What They Can Do: Performance Indicators	• Listen • Point • Illustrate • Match • Choose	• Name • List and group • Categorize • Label • Demonstrate	• Compare and contrast • Recall and retell • Summarize • Explain	• Higher-order thinking skills • Analyze, debate, justify	• All performance indicators
Instructional Ideas for Teachers	• Visual cues • Tape passages • Pair students • Total Physical Response activities • Concrete objects • Graphic organizers	• Short homework assignments • Short-answer quizzes • Open-ended sentences	• Graphs • Tables • Group discussions • Student-created books • Cloze activities	• Group panels • Paraphrasing • Defending and debating	• Lessons on writing mechanics • Free reading of appropriate books • Cooperative learning groups

Customize Literacy on Reading Street

Each day begins with a greeting to your second graders. Your welcome also extends to their varying literacy experiences. Like many teachers, you appreciate that not all children learn at the same rate or level. You customize your literacy program because it's a responsive and rewarding way to teach. Your way is to plan for different approaches that develop children's strengths and support their needs. At the same time, you carefully balance your plan to build in required skills.

Section 7 shows how *Scott Foresman Reading Street* provides just what you need to organize and carry out your customized literacy program. You'll find planning guides and instructional lessons to help you plan and implement your lessons. You can select from a rich array of readers to match texts to your second graders.

Keep your expectations high as you customize your literacy program. *Reading Street* is here to help!

What Are Goals for Customizing a Literacy Program?

When you customize literacy, you create a program that balances direct skill instruction with a variety of approaches to meet children's needs. Your goal is to allow children to be increasingly in charge of their own learning, so you use flexible grouping and organize your literacy materials and practice stations in specific ways. The decisions you make about setting up your classroom and your use of a variety of assessments support the overall goals you've set. You want to know the most effective ways to:

- assess children to determine their strengths and learning needs.
- meet state standards for reading, writing, speaking, and listening.
- plan lessons to focus on areas of instructional need, based on assessment.
- match books to meet readers at their instructional level.
- build a community of learners.

How Can You Customize Literacy with *Reading Street*?

Lesson plans can be thought out in broad strokes in advance. Yet, if instruction is to be truly effective, lesson plans need to be revised constantly to accommodate new assessment information, and lessons need to be customized to suit the learning needs of individual children. At the same time, your plan must include district and state standards.

How Should You Group Children for Reading Instruction?

As you conduct a variety of assessments, you learn about children as individuals. You come to know a great deal about their achievement levels, their interests, and their ability to interact with other children. The results of these observations and performance-based assessments help you determine children's instructional needs and make grouping decisions. Your flexible groups will vary depending on the different instructional purpose you want to address for each. You may address DRA2 Level instruction, strategy and skill instruction, children's interests, or their social abilities. Your guided reading groups may be based on specific areas of need from the DRA2 continuum and Focus for Instruction.

Grouping to Meet Children's Needs	
Grouping Pattern	**Instructional Purpose**
Strategy/Skill Instruction	To work with children who need instruction on a specific reading strategy
Interest	To provide an opportunity for children with the same interests to learn together
Social Skills	To give children an opportunity to build and practice skills for collaboration and cooperation

How Do I Connect with DRA2 Results When I Customize Literacy?

As you customize your literacy program, detailed planning is needed for grouping children based on DRA2 Levels or strategy and skill instruction. For DRA2 Levels, use the chart that begins on the next page to determine the DRA2 instructional strand you plan to teach. The accompanying Focus for Instruction is shown along with the DRA benchmark levels. You'll also want to use lessons in *Reading Street* and leveled readers for practicing the key skills. Those materials are listed for you as well.

What Tools Help Me Teach Skills and Strategies?

For other groups, you may want to teach based on comprehension skill and strategy instruction. The chart that begins on the next page will help you choose leveled readers based on comprehension skill and strategy instruction for these groups. This chart also shows the Fountas and Pinnell leveling criteria, the corresponding DRA benchmark levels, and the genres and content connections of the leveled readers available on *Reading Street*.

The Customize Literacy section in the *Reading Street* Teacher's Edition provides strategies and support as you plan groups, pacing, and the purpose of your instruction. You'll always be able to match your young readers with the right books. To be assured you are providing consistent instruction, you can incorporate the routines from the Teacher Edition in your customized lessons. The flexibility of *Reading Street* resources provides the structure you need when you customize your literacy program. Overall, you're in the driver's seat, always doing your own thinking and planning.

A Rich Array of Leveled Text Sets

You choose the texts when you customize your literacy program. Select from Below-Level, On-Level, and Advanced Readers in *Reading Street*. Specific text sets are also available for your ELD and ELL groups. For struggling readers who need to practice independent reading as they build understanding and develop concept knowledge, choose the Concept Literacy Leveled Readers.

Grade 2 Alignment with DRA2

Many educators use the Developmental Reading Assessment, or DRA2, to assess students' reading achievement. This chart shows how *Reading Street* aligns with DRA2.

GRADE TWO Instructional Strand	Focus for Instruction	DRA2 Benchmark	*Reading Street* Unit/ Week Lesson Plan	Materials
Phonics				
	Short vowels	16–28	1/1	DI pages: U1v1 DI1–DI11 Decodable Readers: 1A, 1C Leveled Readers*
	Long vowels	16–28	1/2	DI pages: U1v1 DI22–DI32 Decodable Readers: 2A, 2C Leveled Readers*
	Consonant blends	16–28	1/3	DI pages: U1v1 DI43–DI53 Decodable Readers: 3A, 3C Leveled Readers*
	Endings	16–28	1/4, 3/5, 6/1	DI pages: U1v2 DI64–DI74, U3v2 DI85–DI95, U6v1 DI1–DI11 Decodable Readers: 4A, 4C, 15A, 15C, 26A, 26C Leveled Readers*
	Consonant digraphs	16–28	1/4	DI pages: U1v2 DI64–DI74 Decodable Readers: 4A, 4C Leveled Readers*
	r-controlled vowels	16–28	2/1, 2/2	DI pages: U2v1 DI1–DI11, U2v1 DI22–DI32 Decodable Readers: 6A, 6C, 7A, 7C Leveled Readers*
	Contractions	16–28	2/2	DI pages: U2v1 DI22–DI32 Decodable Readers: 7A, 7C Leveled Readers*
	Plurals	16–28	2/4	DI pages: U2v2 DI64–DI74 Decodable Readers: 9A, 9C Leveled Readers*

* See following pages for a list of Leveled Readers.

GRADE TWO Instructional Strand	Focus for Instruction	DRA2 Benchmark	*Reading Street* Unit/ Week Lesson Plan	Materials
	Vowel patterns	16–28	2/5, 3/1, 3/2, 3/4, 4/2, 5/5	DI pages: U2v2 DI85–DI95, U3v1 DI1–DI11, U3v1 DI22–DI32, U3v2 DI64–DI74, U4v1 DI22–DI32, U5v2 DI85–DI95 Decodable Readers: 10A, 10C, 11A, 11C, 12A, 12C, 14A, 14C, 17A, 17C, 25A, 25C Leveled Readers*
	Syllable patterns	16–28	4/1, 4/4, 6/3	DI pages: U4v1 DI1–DI11, U4v2 DI64–DI74, U6v1 DI43–DI53 Decodable Readers: 16A, 16C, 19A, 19C, 28A, 28C Leveled Readers*
	Diphthongs	16–28	4/3	DI pages: U4v1 DI43–DI53 Decodable Readers: 18A, 18C Leveled Readers*
	Vowel digraphs	16–28	4/5	DI pages: U4v2 DI85–DI95 Decodable Readers: 20A, 20C Leveled Readers*
	Consonant patterns	16–28	5/3, 5/4	DI pages: U5v1 DI43–DI53, U5v2 DI64–DI74 Decodable Readers: 23A, 23C, 24A, 24C Leveled Readers*
	Suffixes -ly, -ful, -er, -or, -ish, -ness, -less, -able, -ible	16–28	5/1, 6/4	DI pages: U5v1 DI1–DI11, U6v2 DI64–DI74 Decodable Readers: 21A, 21C, 29A, 29C Leveled Readers*
	Prefixes un-, re-, pre-, dis-, mis-, mid-, micro-, non-	16–28	5/2, 6/5	DI pages: U5v1 DI22–DI32, U6v2 DI85–DI95 Decodable Readers: 22A, 30A, 30C Leveled Readers*
	Abbreviations	16–28	6/2	DI pages: U6v1 DI22–DI32 Decodable Readers: 27A, 27C Leveled Readers*
Comprehension				
Questioning	Model asking questions	18–28	3/1, 4/3, 6/3	DI pages: U3v1 DI1–DI11, U4v1 DI43–DI53, U6v1 DI43–DI53 Leveled Readers*

* See following pages for a list of Leveled Readers.

GRADE TWO Instructional Strand	Focus for Instruction	DRA2 Benchmark	*Reading Street* Unit/ Week Lesson Plan	Materials
Prediction	Model how to preview a text based on prior knowledge and oral introduction	18–28	1/5, 3/4, 6/5	DI pages: U1v2 DI85–DI95, U3v2 DI64–DI74, U6v2 DI85–DI95 Leveled Readers*
Story Structure	Model the retelling of a story or information sequentially	18–28	1/3, 2/4, 5/4, 6/4	DI pages: U1v1 DI43–DI53, U2v2 DI64–DI74, U5v2 DI64–DI74, U6v2 DI64–DI74 Leveled Readers*
Monitor and Clarify	Demonstrate how to read for meaning, self-correcting when a word doesn't make sense	18–28	1/1, 4/5, 6/1	DI pages: U1v1 DI1–DI11, U4v2 DI85–DI95, U6v1 DI1–DI11 Leveled Readers*
Background Knowledge	Model connecting text to self	18–28	2/3, 4/1, 5/3	DI pages: U2v1 DI43–DI53, U4v1 DI1–DI11, U5v1 DI43–DI53 Leveled Readers*
Summarize	Teach how to identify important details to include in a retelling	18–28	2/1, 3/3, 6/2	DI pages: U2v1 DI1–DI11, U3v1 DI43–DI53, U6v2 DI22–DI32 Leveled Readers*
	Identify story elements (e.g., characters, setting, problem, solution)	18–28	2/1, 3/3, 6/2	DI pages: U2v1 DI1–DI11, U3v1 DI43–DI53, U6v1 DI22–DI32 Leveled Readers*
Visualize	Model sensory images to determine word meaning	18–28	3/2, 4/4, 5/2	DI pages: U3v1 DI22–DI32, U4v2 DI64–DI74, U5v1 DI22–DI32 Leveled Readers*
Important Ideas	Model how to use graphic organizers to present ideas	18–28	1/4, 4/2, 5/1	DI pages: U1v2 DI64–DI74, U4v1 DI22–DI32, U5v1 DI1–DI11 Leveled Readers*
Text Structure	Teach how to identify text features	18–28	1/2, 2/2, 6/4	DI pages: U1v2 DI22–DI32, U2v2 DI22–DI32, U6v2 DI64–DI74 Leveled Readers*
Inferring	Model responding to why questions about inferences	18–28	2/5, 3/5	DI pages: U2v2 DI85–DI95, U3v2 DI85–DI95 Leveled Readers*

* See following pages for a list of Leveled Readers.

Leveled Reader Skills Chart

How do I find the right reader for every student?

The books in this list were leveled using the criteria suggested in Matching Books to Readers *and* Leveled Books for Readers, Grades 3–6 *by Irene C. Fountas and Gay Su Pinnell. For more on leveling, see the* Reading Street Leveled Readers Leveling Guide. *Complete books may also be found on the Leveled Readers Database.*

grade 2 Title	Level*	DRA Level*	Genre	Target Comprehension Skill	
The Rescue Dogs	C	3	Narrative Nonfiction	Cause and Effect	
Country Mouse and City Mouse	D	4	Traditional Tales	Character and Setting	
All About Astronauts	D	4	Expository Nonfiction	Main Idea	
Camping with Pup	D	4	Animal Fantasy	Character and Setting	
Deserts	D	4	Expository Nonfiction	Main Idea	
Too Many Rabbit Holes	D	4	Fantasy/Play	Facts and Details	
A Class Play	D	4	Realistic Fiction	Author's Purpose	
The Barn Raising	D	4	Nonfiction	Facts and Details	
Working Dogs	D	4	Expository Nonfiction	Cause and Effect	
Where is Fish?	D	4	Fantasy	Compare and Contrast	
Our School Science Fair	D	4	Realistic Fiction	Author's Purpose	
Let's Send a Letter!	D	4	Narrative Nonfiction	Draw Conclusions	
Using a Net	D	4	Expository Nonfiction	Compare and Contrast	
Ana Is Shy	E	6–8	Realistic Fiction	Sequence	
Sink or Float?	E	6–8	Narrative Nonfiction	Fact and Opinion	
The Camping Trip	E	6–8	Realistic Fiction	Draw Conclusions	
How to Grow Tomatoes	E	6–8	How-to	Sequence	
How a Seed Grows	E	6–8	Expository Nonfiction	Fact and Opinion	
Snakeskin Canyon	E	6–8	Realistic Fiction	Plot and Theme	
Blizzard!	E	6–8	Realistic Fiction	Plot and Theme	
The New Kid in Bali	F	10	Realistic Fiction	Character and Setting	
An Astronaut Space Walk	F	10	Expository Nonfiction	Character and Setting	
Camping at Crescent Lake	F	10	Realistic Fiction	Character and Setting	
Desert Animals	F	10	Expository Nonfiction	Main Idea	
Service Workers	F	10	Expository Nonfiction	Fact and Opinion	
What Can You Do?	F	10	Narrative Nonfiction	Cause and Effect	
Sally and the Wild Puppy	F	10	Humorous Fiction	Plot and Theme	
Join an Adventure Club!	F	10	Narrative Nonfiction	Character and Setting	
Andrew's Mistake	F	10	Realistic Fiction	Main Idea	

* Suggested Guided Reading level. Use your knowledge of children's abilities to adjust levels as needed.

Additional Comprehension Instruction	Comprehension Strategy	Vocabulary	Content Connection
Fact and Opinion	Summarize	High-Frequency Words	Citizenship
Fact and Opinion	Monitor and Clarify	High-Frequency Words	Economics/Geography
Author's Purpose	Text Structure	High-Frequency Words	Space and Technology/ Life Science
Main Idea	Story Structure	High-Frequency Words	Citizenship/Culture
Compare and Contrast	Important Ideas	High-Frequency Words	Earth Science
Character and Setting	Predict and Set Purpose	High-Frequency Words	Life Science
Fact and Detail	Text Structure	High-Frequency Words	History
Cause and Effect	Background Knowledge	High-Frequency Words	Citizenship
Compare and Contrast	Story Structure	High-Frequency Words	Citizenship
Author's Purpose	Inferring	High-Frequency Words	Life Science
Plot and Theme	Questioning	High-Frequency Words	Physical Science/ Earth Science
Sequence	Visualize	High-Frequency Words	Government
Draw Conclusions/ Make Inferences	Summarize	High-Frequency Words	Citizenship
Cause and Effect	Predict and Set Purpose	High-Frequency Words	Culture
Sequence	Inferring	High-Frequency Words	Physical Science
Character and Setting	Background Knowledge	Word Structure/Prefixes	Culture
Fact and Opinion	Important Ideas	Context Clues/Antonyms	Life Science
Facts and Details	Questioning	Context Clues/Unfamiliar Words	Life Science
Draw Conclusions/ Make Inferences	Visualize	Context Clues/Multiple Meanings	Economics/Geography
Main Idea	Monitor and Clarify	Picture Clues/Multiple Meanings	Earth Science
Plot and Theme	Monitor and Clarify	High-Frequency Words	Culture
Sequence	Story Structure	High-Frequency Words	Science and Technology
Main Idea	Story Structure	High-Frequency Words	Life Science
Compare and Contrast	Important Ideas	High-Frequency Words	Space and Technology/ Earth Science
Author's Purpose	Important Ideas	Word Structure/Suffixes	Citizenship
Facts and Details	Visualize	Dictionary Skills/Unfamiliar Words	Citizenship
Sequence	Background Knowledge	Dictionary Skills/Unfamiliar Words	Citizenship
Plot and Theme	Story Structure	Dictionary Skills/Unfamiliar Words	Citizenship
Character and Setting	Inferring	Word Structure/Compound Words	Citizenship

Leveled Reader Skills Chart (*continued*)

grade 2 — Title	Level*	DRA Level*	Genre	Target Comprehension Skill	
Glooskap and the First Summer: An Algonquin Tale	G	12	Folk Tale	Facts and Details	
Be Ready for an Emergency	G	12	Narrative Nonfiction	Cause and Effect	
Let's Work Together!	G	12	Realistic Fiction	Author's Purpose	
Farming Families	G	12	Expository Nonfiction	Facts and Details	
Growing Up	G	12	Realistic Fiction	Cause and Effect	
Three Great Ballplayers	G	12	Autobiography/Biography	Compare and Contrast	
America's Birthday	G	12	Expository Nonfiction	Author's Purpose	
Special Chinese Birthdays	G	12	Narrative Nonfiction	Draw Conclusions	
Down on the Ranch	G	12	Historical Fiction	Sequence	
Just Like Grandpa	G	12	Realistic Fiction	Facts and Details	
Showing Good Manners	H	14	Nonfiction	Compare and Contrast	
Dotty's Art	H	14	Realistic Fiction	Author's Purpose	
Living in Seoul	H	14	Narrative Nonfiction	Draw Conclusions	
Arachnid or Insect?	H	14	Expository Nonfiction	Compare and Contrast	
The International Food Fair	H	14	Realistic Fiction	Sequence	
Thomas Adams: Chewing Gum Inventor	I	16	Biography	Fact and Opinion	
Making Travel Fun	I	16	Expository Nonfiction	Draw Conclusions	
How Do Plants Grow?	I	16	Expository Nonfiction	Sequence	
A Slice of Mud Pie	I	16	Realistic Fiction	Fact and Opinion	
Too Many Frogs!	I	16	Humorous Fiction	Plot and Theme	
Rainbow Crow Brings Fire to Earth	J	18	Narrative Nonfiction	Plot and Theme	
Keeping Our Community Safe	J	18	Expository Nonfiction	Fact and Opinion	
Annie Makes a Big Change	J	18	Realistic Fiction	Cause and Effect	
Hubert and Frankie	J	18	Animal Fantasy	Plot and Theme	
Everyone Can Make a Difference!	K	20	Narrative Nonfiction	Character and Setting	
Freda the Signmaker	K	20	Humorous Fiction	Main Idea	
Women Play Baseball	K	20	Narrative Nonfiction	Compare and Contrast	
American Revolution Heroes	K	20	Biography	Author's Purpose	
Country Friends, City Friends	L	24	Realistic Fiction	Character and Setting	
Look at Our Galaxy	L	24	Expository Nonfiction	Main Idea	
At Home in the Wilderness	L	24	Historical Fiction	Character and Setting	

* Suggested Guided Reading level. Use your knowledge of children's abilities to adjust levels as needed.

Additional Comprehension Instruction	Comprehension Strategy	Vocabulary	Content Connection
Character and Setting	Predict and Set Purpose	High-Frequency Words	Culture
Fact and Opinion	Summarize	High-Frequency Words	Citizenship
Facts and Details	Text Structure	High-Frequency Words	Citizenship
Cause and Effect	Background Knowledge	High-Frequency Words	Life Science
Compare and Contrast	Story Structure	High-Frequency Words	Life Science
Draw Conclusions/ Make Inferences	Monitor and Clarify	Context Clues/Homophones	History
Fact and Opinion	Summarize	Context Clues/Unfamiliar Words	Citizenship
Cause and Effect	Questioning	Context Clues/Synonyms	Culture
Main Idea	Story Structure	Word Structure/Suffixes	History
Compare and Contrast	Predict and Set Purpose	Word Structure/Compound Words	Culture
Author's Purpose	Inferring	High-Frequency Words	Culture
Plot and Theme	Questioning	High-Frequency Words	Culture
Sequence	Visualize	High-Frequency Words	Culture
Draw Conclusions/ Make Inferences	Summarize	High-Frequency Words	Life Science
Cause and Effect	Predict and Set Purpose	High-Frequency Words	Culture
Sequence	Inferring	High-Frequency Words	History
Character and Setting	Background Knowledge	Word Structure/Prefixes	History
Fact and Opinion	Important Ideas	Context Clues/Antonyms	Life Science
Fact and Details	Questioning	Context Clues/Unfamiliar Words	Earth Science
Draw Conclusions/ Make Inferences	Visualize	Context Clues/Multiple Meanings	Citizenship
Main Idea	Monitor and Clarify	Context Clues/Multiple Meanings	Earth Science
Author's Purpose	Important Ideas	Word Structure/Suffixes	Citizenship
Facts and Details	Visualize	Dictionary Skills/Unfamiliar Words	Life Science/Citizenship
Sequence	Background Knowledge	Dictionary Skills/Unfamiliar Words	Citizenship
Plot and Theme	Story Structure	Dictionary Skills/Unfamiliar Words	Citizenship
Character and Setting	Inferring	Word Structure/Compound Words	Citizenship
Draw Conclusions/ Make Inferences	Monitor and Clarify	Context Clues/Homophones	History
Fact and Opinion	Summarize	Context Clues/Unfamiliar Words	History
Plot and Theme	Monitor and Clarify	Amazing Words	Culture
Author's Purpose	Text Structure	Amazing Words	Space and Technology
Main Idea	Story Structure	Amazing Words	History

Leveled Reader Skills Chart (*continued*)

grade 2 Title	Level*	DRA Level*	Genre	Target Comprehension Skill	
The First People to Fly	L	24	Realistic Fiction	Facts and Details	
A World of Birthdays	L	24	Narrative Nonfiction	Draw Conclusions	
A Cowboy's Life	L	24	Historical Fiction	Sequence	
Voting Day	L	24	Realistic Fiction	Facts and Details	
The Hummingbird	M	28	Expository Nonfiction	Main Idea	
Special Animal Helpers	M	28	Narrative Nonfiction	Cause and Effect	
The Hoover Dam	M	28	Expository Nonfiction	Author's Purpose	
Many Types of Energy	M	28	Expository Nonfiction	Facts and Details	
Stripes and Silver	M	28	Play	Cause and Effect	
Saint Bernards and Other Working Dogs	N	30	Nonfiction	Compare and Contrast	
Maggie's New Sidekick	N	30	Fantasy	Author's Purpose	
Communicating Then and Now	N	30	Expository Nonfiction	Draw Conclusions	
How Can Animals Help?	N	30	Narrative Nonfiction	Compare and Contrast	
Hank's Tortilla Factory	N	30	Realistic Fiction	Sequence	
A Few Nifty Inventions	N	30	Expository Nonfiction	Fact and Opinion	
Starting a New Life	N	30	Expository Nonfiction	Draw Conclusions	
Plants Grow Everywhere	O	34	Expository Nonfiction	Sequence	
Compost: Recycled Waste	O	34	Narrative Nonfiction	Fact and Opinion	
A Quiet Place	O	34	Realistic Fiction	Plot and Theme	
Hurricane!	O	34	Expository Nonfiction	Plot and Theme	
Services and Goods	O	34	Narrative Nonfiction	Fact and Opinion	
A Vet for All Animals	O	34	Narrative Nonfiction	Cause and Effect	
Training Peanut	O	34	Realistic Fiction	Plot and Theme	
Protect the Earth	P	38	Narrative Nonfiction	Character and Setting	
Marty's Summer Job	P	38	Realistic Fiction	Main Idea	
Baseball Heroes Make History	P	38	Autobiography/Biography	Compare and Contrast	
Living in a Democracy	P	38	Expository Nonfiction	Author's Purpose	
Celebrations and Family Traditions	P	38	Narrative Nonfiction	Draw Conclusions	
Living on a Ranch	P	38	Realistic Fiction	Sequence	
Happy New Year!	P	38	Realistic Fiction	Facts and Details	

* Suggested Guided Reading level. Use your knowledge of children's abilities to adjust levels as needed.

Additional Comprehension Instruction	Comprehension Strategy	Vocabulary	Content Connection
Character and Setting	Predict and Set Purpose	Amazing Words	Culture
Cause and Effect	Questioning	Context Clues/Synonyms	Culture
Main Idea	Text Structure	Word Structure/Suffixes	History
Compare and Contrast	Predict and Set Purpose	Word Structure/Compound Words	Culture
Compare and Contrast	Important Ideas	Amazing Words	Physical Science
Cause and Effect	Summarize	Amazing Words	Citizenship
Fact and Detail	Text Structure	Amazing Words	History
Cause and Effect	Background Knowledge	Amazing Words	Physical Science
Compare and Contrast	Story Structure	Amazing Words	Citizenship/Life Science
Author's Purpose	Inferring	Amazing Words	History
Plot and Theme	Questioning	Amazing Words	Space and Technology
Sequence	Visualize	Amazing Words	Government
Draw Conclusions/ Make Inferences	Summarize	Amazing Words	Life Science
Cause and Effect	Predict and Set Purpose	Amazing Words	History
Sequence	Inferring	Amazing Words	History
Character and Setting	Background Knowledge	Word Structure/Prefixes	History
Fact and Opinion	Important Ideas	Context Clues/Antonyms	Life Science
Fact and Details	Questioning	Context Clues/Unfamiliar Words	Life Science
Draw Conclusions/ Make Inferences	Visualize	Context Clues/Multiple Meanings	Economics/Geography
Main Idea	Monitor and Clarify	Context Clues/Multiple Meanings	Earth Science
Author's Purpose	Important Ideas	Word Structure/Suffixes	Economics/Geography
Facts and Details	Visualize	Dictionary Skills/Unfamiliar Words	Life Science
Sequence	Background Knowledge	Dictionary Skills/Unfamiliar Words	Citizenship
Plot and Theme	Story Structure	Dictionary Skills/Unfamiliar Words	Citizenship
Character and Setting	Inferring	Word Structure/Compound Words	Citizenship
Draw Conclusions/ Make Inferences	Monitor and Clarify	Context Clues/Homophones	History
Fact and Opinion	Summarize	Context Clues/Unfamiliar Words	History
Cause and Effect	Questioning	Context Clues/Synonyms	Culture
Main Idea	Text Structure	Word Structure/Suffixes	Culture
Compare and Contrast	Predict and Set Purpose	Word Structure/Compound Words	Culture

Leveled Reader Skills Chart (*continued*)

Need more choices? Look back to Grade 1.

Grade 1 — Title	Level*	DRA Level*	Genre	Target Comprehension Skill	
Bix the Dog	A	1	Realistic Fiction	Plot	
Time for Dinner	B	2	Realistic Fiction	Main Idea and Details	
Sam	B	2	Realistic Fiction	Character and Setting	
Mack and Zack	B	2	Realistic Fiction	Character and Setting	
The Sick Pets	B	2	Realistic Fiction	Plot	
On the Farm	B	2	Realistic Fiction	Character and Setting	
At Your Vet	B	2	Realistic Fiction	Main Idea and Details	
Fun in the Sun	B	2	Expository Nonfiction	Cause and Effect	
We Are a Family	B	2	Nonfiction	Sequence	
Where They Live	C	3	Realistic Fiction	Character and Setting	
Which Fox?	C	3	Realistic Fiction	Main Idea and Details	
Which Animals Will We See?	C	3	Realistic Fiction	Cause and Effect	
Let's Go to the Zoo	C	3	Nonfiction	Sequence	
A Play	C	3	Realistic Fiction	Cause and Effect	
A Class	C	3	Nonfiction	Cause and Effect	
Here in My Neighborhood	C	3	Nonfiction	Author's Purpose	
Look at My Neighborhood	C	3	Realistic Fiction	Author's Purpose	
Look at Dinosaurs	C	3	Expository Nonfiction	Sequence	
Around the Forest	C	3	Nonfiction	Author's Purpose	
Learn About Worker Bees	C	3	Expository Nonfiction	Compare and Contrast	
In My Room	C	3	Nonfiction	Sequence	
Hank's Song	C	3	Fantasy	Compare and Contrast	
Gus the Pup	C	3	Realistic Fiction	Fact and Opinion	
What Animals Can You See?	D	4	Expository Nonfiction	Main Idea and Details	
The Dinosaur Herds	D	4	Expository Nonfiction	Sequence	
People Help the Forest	D	4	Expository Nonfiction	Author's Purpose	
Honey	D	4	Nonfiction	Compare and Contrast	
Let's Build a Park!	D	4	Fiction	Sequence	
Mac Can Do It!	D	4	Fantasy	Compare and Contrast	
The Seasons Change	D	4	Nonfiction	Author's Purpose	
Animals Change and Grow	D	4	Nonfiction	Fact and Opinion	
Ready for Winter?	D	4	Expository Nonfiction	Draw Conclusions	

* Suggested Guided Reading level. Use your knowledge of children's abilities to adjust levels as needed.

Additional Comprehension Instruction	Comprehension Strategy	Vocabulary	Content Connection
Sequence	Summarize	High-Frequency Words	Life Science
Compare and Contrast	Important Ideas	High-Frequency Words	Life Science
Draw Conclusions	Monitor and Clarify	High-Frequency Words	Life Science
Main Idea	Monitor and Clarify	High-Frequency Words	Life Science
Draw Conclusions	Summarize	High-Frequency Words	Life Science/Citizenship
Plot	Visualize	High-Frequency Words	Citizenship
Theme	Story Structure	High-Frequency Words	Citizenship
Author's Purpose	Text Structure	High-Frequency Words	Life Science
Draw Conclusions	Predict and Set Purpose	High-Frequency Words	Culture
Theme and Plot	Visualize	High-Frequency Words	Geography/Culture
Compare and Contrast	Important Ideas	High-Frequency Words	Life Science
Setting and Plot	Text Structure	High-Frequency Words	Life Science
Compare and Contrast	Predict and Set Purpose	High-Frequency Words	Life Science
Main Idea	Monitor and Clarify	High-Frequency Words	Citizenship
Author's Purpose	Monitor and Clarify	High-Frequency Words	Citizenship/Culture
Draw Conclusions	Important Ideas	High-Frequency Words	Citizenship/Culture
Compare and Contrast	Important Ideas	High-Frequency Words	Citizenship
Cause and Effect	Inferring	High-Frequency Words	Life Science
Cause and Effect	Background Knowledge	High-Frequency Words	Life Science
Sequence	Questioning	High-Frequency Words	Life Science
Author's Purpose	Summarize	High-Frequency Words	Life Science
Realism and Fantasy	Inferring	High-Frequency Words	Citizenship
Cause and Effect	Monitor and Clarify	High-Frequency Words	Culture
Compare and Contrast	Text Structure	High-Frequency Words	Life Science
Draw Conclusions	Inferring	High-Frequency Words	Life Science
Cause and Effect	Background Knowledge	High-Frequency Words	Life Science
Draw Conclusions	Questioning	High-Frequency Words	Life Science
Author's Purpose	Summarize	High-Frequency Words	Citizenship
Realism and Fantasy	Inferring	High-Frequency Words	Life Science
Draw Conclusions	Visualize	High-Frequency Words	Life Science
Sequence	Text Structure	High-Frequency Words	Life Science
Sequence	Background Knowledge	High-Frequency Words	Earth Science

Leveled Reader Skills Chart (continued)

Grade 1 Title	Level*	DRA Level*	Genre	Target Comprehension Skill	
A Party for Pedro	D	4	Realistic Fiction	Draw Conclusions	
Space Star	D	4	Realistic Fiction	Theme	
Our Leaders	D	4	Nonfiction	Facts and Details	
Grandma's Farm	D	4	Realistic Fiction	Facts and Details	
A New Baby Brother	D	4	Realistic Fiction	Theme	
My Babysitter	D	4	Narrative Nonfiction	Cause and Effect	
What Brown Saw	D	4	Animal Fantasy	Character, Setting, and Plot	
Fly Away Owl!	D	4	Realistic Fiction	Draw Conclusions	
What A Detective Does	D	4	Realistic Fiction	Compare and Contrast	
The Inclined Plane	D	4	Expository Nonfiction	Main Idea and Details	
Using the Telephone	D	4	Expository Nonfiction	Sequence	
A Garden for All	D	4	Nonfiction	Theme	
Big Wishes and Her Baby	E	6–8	Realistic Fiction	Fact and Opinion	
Plans Change	E	6–8	Realistic Fiction	Author's Purpose	
Let's Visit a Butterfly Greenhouse	E	6–8	Nonfiction	Fact and Opinion	
Seasons Come and Go	E	6–8	Expository Nonfiction	Draw Conclusions	
Special Days, Special Food	E	6–8	Expository Nonfiction	Draw Conclusions	
The Art Show	F	10	Realistic Fiction	Theme	
Treasures of Our Country	F	10	Nonfiction	Facts and Details	
A Visit to the Ranch	F	10	Realistic Fiction	Facts and Details	
My Little Brother Drew	F	10	Realistic Fiction	Theme	
The Story of the Kids Care Club	F	10	Expository Nonfiction	Cause and Effect	
Squirrel and Bear	G	12	Animal Fantasy	Character, Setting, and Plot	
Puppy Raiser	G	12	Expository Nonfiction	Draw Conclusions	
A Mighty Oak Tree	G	12	Expository Nonfiction	Compare and Contrast	
Simple Machines at Work	G	12	Expository Nonfiction	Main Idea and Details	
Carlos Picks a Pet	H	14	Realistic Fiction	Character and Setting	
That Cat Needs Help!	H	14	Realistic Fiction	Plot	
Loni's Town	H	14	Realistic Fiction	Character and Setting	
Baby Animals in the Rain Forest	H	14	Expository Nonfiction	Main Idea and Details	
Cary and the The Wildlife Shelter	H	14	Realistic Fiction	Main Idea and Details	
Around the World	H	14	Narrative Nonfiction	Cause and Effect	

* Suggested Guided Reading level. Use your knowledge of children's abilities to adjust levels as needed.

Additional Comprehension Instruction	Comprehension Strategy	Vocabulary	Content Connection
Author's Purpose	Monitor and Clarify	High-Frequency Words	Culture
Realism and Fantasy	Visualize	High-Frequency Words	Citizenship/Culture
Cause and Effect	Important Ideas	High-Frequency Words	Government
Plot	Questioning	High-Frequency Words	Culture
Realism and Fantasy	Story Structure	High-Frequency Words	Culture
Main Idea	Predict and Set Purpose	High-Frequency Words	Culture
Realism and Fantasy	Monitor and Clarify	High-Frequency Words	Life Science
Cause and Effect	Background Knowledge	High-Frequency Words	Citizenship
Cause and Effect	Monitor and Clarify	High-Frequency Words	Earth Science/Life Science
Cause and Effect	Summarize	High-Frequency Words	Physical Science
Author's Purpose	Text Structure	High-Frequency Words	Space and Technology
Sequence	Inferring	High-Frequency Words	Citizenship
Setting	Monitor and Clarify	High-Frequency Words	Citizenship
Setting	Visualize	High-Frequency Words	Life Science
Author's Purpose	Text Structure	High-Frequency Words	Life Science
Compare and Contrast	Background Knowledge	High-Frequency Words	Life Science
Author's Purpose	Monitor and Clarify	High-Frequency Words	Culture
Plot	Visualize	High-Frequency Words	Citizenship/Culture
Cause and Effect	Important Ideas	High-Frequency Words	History/Geography
Compare and Contrast	Questioning	High-Frequency Words	Culture
Realism and Fantasy	Story Structure	High-Frequency Words	Citizenship
Author's Purpose	Predict and Set Purpose	High-Frequency Words	Citizenship
Realism and Fantasy	Monitor and Clarify	High-Frequency Words	Citizenship
Main Idea	Background Knowledge	High-Frequency Words	Citizenship
Draw Conclusions	Monitor and Clarify	High-Frequency Words	Life Science
Compare and Contrast	Summarize	High-Frequency Words	Physical Science
Compare and Contrast	Monitor and Clarify	Amazing Words	Life Science
Sequence	Summarize	Amazing Words	Citizenship
Theme	Visualize	Amazing Words	History
Author's Purpose	Important Ideas	Amazing Words	Life Science
Sequence	Story Structure	Amazing Words	Life Science
Main Idea	Text Structure	Amazing Words	Life Science

Leveled Reader Skills Chart (*continued*)

grade 1 Title	Level*	DRA Level*	Genre	Target Comprehension Skill	
The Communication Story	H	14	Expository Nonfiction	Sequence	
Marla's Good Idea	H	14	Realistic Fiction	Theme	
Rules at School	I	16	Animal Fantasy	Sequence	
School: Then and Now	I	16	Expository Nonfiction	Cause and Effect	
Mom the Mayor	I	16	Realistic Fiction	Author's Purpose	
The Dinosaur Detectives	I	16	Expository Nonfiction	Sequence	
All About Food Chains	I	16	Expository Nonfiction	Author's Purpose	
Bees and Beekeepers	I	16	Expository Nonfiction	Compare and Contrast	
A New Library	I	16	Narrative Nonfiction	Sequence	
Paul's Bed	J	18	Traditional Tales	Compare and Contrast	
Britton Finds a Kitten	J	18	Realistic Fiction	Fact and Opinion	
All About the Weather	J	18	Expository Nonfiction	Author's Purpose	
Learn About Butterflies	J	18	Expository Nonfiction	Fact and Opinion	
Monarchs Migrate South	J	18	Narrative Nonfiction	Draw Conclusions	
Cascarones Are for Fun	J	18	Expository Nonfiction	Draw Conclusions	
Jamie's Jumble of Junk	J	18	Realistic Fiction	Theme	
America's Home	K	20	Nonfiction	Facts and Details	
Go West!	K	20	Legend	Facts and Details	
Double Trouble Twins	K	20	Realistic Fiction	Theme	
What Makes Buildings Special?	K	20	Expository Nonfiction	Cause and Effect	
Grasshopper and Ant	K	20	Fable	Character, Setting, and Plot	
Ways to be a Good Citizen	K	20	Expository Nonfiction	Draw Conclusions	
Great Scientists: Detectives at Work	L	24	Expository Nonfiction	Compare and Contrast	
Simple Machines in Compound Machines	L	24	Nonfiction	Main Idea and Details	
Over the Years	L	24	Expository Nonfiction	Sequence	
Cody's Adventure	L	24	Realistic Fiction	Theme	

* Suggested Guided Reading level. Use your knowledge of children's abilities to adjust levels as needed.

Additional Comprehension Instruction	Comprehension Strategy	Vocabulary	Content Connection
Compare and Contrast	Text Structure	High-Frequency Words	Space and Technology
Sequence	Inferring	High-Frequency Words	Space and Technology
Character	Predict and Set Purpose	Amazing Words	Citizenship
Draw Conclusions	Monitor and Clarify	Amazing Words	History
Cause and Effect	Important Ideas	Amazing Words	Government
Draw Conclusions	Inferring	Amazing Words	Life Science
Cause and Effect	Background Knowledge	Amazing Words	Life Science
Main Idea	Questioning	Amazing Words	Life Science
Author's Purpose	Summarize	Amazing Words	Citizenship
Character	Inferring	Amazing Words	Citizenship
Setting	Monitor and Clarify	Amazing Words	Life Science
Plot	Visualize	Amazing Words	Earth Science
Cause and Effect	Text Structure	Amazing Words	Life Science
Author's Purpose	Background Knowledge	Amazing Words	LIfe Science
Sequence	Monitor and Clarify	Amazing Words	Culture/History
Character, Setting, and Plot	Visualize	Amazing Words	Culture
Cause and Effect	Important Ideas	Amazing Words	Government
Theme	Questioning	Amazing Words	Culture
Realism and Fantasy	Story Structure	Amazing Words	Citizenship
Draw Conclusions	Predict and Set Purpose	Amazing Words	Culture
Cause and Effect	Monitor and Clarify	Amazing Words	Citizenship
Compare and Contrast	Background Knowledge	Amazing Words	Citizenship
Compare and Contrast	Monitor and Clarify	Amazing Words	Citizenship
Cause and Effect	Summarize	Amazing Words	Physical Science
Draw Conclusions	Text Structure	Amazing Words	Space and Technology
Sequence	Inferring	Amazing Words	Science

Leveled Reader Skills Chart (*continued*)

Need more choices? Look ahead to Grade 3.

Grade 3 Title	Level*	DRA Level*	Genre	Target Comprehension Skill	
The Opposite Cousins	F	10	Realistic Fiction	Character, Setting, and Theme	
It's a Fair Swap!	F	10	Expository Nonfiction	Sequence	
Life in the Arctic	F	10	Nonfiction	Sequence	
Let's Surprise Mom	F	10	Realistic Fiction	Compare and Contrast	
E-mail Friends	F	10	Realistic Fiction	Author's Purpose	
The Frozen Continent: Antarctica	F	10	Expository Nonfiction	Main Idea and Details	
Buddy Goes to School	G	12	Realistic Fiction	Compare and Contrast	
The Metal Detective	G	12	Realistic Fiction	Draw Conclusions	
Growing Vegetables	G	12	Narrative Nonfiction	Author's Purpose	
All About Birds	G	12	Nonfiction	Main Idea and Details	
Raisins	G	12	Nonfiction	Draw Conclusions	
The Hunters and the Elk	G	12	Fiction	Character, Setting, and Plot	
Pictures in the Sky	H	14	Expository Nonfiction	Graphic Sources	
Rescuing Whales	H	14	Expository Nonfiction	Generalize	
The Field Trip	H	14	Expository Nonfiction	Cause and Effect	
The Winning Point	H	14	Realistic Fiction	Generalize	
How to Measure the Weather	H	14	Expository Nonfiction	Graphic Sources	
Grandpa's Rock Kit	H	14	Narrative Nonfiction	Fact and Opinion	
Across the English Channel	H	14	Expository Nonfiction	Fact and Opinion	
Swimming Like Buck	I	16	Animal Fantasy	Cause and Effect	
A Tea Party with Obâchan	I	16	Realistic Fiction	Compare and Contrast	
Celebrate Independence Day/ Celebra el Día de la Independencia	I	16	Nonfiction	Main Idea and Details	
A Child's Life in Korea	I	16	Expository Nonfiction	Sequence	
The World of Bread!	I	16	Expository Nonfiction	Draw Conclusions	
A Walk Around the City	I	16	Expository Nonfiction	Author's Purpose	
The Statue of Liberty: A Gift From France	I	16	Expository Nonfiction	Fact and Opinion	
Camping with Aunt Julie	J	18	Realistic Fiction	Character and Setting	
Let's Make a Trade!	J	18	Expository Nonfiction	Sequence	
Ice Fishing in the Arctic	J	18	Nonfiction	Sequence	
The Shopping Trip	J	18	Fiction	Compare and Contrast	

* Suggested Guided Reading level. Use your knowledge of children's abilities to adjust levels as needed.

Additional Comprehension Instruction	Comprehension Strategy	Vocabulary	Content Connection
Draw Conclusions	Background Knowledge	Context Clues/Homonyms	Social Studies
Fact and Opinion	Summarize	Word Structure/Compound Words	Economics/Geography
Generalize	Visualize	Dictionary/Glossary/Unfamiliar Words	Life Science
Main Idea	Background Knowledge	Context Clues/Multiple Meanings	Social Studies
Compare and Contrast	Story Structure	Word Structure/Prefixes and Suffixes	Culture
Generalize	Monitor and Clarify	Context Clues/Synonyms	Earth Science
Sequence	Visualize	Context Clues/Unfamiliar Words	Social Studies
Realism and Fantasy	Questioning	Compound Words/Word Structure	Economics
Generalize	Predict and Set Purpose	Context Clues/Antonyms	Life Science
Compare and Contrast	Text Structure	Context Clues/Unfamiliar Words	Life Science
Generalize	Important Ideas	Homophones/Context Clues	Life Science
Theme	Inferring	Unknown Words/Dictionary/Glossary	Life Science
Author's Purpose	Text Structure	Unknown Words/Dictionary/Glossary	Earth Science
Sequence	Story Structure	Context Clues/Unfamiliar Words	Life Science
Draw Conclusions	Predict and Set Purpose	Prefixes/Suffixes/Word Structure	Life Science
Plot	Summarize	Unfamiliar Words/Context Clues	Social Studies
Main Idea	Important Ideas	Unknown Words/Dictionary/Glossary	Earth Science
Fact and Opinion	Inferring	Context Clues/Multiple Meanings	Earth Science
Generalize	Questioning	Context Clues/Multiple Meanings	History
Character	Monitor and Clarify	Unknown Words/Dictionary/Glossary	Life Science
Generalize	Visualize	Context Clues/Synonyms	Culture
Draw Conclusions	Inferring	Context Clues/Antonyms	History
Author's Purpose	Monitor and Clarify	Word Structure/Compound Words	Culture
Main Idea	Summarize	Context Clues/Unfamiliar Words	Culture
Generalize	Background Knowledge	Context Clues/Homonyms	Culture
Fact and Opinion	Questioning	Word Structure/Prefixes	History
Theme	Background Knowledge	Context Clues/Homonyms	Social Studies
Draw Conclusions	Summarize	Word Structure/Compound Words	Economics/Geography
Author's Purpose	Visualize	Dictionary/Glossary/Unfamiliar Words	Life Science/Economics
Character	Background Knowledge	Context Clues/Multiple Meanings	Economics

Leveled Reader Skills Chart (*continued*)

Grade 3 Title	Level*	DRA Level*	Genre	Target Comprehension Skill	
New York's Chinatown	J	18	Expository Nonfiction	Cause and Effect	
One Forest, Different Trees	J	18	Realistic Fiction	Graphic Sources	
Swimming in a School	J	18	Animal Fantasy	Plot and Theme	
Greek Myths	J	18	Nonfiction	Generalize	
The Market Adventure	K	20	Realistic Fiction	Author's Purpose	
These Birds Can't Fly!	K	20	Expository Nonfiction	Main Idea and Details	
Iguana Takes a Ride	K	20	Animal Fantasy	Compare and Contrast	
The Last Minute	K	20	Realistic Fiction	Draw Conclusions	
Our Garden	K	20	Realistic Fiction	Author's Purpose	
Bills and Beaks	L	24	Historical Fiction	Main Idea and Details	
In the Fields	L	24	Historical Fiction	Draw Conclusions	
The Thunder and Lightning Men	L	24	Folktale	Character, Setting, and Plot	
Meet the Stars	L	24	Realistic Fiction	Graphic Sources	
What a Day!	L	24	Realistic Fiction	Generalize	
Desert Life	L	24	Expository Nonfiction	Cause and Effect	
A Trip	M	28	Realistic Fiction	Generalize	
Measuring the Earth	M	28	Expository Nonfiction	Graphic Sources	
Fun with Hobbies and Science!	M	28	Expository Nonfiction	Fact and Opinion	
Great Women in U.S. History	M	28	Biography	Fact and Opinion	
Buddy Ran Away	M	28	Realistic Fiction	Cause and Effect	
Cowboy Slim's Dude Ranch	M	28	Realistic Fiction	Compare and Contrast	
Celebrate Around the World	N	30	Nonfiction	Main Idea and Details	
Joanie's House Becomes a Home	N	30	Realistic Fiction	Sequence of Events	
Kapuapua's Magic Shell	N	30	Folktale	Draw Conclusions	
Bobby's New Apartment	N	30	Realistic Fiction	Author's Purpose	
Symbols, Signs, and Songs of America	N	30	Narrative Nonfiction	Main Idea	
A Pet Bird	O	34	Expository Nonfiction	Cause and Effect	
Lily's Adventure Around the World	O	34	Realistic Fiction	Graphic Sources	
The Three Bears and Goldilocks	O	34	Animal Fantasy	Plot and Theme	
Sweet Freedom!	O	34	Nonfiction	Generalize	

* Suggested Guided Reading level. Use your knowledge of children's abilities to adjust levels as needed.

Additional Comprehension Instruction	Comprehension Strategy	Vocabulary	Content Connection
Generalize	Inferring	Context Clues/Antonyms	Culture
Generalize	Important Ideas	Dictionary/Glossary/Unknown Words	Culture
Realism and Fantasy	Story Structure	Word Structure/Prefixes and Suffixes	Life Science
Compare and Contrast	Inferring	Homographs/Context Clues	History/Culture
Generalize	Story Structure	Word Structure/Prefixes and Suffixes	Economics/Geography
Compare and Contrast	Monitor and Clarify	Context Clues/Synonyms	Life Science
Draw Conclusions	Visualize	Context Clues/Unfamiliar Words	Culture
Sequence	Questioning	Compound Words/Word Structure	Culture
Plot	Predict and Set Purpose	Context Clues/Antonyms	Citizenship
Setting	Text Structure	Context Clues/Unfamiliar Words	Life Science
Author's Purpose	Important Ideas	Homophones/Context Clues	Life Science
Main Idea	Inferring	Unknown Words/Dictionary/Glossary	Culture
Plot	Text Structure	Unknown Words/Dictionary/Glossary	Science and Technology
Character	Story Structure	Context Clues/Unfamiliar Words	Earth Science
Generalize	Predict and Set Purpose	Dictionary/Glossary/Unfamiliar Words	Life Science
Author's Purpose	Summarize	Unfamiliar Words/Context Clues	History
Fact and Opinion	Important Ideas	Unknown Words/Dictionary/Glossary	Earth Science
Draw Conclusions	Inferring	Context Clues/Multiple Meanings	Earth Science
Main Idea and Details	Questioning	Context Clues/Multiple Meanings	History
Sequence	Monitor and Clarify	Unknown Words/Dictionary/Glossary	Life Science
Main Idea	Visualize	Context Clues/Synonyms	Culture
Compare and Contrast	Inferring	Homophones/Context Clues	Culture
Draw Conclusions	Monitor and Clarify	Word Structure/Compound Words	Economics/Geography
Theme	Summarize	Context Clues/Unfamiliar Words	Culture
Realism and Fantasy	Background Knowledge	Context Clues/Homonyms	Culture
Fact and Opinion	Text Structure	Word Structure/Prefixes	Citizenship/Culture
Main Idea	Inferring	Context Clues/Antonyms	Life Science
Compare and Contrast	Important Ideas	Unknown Words/Dictionary/Glossary	Culture/Geography
Character	Story Structure	Word Structure/Prefixes and Suffixes	Culture
Author's Purpose	Inferring	Homographs/Context Clues	Citizenship

Leveled Reader Skills Chart (*continued*)

grade 3 Title	Level*	DRA Level*	Genre	Target Comprehension Skill	
Mr. Post's Project	P	38	Realistic Fiction	Character and Setting	
What's Money All About?	P	38	Expository Nonfiction	Sequence	
Journey Across the Arctic	P	38	Fiction	Sequence	
The Road to New York	P	38	Realistic Fiction	Compare and Contrast	
With a Twist	P	38	Fantasy	Author's Purpose	
All About Penguins	P	38	Expository Nonfiction	Main Idea and Details	
Puppy Problems	Q	40	Realistic Fiction	Compare and Contrast	
A Family of Collectors	Q	40	Realistic Fiction	Graphic Sources	
The Magic of Coyote	Q	40	Realistic Fiction	Author's Purpose	
Animals of the Concrete Jungle	Q	40	Expository Nonfiction	Main Idea and Details	
Grape Season	Q	40	Realistic Fiction	Draw Conclusions	
Grandmother Spider Steals the Sun	Q	40	Folktale	Character, Setting, and Plot	
Animal Tracking: Learn More About Animals	Q	40	Expository Nonfiction	Graphic Sources	
Whales and Other Amazing Animals	R	40	Expository Nonfiction	Generalize	
Coral Reefs	R	40	Expository Nonfiction	Cause and Effect	
Extraordinary Athletes	R	40	Biography	Generalize	
Largest, Fastest, Lightest, Longest	R	40	Expository Nonfiction	Compare and Contrast	
Gemstones Around the World	R	40	Expository Nonfiction	Fact and Opinion	
Changing Times: Women in the Early Twentieth Century	R	40	Expository Nonfiction	Fact and Opinion	
Toby the Smart Dog	R	40	Humorous Fiction	Cause and Effect	
His Favorite Sweatshirt	S	40	Realistic Fiction	Compare and Contrast	
Life Overseas	S	40	Expository Nonfiction	Main Idea and Details	
It's a World of Time Zones	S	40	Expository Nonfiction	Sequence	
Mixing, Kneading, and Baking: The Baker's Art	S	40	Narrative Nonfiction	Draw Conclusions	
Let's Go Have Fun!	S	40	Expository Nonfiction	Author's Purpose	
The French Connection	S	40	Narrative Nonfiction	Fact and Opinion	
China's Special Gifts to the World	T	50	Expository Nonfiction	Cause and Effect	
Thomas Hart Benton: Painter of Murals	T	50	Biography	Graphic Sources	
The Best Field Trip Ever!	T	50	Expository Fiction	Plot and Theme	
Free in the Sea	T	50	Expository Nonfiction	Generalize	

* Suggested Guided Reading level. Use your knowledge of children's abilities to adjust levels as needed.

Additional Comprehension Instruction	Comprehension Strategy	Vocabulary	Content Connection
Theme	Background Knowledge	Context Clues/Homonyms	Economics
Draw Conclusions	Summarize	Word Structure/Compound Words	Economics/Geography
Setting	Visualize	Dictionary/Glossary/Unfamiliar Words	Earth Science
Character	Background Knowledge	Context Clues/Multiple Meanings	Culture
Sequence	Story Structure	Word Structure/Prefixes and Suffixes	History
Compare and Contrast	Monitor and Clarify	Context Clues/Synonyms	Social Studies
Cause and Effect	Visualize	Context Clues/Unfamiliar Words	Social Studies
Realism and Fantasy	Important Ideas	Compound Words/Word Structure	Economics
Sequence	Predict	Context Clues/Antonyms	Culture/History
Fact and Opinion	Text Structure	Context Clues/Unfamiliar Words	Life Science
Main Idea	Important Ideas	Homophones/Context Clues	Life Science
Fact and Opinion	Inferring	Dictionary/Glossary/Unfamiliar Words	Culture
Compare and Contrast	Text Structure	Unknown Words/Dictionary/Glossary	Life Science
Author's Purpose	Story Structure	Context Clues/Unfamiliar Words	Life Science
Draw Conclusions	Predict and Set Purpose	Prefixes and Suffixes/Word Structure	Life Science
Draw Conclusions	Summarize	Unfamiliar Words/Context Clues	History
Author's Purpose	Ask Questions	Word Structure/Compound Words	Life Science
Cause and Effect	Inferring	Context Clues/Multiple Meanings	Earth Science
Generalize	Questioning	Context Clues/Multiple Meanings	History
Character and Setting	Monitor and Clarify	Unknown Words/Dictionary/Glossary	Life Science
Draw Conclusions	Visualize	Context Clues/Synonyms	Culture
Cause and Effect	Inferring	Homophones/Context Clues	Culture/Geography
Draw Conclusions	Monitor and Clarify	Word Structure/Compound Words	Economics/Geograpy
Main Idea	Summarize	Context Clues/Unfamiliar Words	Culture
Compare and Contrast	Background Knowledge	Context Clues/Homonyms	Culture
Generalize	Questioning	Word Structure/Prefixes	Culture/Geography
Generalize	Graphic Organizers	Context Clues/Antonyms	Culture/Geography
Author's Purpose	Important Ideas	Unknown Words/Dictionary/Glossary	History
Realism and Fantasy	Story Structure	Word Structure/Prefixes and Suffixes	Life Science
Compare and Contrast	Predict	Context Clues/Synonyms	Life Science

Concept Literacy Leveled Reader Chart

Concept Literacy Leveled Readers align with the weekly concepts in each unit. Each book is written at a lower level than the Below-Level Reader for the week to provide struggling readers with a way to practice independent reading as they build understanding and develop concept knowledge. Concept Literacy Readers play a role in the instruction for the Strategic Intervention group, but they can be used for independent reading practice for any struggling readers.

grade 2 Title	Level*	DRA Level*	Concept	Content Connection
The Country and the City	A	1	Exploration	Culture
How Do We Explore Space?	A	1	Exploration	Space and Technology
Our Camping Trip	A	1	Exploration	Life Science
In the Dry Desert	A	1	Exploration	Life Science
How Can You Find Animals?	A	1	Exploration	Life Science
Who Helps?	A	1	Working Together	Citizenship
Working Together	A	1	Working Together	Citizenship
What a School Needs	A	1	Working Together	Economics
Let's Clean Up the Park!	A	1	Working Together	Citizenship
We Make Soup!	A	1	Working Together	Social Studies
Help from a Friend	B	2	Creative Ideas	CItizenship
How I Feel	B	2	Creative Ideas	Social Studies
What Should We Do?	B	2	Creative Ideas	Social Studies
Good Ideas!	B	2	Creative Ideas	Culture
What Can You Make?	B	2	Creative Ideas	Science
When Things Change	B	2	Our Changing World	Social Studies
Harvest Time	B	2	Our Changing World	Life Science
Who Needs Soil?	B	2	Our Changing World	Life Science
New Faces and Places	B	2	Our Changing World	Social Studies
All Kinds of Weather	B	2	Our Changing World	Physical Science
Who Helps on Your Street?	C	3	Responsibility	Citizenship
Helping Our World	C	3	Responsibility	Citizenship
Our Dog Buster	C	3	Responsibility	Citizenship
Neighbors Help Neighbors	C	3	Responsibility	Citizenship
I Follow the Rules	C	3	Responsibility	Citizenship
At the Ballpark	C	3	Traditions	Social Studies
Flag Day	C	3	Traditions	History
Happy Birthday!	C	3	Traditions	Social Studies
Cowboys	C	3	Traditions	Culture/History
Election Day	C	3	Traditions	History

* Suggested Guided Reading level. Use your knowledge of children's abilities to adjust levels as needed.

Concept Literacy Leveled Reader
Skills Chart (continued)

Need more choices? Look back to Grade 1.

Grade 1 Title	Level*	DRA Level*	Concept	Content Connection
In My Room	A	1	Home and Families	Culture
My Family	A	1	Home and Families	Culture
Outside My Door	A	1	Home and Families	Social Studies
My Friends	A	1	Neighborhoods	Social Studies
My School	A	1	Neighborhoods	Social Studies
Around My Neighborhood	A	1	Neighborhoods	Social Studies
The Dog	A	1	Animal Friends	Life Science
Helping Pets	A	1	Animal Friends	Citizenship
Animals Help	A	1	Animal Friends	Citizenship
We See Animals	A	1	Wild Animals	Life Science
Neighborhood Animals	A	1	Wild Animals	Life Science
Wild Animals	A	1	Wild Animals	Life Science
My Family	A	1	People in Communities	Culture
At School	A	1	People in Communities	Social Studies
In My Neighborhood	A	1	People in Communities	Social Studies
Animals Work Together	A	1	Communities in Nature	Life Science
In the Forest	A	1	Communities in Nature	Life Science
Ants and People	A	1	Communities in Nature	Science
Gardens Change	A	1	Growing and Changing	Life Science
I Can Read	A	1	Growing and Changing	Social Studies
Animals Change	A	1	Growing and Changing	Life Science
Changes in Gardens	A	1	Changes in Nature	Life Science
Caterpillars Change	A	1	Changes in Nature	Life Science
In the Winter	A	1	Changes in Nature	Life Science
Surprise! Surprise!	B	2	Surprising Treasures	Social Studies
Special Stories	B	2	Surprising Treasures	Culture
Our Country's Treasures	B	2	Surprising Treasures	History
Places We Treasure	B	2	Treasures to Share	Social Studies
Treasures We Share	B	2	Treasures to Share	Culture
My Town	B	2	Treasures to Share	Social Studies
Great Ideas	B	2	Clever Solutions	Social Studies
Ways We Learn	B	2	Clever Solutions	Social Studies
Who Likes the Old Tree?	B	2	Clever Solutions	Life Science
Simple Machines	B	2	Ideas That Change Our World	Physical Science
Telephones Help Us Every Day	B	2	Ideas That Change Our World	Space & Technology
Let's Plant A Garden	B	2	Ideas That Change Our World	Life Science

* Suggested Guided Reading level. Use your knowledge of children's abilities to adjust levels as needed.

Concept Literacy Leveled Reader Skills Chart (*continued*)

Need more choices? Look ahead to Grade 3.

Title	Level*	DRA Level*	Concept	Content Connection
Learning New Things!	B	2	Living and Learning	Social Studies
Trading This for That	B	2	Living and Learning	Economics
We Want Soup!	B	2	Living and Learning	Social Studies
The Supermarket	B	2	Living and Learning	Economics
I Have a Dollar	B	2	Living and Learning	Economics
Keeping Warm	B	2	Smart Solutions	Life Science
Which Way Is Better?	B	2	Smart Solutions	Social Studies
You Can Solve It!	B	2	Smart Solutions	Citizenship
Let's Be Fair!	B	2	Smart Solutions	Citizenship
Birds' Nests	B	2	Smart Solutions	Life Science
Grapes into Raisins	C	3	People and Nature	Life Science
Explaining Nature	C	3	People and Nature	Culture
Take a Look!	C	3	People and Nature	Space and Technology
Helping Whales	C	3	People and Nature	Life Science
The Hot Desert	C	3	People and Nature	Life Science
What Can Athletes Do?	C	3	One of a Kind	Social Studies
Extremes	C	3	One of a Kind	Earth Science
I Collect Rocks	C	3	One of a Kind	Earth Science
Women Who Were First!	C	3	One of a Kind	History
What Can Animals Do?	C	3	One of a Kind	Life Science
Kiko's Kimono	D	4	Cultures	Culture
Happy New Year!	D	4	Cultures	Culture
Our New Home	D	4	Cultures	Culture
Bread!	D	4	Cultures	Culture
From Country to City	D	4	Cultures	Culture
The Statue of Liberty	D	4	Freedom	History/Citizenship
The Eagle Is Free	D	4	Freedom	Citizenship/Life Science
Many Voices	D	4	Freedom	Social Studies
We Have Rules	D	4	Freedom	Citizenship
Freedom for All!	D	4	Freedom	Citizenship

* Suggested Guided Reading level. Use your knowledge of children's abilities to adjust levels as needed.

21st Century Skills
on Reading Street

Your second graders are "digital natives." So when you tell them to *Get Online!* they jump at the chance. The world of information and communication technology (ICT) is a natural part of their everyday lives.

In **Section 8**, you'll discover the visually engaging and entertaining Digital Path locations on *Scott Foresman Reading Street*. These exciting, research-based tools motivate children to explore the new literacies of the 21st Century and their own ideas through technology.

The next step is easy. To begin exploring content and features, just visit www.ReadingStreet.com!

21st Century Skills

The world today is one of rapid technological advancement and change. The second graders in your classroom now will quickly become part of tomorrow's workforce. As a teacher of literacy, you are providing them valuable literacy skills as they grow up in this information, media, and information-rich context.

Technology on *Scott Foresman Reading Street* can be used both for enhancing children's experiences and preparing them for the future. Throughout the year, you can choose from research-based technology options that enrich your instruction and assist you in the management of classroom learning.

What Are New Literacies?

Right before our eyes, the nature of reading and learning is changing. The Internet and other technologies create new opportunities, new solutions, and new literacies—new ways to make meaning out of what we see and read onscreen. Each new technology for reading, writing, and communicating requires new literacies to take full advantage of its potential. The future calls for new comprehension skills too. Children must adapt and use new reading comprehension skills when they are online. These literacies are increasingly important to our children and our society.

Research has shown that technology is a powerful motivational tool as well as a critical literacy area for the future. It has the power to engage and hold children's attention, maximize time on task, and help you scaffold children's learning. Child engagement leads to willingness to practice and practice leads to real learning. To be effective, technology and digital media for literacy learning must be carefully designed to include instructionally effective visuals, audio, and interactivity.

"Locating information on the Internet requires very different reading skills from locating information in a book."
Donald J. Leu, Jr., 2008

How Can I Help Children Adjust to Changing Technology?

Technology is part of our lives, so what we are used to now changes rapidly. New uses for technology are constantly being envisioned, and teachers respond by changing their instruction. They see the benefits of child-centered learning that technology makes possible. In the future, technology will foster even more learner-based instruction. Your second graders don't have to wait for opportunities to control how they will achieve certain learning goals. *Scott Foresman Reading Street* has multiple destinations on its Digital Path that help make the transition to child-centered instruction effective. With these research-based multimedia tools, you can guide children to See It!, Hear It!, and Do It!

Big Question Videos introduce the unit level Big Question that children explore throughout the unit. Children use the Journal activity to capture their questions and ideas in a graphic organizer.

Concept Talk Videos support you in providing critical background building information. Children learn background about text topics before they begin to read. Seeing and hearing concept vocabulary prepares children to talk about the topic with others in the class.

Envision It! Animations make cause and effect, compare and contrast, and other comprehension skills come to life in an animated context. After children watch, they can talk about and understand the skill. The next stop, learning the academic vocabulary for each comprehension skill, comes more easily. Children can click on to retellings, which include concept vocabulary, and access definitions. The picture prompts help children retell. Envision It! also includes a paired selection, with audio, that expands on the theme or topic in a new way.

Amazing Words Sing With Me allows children to develop oral language as they sing and use Amazing Words vocabulary. Animated text scrolls and lines are highlighted in time to the song as children hear it. Children practice and then use the words in class conversations. The video images provide English language learners with comprehensible input. English learners feel more comfortable participating when they use the engaging technology, which lowers the affective filter.

What Skills Do Children Need for New Literacies?

Five comprehension skill areas are important for children to develop as they read online. These skills build on the decoding, vocabulary, and text comprehension skills that are also necessary for reading on the Internet.

1. **Ask, identify, and generate important questions.**

   What motivates children to read on the Internet? Most begin with a question or another need to find information. Children need to know how to ask important questions. They also need to use the Internet to generate questions.

2. **Use multiple comprehension skills to locate information.**

   Children encounter separate search engines to find information. Then they read search results and make inferences to select the best links for their needs.

3. **Critically evaluate information on the Internet.**

   Children read information that anyone may have published on the Internet, so they must pay attention to accuracy. Children need to determine who created the information and consider why and when it was published. They need to detect bias in the information. They must also know how to use other sources to check if information is accurate for their own purposes.

4. **Synthesize information to create unique answers.**

   Readers on the Internet are putting together a new, or external, text as they find information in different places. A critical new comprehension skill is learning to make wise choices as they select links and add information. Each child's synthesis may be different because different links may be chosen. Children also must learn to create the external text that answers their question, or answers additional questions that arose as they searched.

5. **Communicate the answers to others.**

   Reading and writing are integrated when using the Internet. Children must learn to compose texts through the links that they select during reading. They use blogs, e-mail, text messaging, and other communication technologies to send the new information.

When children follow the Digital Path in *Scott Foresman Reading Street*, they are learning 21st Century literacy skills. As children read Paired eSelections, which extend concepts, vocabulary, and the topic of the main selection, they can select the Read Online feature. This interactive lesson is like a private tutor that teaches children information and communication technology (ICT) comprehension skills and strategies for e-mail, Web sites, and media awareness.

How Does Technology Help Children Acquire Vocabulary?

Have you observed that children who use academic vocabulary in classroom conversations—even before they can read the words—are at an advantage? Later, when children see the words in print, you notice that they comprehend more quickly. Your observations align with what research is pointing to. Children who view images, video, and animation while listening to audio gain important information. But they won't use those sources alone. In the 21ˢᵗ century, children will use multimedia information sources and read traditional text often. The reason is obvious: we can read text far faster than we can listen to or view it. The need for speed and information management will require all readers to depend on a balance of technological and traditional text sources—as well as their expanded knowledge of literacy skills.

eReaders Leveled books are available as audio books. Teachers can assign the book matched to each child based on his or her reading profile, or choose another book based on a different instructional purpose.

Vocabulary Activities on the Digital Path show children that words are fun. Activities include Vocabulary Flashcards, Crossword Puzzle, Memory Match, Trivia, and Poetry.

Journal Word Bank is a rich source of vocabulary practice. Children respond to prompts and use weekly tested vocabulary as they write in complete sentences.

Grammar Jammer has songs and rhymes that help children remember the weekly conventions skills.

Interactive Sound-Spelling Cards are engaging activities for phonemic awareness and phonics skills. Children select images and hear words with target spelling patterns. They see, hear and do as they select and see images—and hear and read words.

What Makes Technology Powerful?

Watch children as they engage in technology. They have a "Do It!" attitude and seem to be aware that they're actively learning. Your second graders are eager to make choices in response to reading prompts. They become motivated when they receive immediate feedback and are receptive to thought-provoking questions about their use of strategies. Technology is also a powerful tool for the learning writer. Research shows that technology for writing instruction helps children think as they write, especially when the technology has prompts to support reflection on writing, spelling, and grammar. When you use carefully designed technology, your instruction has more power because it's more child-centered.

While these literacy and learning outcomes are important, new literacies can also lead to important new realizations for children. When you use the Internet, children have the potential to travel across information bridges and interact with authors, experts, communities, and children from around the globe. Meaningful interactions with other children from diverse communities spark new questions about the larger world. As children search for answers, their insights and understanding broaden too.

How Does Technology Support Teachers?

As a teacher in the 21st century, you want to be skilled in the effective use of information and communication technology (ICT) for teaching and learning. You expect a literacy curriculum that integrates the new literacies of ICT into your instructional programs. You need assessment practices in literacy that include reading on the Internet and writing using word-processing. When you go to the Student and Teacher Resources and Download Center in the *Scott Foresman Reading Street* Digital Path, you can choose digital supports for all your needs. The Teacher's Edition, Student Edition, and practice books are available online. You'll also find a variety of online assessment tools that help you adjust your instruction and make grouping decisions. You can search by standards or skill key word to find additional resources that target children's needs. Children will get the specific extra practice they need before reassessment. You'll also find many other teacher and student materials in CD and CD-ROM formats.

Online Assessment has weekly tests, Fresh Reads Tests, Unit Tests, and more for data-driven decision-making. When you need to customize a test, use the Teacher Build-a-Test.

Story Sort allows children to drag and drop retelling cards and place them in correct order. This interactive sequencing is a visual way to practice retelling stories, a critical comprehension skill. Children build comprehension as they write an Image Essay about one picture.

Decodable eBooks show children word-by-word highlighting as they hear the decodable text read aloud. You can use underlining and highlighting tools for group or one-on-one instruction.

Letter Tile Drag and Drop is a word building game that teachers can use whenever children are ready to extend vocabulary and explore words. They manipulate the familiar yellow tiles that appear in Teacher Edition lessons for word work.

New Literacies on *Reading Street*

Did you know that many nations are preparing their children for the reading demands of the Internet? Students need to be prepared for a global information economy. The ability to read information online to learn, solve problems, and communicate solutions is central to success.

As our reliance on technology increases, it is essential that children learn digital skills. Starting in First Grade, *Reading Street* weaves these basic digital skills—e-mail, Web sites, parts of a computer—with the core knowledge. More than ever, America's children require an emphasis on 21st century skills and basic digital know-how. Writing e-mail weekly or daily, children practice the comprehension and writing skills taught in *Reading Street*. School projects call students to search engines, online directories, and reference sources that support the research skills taught in *Reading Street* Teacher Editions.

As students progress in school, *Reading Street* teaches increasingly important ways to write e-mail, browse Web sites, research with online directories and search engines, and evaluate online sources using easily understood and fun-to-read selections. *Reading Street* prepares our youth for the success that they deserve as they enter middle school and high school.

You change the world when you teach a child to read. And now, with the new literacies of the Internet, this can happen in profoundly powerful ways. The Internet opens your classroom windows to the world.

Parts of a Computer Using a computer for the first time might be a puzzling experience for children. That's why *Reading Street* provides a "Read Together" selection called "My Computer." Colorful illustrations of a basic desktop point out the essential parts of a computer, including the cursor, mouse, keyboard, printer, CD-ROM, and monitor. In just a few minutes, children will be familiar with a few of the devices that they'll use as they approach higher grades!

E-mail E-mail is one of the quickest and easiest ways to teach young children how to interact with people using the written word. *Reading Street* teaches first and second graders how to write e-mail to family and friends. By writing and mastering e-mail, children practice comprehension and

vocabulary skills, exchange ideas, engage in dialogue with peers, and gain the electronic skills vital to their future.

Web Sites With almost every click of a mouse button, children encounter information on Web sites. Children browse Web sites for fun, for researching school projects, and for learning about other nations and cultures. *Reading Street* shows first and second graders that they can use Web sites for learning more about what they read in class. Browsing the Internet is one of the easiest ways for a child to improve comprehension and develop a thirst for learning. Encourage students to keep on clicking!

Online Directories Students browse online directories when they want to find information about specific topics. Using the same set of skills they hone while browsing Web sites, students punch key words into directories to discover organized information and articles that assist them in research and broaden their view of the environment around them.

Evaluating Online Sources Two questions to listen for from Web-browsing students: *Who wrote that? Can I trust them?* As students learn to research information on the Internet, they also must learn to evaluate online sources. Information on the Internet can be inaccurate or even false. Successful students evaluate online information for accuracy and reliability by checking URL extensions, a crucial step in children's development.

Search Engines When kids use the Internet for research, they are amateur sleuths, clicking links and typing in key words to hunt down the information they need. One of the best tools for Internet information-hunting is the search engine. Learning to use a search engine helps students identify questions and frame information in ways that help them solve problems.

Online Reference Sources Dictionaries, almanacs, encyclopedias: These are the essential tools at our fingertips to complete projects and learn about our world. In *Reading Street*, students learn to access online reference sources to learn about topics in science and social studies. They analyze information to answer questions. By learning to navigate these sources, students gain research skills and learn how to construct better solutions to problems.

Teacher Resources
for Grade 2

Oral Vocabulary/Amazing Words

UNIT 1

WEEK 1

downy
founders
investigate
muttered
perch
rural
unanimous
urban

WEEK 2

ascend
descend
enormous
journey
launch
meteorite
orbit
universe

WEEK 3

detective
fascinating
fledglings
galaxy
secure
slimy
tranquil
wildlife

WEEK 4

arid
dunes
extinct
forbidding
haven
landform
ledge
precipitation

WEEK 5

delicate
exhibit
genius
inquire
resist
satisfaction
stun
sturdy

UNIT 2

WEEK 1

avalanche
blustery
courageous
fast-paced
hazard
instinct
rescue
skittish

WEEK 2

aloft
architect
ingenious
identify
participate
scour
significant
tinker

WEEK 3

consumer(s)
decision(s)
extraordinary
fiber
lack
producer(s)
strand
typical

WEEK 4

depend
familiar
insist
miserable
partnership
solution
struggle
survival

WEEK 5

coax
conflict
deserve
mope
pursue
ramp
resolve
startle

UNIT 3

WEEK 1

construct
contraption
daydream
foolproof
project
scrap
sidekick
unique

WEEK 2

correspond
cove
deaf
footprint
imitate
postage
sign language
transport

WEEK 3

boast
consume
contentment
cure
gloat
incident
prey
shrewd
snicker

WEEK 4

abundant
assist
beam
dismay
efficient
forever
generous
situation

WEEK 5

accomplish
excel
opportunity
original
process
research
scientist
unusual

| UNIT 4 | UNIT 5 | UNIT 6 |

UNIT 4

WEEK 1

concentration
frown
homeland
patient
preserve
represent
tough
valuable

WEEK 2

adapt
ancient
annual
blazing
drought
massive
nutrients
sprout

WEEK 3

blizzard
discovery
fine
incredible
landscape
molten
transform
underneath

WEEK 4

accent
adjust
foreign
forlorn
landmark
quiver
tease
unexpected

WEEK 5

breeze
condition
funnel
predict
sparkle
swirl
terrifying
whip

UNIT 5

WEEK 1

caretaker
community
instrument
lug
operation
responsible
supplies
teamwork

WEEK 2

concern
contribute
fragile
litter
pellets
persuade
pollute
release

WEEK 3

behavior
companion
confident
consider
cooperate
obedient
properly
reprimand

WEEK 4

advantage
appreciate
communicate
defiant
demand
ferocious
firmly
respect

WEEK 5

apologize
citizen
hoard
interrupt
judgment
protest
scold
troublemaker

UNIT 6

WEEK 1

athlete
challenge
champion
dainty
disguise
effort
professional
shortstop

WEEK 2

allegiance
frayed
history
independence
indivisible
patriotic
symbol
unfurl

WEEK 3

angle
brilliant
celebration
create
custom
inspect
snapshot
tradition

WEEK 4

buckaroo
climate
drover
lariat
legend
livestock
occupation
rawhide

WEEK 5

ceremony
compliment
culture
evergreen
festival
fidget
multicolored
sash

You've learned 241 **Amazing Words** this year!

Word Lists for Unit 1

The Twin Club

Short Vowels

back	sad	well	rib	sock	run
camp	tag	yell	rip	tock	tub
cap	van	big	sick	top	tuck
cat	bed	fill	six	but	tug
fast	bell	fist	still	cup	
hat	best	fit	this	cut	
lack	desk	fix	tip	duck	
land	get	hill	will	dust	
man	less	his	win	fun	
map	let	hit	box	gum	
pack	peck	kid	dock	hug	
pan	red	lick	got	hum	
pat	sled	list	hot	just	
sack	step	mist	jog	luck	
sat	tell	pick	lock	mug	

Exploring Space with an Astronaut

Long Vowels: vowel_*e*

age	lane	wage	mice	code	vote
ate	late	bite	miles	dose	cube
bake	made	bride	mine	home	cute
brave	make	dice	nice	hope	fuse
cage	mane	dime	pile	hose	huge
cake	pace	file	rice	joke	mule
cape	page	fine	ride	lone	mute
date	race	hike	ripe	nose	rude
erase	rage	ice	size	note	rule
face	rake	kite	time	poke	tube
game	safe	lice	wide	pose	tune
gape	sage	life	wise	rode	use
lace	take	like	bone	rose	
lake	tame	lime	broke	tone	

Spelling Words

chop
desk
drum
dust
job
list
mess
rib
rock
sack
sad
tag

High-Frequency/Tested Words

beautiful
country
friend*
front
someone
somewhere

Story Words

cousins
meadow
parents
promise

Spelling Words

blaze
fine
huge
late
mice
nose
page
race
rice
size
space
vote

High-Frequency/Tested Words

everywhere
live* /liv/
machines
move
woman
work*
world

Story Words

astronaut
experiment
gravity
shuttle
telescope

* = reviewed high-frequency word from Grade 1

Word Lists for Unit 1

Henry and Mudge and the Starry Night

Consonant Blends

act	clam	flock	milk	sleep	stretch
ant	clap	fly	must	slow	string
band	close	frame	next	small	strong
best	crate	frog	past	snack	stung
blame	crept	glad	plan	snap	tent
blank	crust	grace	plant	sound	track
blew	drank	grass	pond	space	tree
brake	drink	gray	pride	split	trunk
branch	drove	help	raft	spread	trust
bread	dump	jump	scrape	spring	twice
bring	dust	just	scrub	stage	went
broke	fast	land	send	stamp	west
brush	felt	last	skate	stick	wind
camp	flat	long	sky	stone	

A Walk in the Desert

Base Words and Endings -s, -ed, -ing

-s	lives	*-ed*	looked	wiped	looking	walking
asks	makes	added	nodded	yelled	making	winning
bakes	pecks	asked	patted		opening	
calls	races	dragged	peeled	*-ing*	patting	
chips	rubs	dropped	placed	asking	playing	
cools	runs	filled	raced	bugging	racing	
drags	seems	gagged	rested	confusing	riding	
eats	uses	grabbed	saved	dining	rubbing	
gets	wags	grinned	smiled	dragging	running	
grows	walks	hiked	tagged	hiding	shaking	
hikes	wipes	hopped	traded	hiking	sleeping	
howls		jogged	wagged	hopping	sliding	
jumps		jumped	walked	jumping	smiling	
lies		lifted	watched	lifting	trading	

The Strongest One

Consonant Digraphs

ch	such	shake	*th*	thick	patch
arch	teach	shape	bath	thin	pitch
bench	watch	shell	forth	third	stitch
bunch		shine	math	those	watch
chase	*sh*	ship	mouth	thumb	
chat	blush	shop	path		*wh*
chin	brush	show	teeth	*tch*	whale
chip	crush	shut	than	batch	when
chop	dash	shy	thank	catch	where
chose	dish	trash	that	clutch	which
each	fish	wash	them	ditch	while
lunch	hush	wish	then	itch	whip
much	mash		there	latch	whisk
pinch	mush		they	match	white

Spelling Words

ask
brave
breeze
clip
hand
mask
nest
state
stop
strap
stream
twin

High-Frequency/Tested Words

bear
build
couldn't
father
love*
mother
straight

Story Words

drooled
lanterns
shivered
snuggled

Spelling Words

dropped
dropping
excited
exciting
hugged
hugging
lifted
lifting
smiled
smiling
talked
talking

High-Frequency/Tested Words

animals
early*
eyes*
full
warm
water*

Story Words

cactus
climate
coyote
desert
harsh

Spelling Words

bunch
chase
itch
math
patch
shape
that
them
whale
what
when
wish

High-Frequency/Tested Words

gone
learn*
often
pieces
though
together*
very*

Story Words

dangerous
gnaws
narrator
relatives

* = reviewed high-frequency word from Grade 1

Word Lists for Unit 2

Tara and Tiree, Fearless Friends

r-Controlled *ar, or, ore, oar*

ar	harm	corner	*ore*	roar
alarm	harp	correct	adore	soar
armies	lark	forget	bore	
art	mark	fork	more	
barber	market	form	shore	
bark	party	morning	store	
barn	shark	north		
car	star	orbit	*oar*	
carpet	target	order	boar	
cart	yard	short	board	
charm		sport	coarse	
dark	*or*	storm	hoard	
darling	border	thorn	hoarse	
garden	born		oar	

Abraham Lincoln

Contractions

aren't	don't	how's	it's	that's	who's
can't	hadn't	I'll	let's	there's	won't
couldn't	haven't	I'm	she'll	they'll	you'll
didn't	he's	isn't	she's	wasn't	
doesn't	he'll	it'll	shouldn't	we'll	

Scarcity

r-Controlled *er, ir, ur*

er	*ir*	thirsty	murmur
clerk	birch	twirl	nurse
fern	bird		purple
germ	birthday	*ur*	return
herd	chirp	blurt	surf
jerk	circus	burden	survive
kernel	confirm	burn	Thursday
nerve	dirty	burst	turkey
perch	girl	church	urge
perk	firm	curler	
stern	first	disturb	
term	shirt	fur	
verse	stir	furry	
	third	hurt	

Spelling Words

before
born
chore
corn
farm
hard
horse
more
part
porch
score
smart

High-Frequency/Tested Words

break
family*
heard
listen
once*
pull*

Story Words

brave
collar
slipped

Spelling Words

aren't
can't
didn't
hadn't
haven't
he's
I'll
I'm
isn't
it's
she's
who's

High-Frequency/Tested Words

certainly
either
great*
laugh*
second
worst
you're

Story Words

fault
honest
lawyer
noticed

Spelling Words

birth
curb
curl
dirt
her
nurse
person
purse
serve
skirt
turn
turtle

High-Frequency/Tested Words

above*
ago
enough*
toward*
whole
word

Story Words

hurricanes
resources
scarce
scarcity
trade-off

* = reviewed high-frequency word from Grade 1

Word Lists for Unit 2

The Bremen Town Musicians

Plurals -s, -es, -ies

-s			-es		-ies
bags	friends	piles	ashes	leashes	jellies
bases	girls	plates	benches	mixes	ladies
books	grapes	purses	boxes	peaches	parties
boys	hands	rocks	branches	ranches	pennies
cards	heels	roses	brushes	scratches	puppies
chores	homes	stamps	buses	watches	
corners	hours	stars	churches	wishes	
cups	houses	things	classes		
desks	jobs	towns	crutches	-ies	
dimes	lamps	toys	dishes	babies	
dogs	lots	years	dresses	buddies	
drinks	nails		foxes	cherries	
farms	papers		glasses	cities	
	pencils			families	

One Good Turn Deserves Another

Long a: a, ai, ay

a		paid	waist	okay
acorns	brain	pail	wait	pay
agent	claim	pain		play
apron	explain	paint	ay	pray
baby	fail	quail	away	ray
famous	faint	rail	bay	say
lady	frail	rain	day	spray
lazy	gain	raised	dismay	stay
paper	grain	sail	gray	stray
table	hail	snail	fray	sway
	laid	stain	hay	today
ai	maid	tail	holiday	stay
aim	mail	train	lay	way
braid	nail		may	

Spelling Words

babies
baby
lunch
lunches
note
notes
stories
story
switch
switches
tune
tunes

High-Frequency/Tested Words

bought
people*
pleasant
probably
scared
shall
sign*

Story Words

excitement
mill
monsters
musicians
robbers

Spelling Words

away
brain
main
paint
play
raise
say
stay
tail
today
tray
wait

High-Frequency/Tested Words

behind*
brought
door*
everybody
minute
promise
sorry

Story Words

armadillo
creature
grateful
groaned
snorted

* = reviewed high-frequency word from Grade 1

Word Lists for Unit 3

Pearl and Wagner: Two Good Friends

Long e: e, ee, ea, y

e	feet	week	neat	happy
be	fifteen		peach	lady
detail	green	**ea**	peak	lucky
he	greet	beach	please	only
me	keep	bean	seal	pony
secret	meet	cheap	teach	pretty
she	need	clean	treat	ready
we	seed	each		really
	seek	ease	**y**	silly
ee	speech	eating	any	story
agree	street	feast	baby	
beet	sweet	heal	bunny	
breeze	tree	heap	city	
feed	weed	mean	funny	

Dear Juno

Long o: o, oa, ow

o	ocean	**oa**	oath	flown	window
almost	old	boast	road	follow	yellow
bold	over	boat	roam	glow	
cold	photograph	coach	roast	grow	
colt	post	coast	throat	know	
fold	postcard	coat	toad	mow	
gold	rotate	croak	toast	mower	
hello	scold	float		own	
hold	sold	goal	**ow**	owner	
host	strolled	goat	below	row	
locate	told	loaf	blow	show	
mold	unfolded	loan	blown	slow	
most		oat	bowl	snow	
notion		oatmeal	flow	throw	

Spelling Words

deep
easy
feet
leave
party
read
seat
sleep
team
teeth
wheel
windy

High-Frequency/Tested Words

guess
pretty
science*
shoe*
village
watch
won

Story Words

electricity
robot
trash
wad

Spelling Words

ago
bowl
float
goat
hold
most
open
show
slow
toad
toast
told

High-Frequency/Tested Words

answer*
company
faraway
parents
picture*
school*
wash

Story Words

envelope
persimmons
photograph
smudged

* = reviewed high-frequency word from Grade 1

Word Lists for Unit 3

Anansi Goes Fishing

Compound Words

afternoon	carpool	grasshoppers	mailbox	rainbow	sunflowers
airplane	cowboy	haircut	maybe	riverbank	sunrise
anything	daylight	halfway	myself	rowboat	sunscreen
babysit	daytime	haystack	nearby	sailboat	sunshine
backpack	driveway	himself	nobody	schoolyard	supermarket
backyard	everybody	homework	nothing	seashore	teacup
baseball	everyone	inside	nowhere	seaweed	teammates
bathtub	everything	landlord	outside	shortstop	thunderstorm
bedroom	everywhere	laptop	paycheck	snowflake	treehouse
bedtime	fireplace	ladybug	peanuts	snowstorm	watermelon
birthday	flashlight	lipstick	playmate	someone	weekend
brainstorm	forever	lookout	railroad	something	wherever
breakfast	goldfish	lunchbox	raindrop	starfish	worksheet
cannot	grandparents	mailbag	rainstorm	streetcar	yourself

Rosa and Blanca

Long *i: i, ie, igh, y*

i	spider	lied	nightlight	fly
behind	tiger	pie	right	hydrant
bind	tiny	tie	sigh	July
blind	title	tried	sight	myself
child	wild		slight	nylon
cider		***igh***	thigh	shy
climb	***ie***	bright	tight	sky
find	cried	flight		sly
hi	cries	fright	***y***	try
kind	die	high	by	why
lilac	dried	knight	cry	
mild	flies	light	cycle	
mind	fries	might	cyclone	
pilot	lie	night	dry	

A Weed Is a Flower

Comparative Endings

-er	hotter	thicker	coldest	littlest	thinnest
bigger	higher	thinner	cutest	longest	tiniest
brighter	lazier	tighter	fairest	nicest	ugliest
colder	littler	tinier	fastest	prettiest	weakest
fairer	longer	uglier	finest	reddest	widest
fancier	nicer	weaker	friendliest	ripest	
faster	prettier	wider	fullest	saddest	
finer	redder		happiest	silliest	
friendlier	sillier	***-est***	heaviest	slowest	
greener	slower	biggest	highest	smallest	
happier	softer	bravest	hottest	smartest	
harder	sooner	brightest	latest	softest	
harsher	stranger	busiest	laziest	sweetest	
heavier	taller	closest	lightest	tallest	

Spelling Words

backyard
basketball
bathtub
bedtime
birthday
driveway
mailbox
raindrop
riverbank
someone
something
weekend

High-Frequency/Tested Words

been
believe
caught
finally
today*
tomorrow
whatever

Story Words

delicious
justice
lazy
weave

Spelling Words

blind
bright
child
cry
find
flight
fly
myself
right
sky
spider
wild

High-Frequency/Tested Words

alone
buy
daughters
half
many*
their*
youngest

Story Words

chiles
luckiest
tortillas

Spelling Words

busier
busiest
fatter
fattest
happier
happiest
hotter
hottest
smaller
smallest
sooner
soonest

High-Frequency/Tested Words

clothes
hours
money
neighbor
only*
question
taught

Story Words

agriculture
college
greenhouse
laboratory

* = reviewed high-frequency word from Grade 1

Word Lists for Unit 4

A Froggy Fable

Syllables: Consonant + _le_

able	cradle	maple	rattle	stable	twinkle
ankle	cuddle	middle	riddle	staple	uncle
apple	dimple	mumble	rifle	startle	whistle
bottle	fable	nibble	ripple	struggle	wiggle
bubble	giggle	noble	sample	stumble	wobble
bugle	gobble	paddle	scribble	table	
bundle	handle	pickle	simple	tickle	
cable	jumble	puddle	snuggle	title	
candle	ladle	purple	sparkle	trouble	
cattle	little	puzzle	sprinkle	tumble	

The Life Cycle of a Pumpkin

Vowels _oo_, _u_

_oo_				_u_	bushy
book	football	notebook	understood	bull	full
bookbag	footstep	overlook	wood	bulldog	fully
brook	good	root	wooden	bullet	pudding
cook	hood	shook	woodpile	bullfrog	pull
cookbook	hoof	soot	wool	bully	pulley
cookie	hook	stood		bush	push
crook	look	textbook		bushel	put
	foot	nook	took		

Soil

Vowel Diphthongs /ou/ _ou_, _ow_; /oi/ _oi_, _oy_

_ou_	ounce	_ow_	growl	_oi_	_oy_
about	our	allow	how	boil	annoy
aloud	out	bow	now	coin	boy
amounts	pouch	brown	owl	join	cowboy
around	pounce	cow	plow	moist	destroy
bounce	pout	cowboy	powder	noisy	employ
cloud	proud	crowd	powerful	oily	enjoy
count	round	crown	rowdy	point	joy
found	shout	down	shower	poison	loyal
grouch	south	downtown	soil	soil	royal
house	sprout	drown	towel	spoil	soy
loud	trout	flower	towers	toil	toy
mouth	without	frown	town	voice	voyage
			vowel		

160

Spelling Words

able
ankle
apple
bubble
bugle
bundle
cable
giggle
purple
sparkle
tickle
title

Selection Vocabulary

clearing
crashed
perfect
pond
spilling
splashing
traveled

High-Frequency Words

ago
family
father
mother
warm

Spelling Words

book
brook
cook
full
hood
July
pull
push
put
shook
stood
wood

Selection Vocabulary

bumpy
fruit
harvest
root
smooth
soil
vine

High-Frequency Words

everywhere
live /liv/
machines
woman
work
world

Spelling Words

around
coil
cow
flower
gown
howl
moist
noise
out
pound
royal
toy

Selection Vocabulary

grains
materials
particles
seeps
substances
texture

High-Frequency Words

bear
build
couldn't
father
love
mother
straight

Word Lists for Unit 4

The Night the Moon Fell

Syllable Patterns

VCV	VCCV
donate	boathouse
favor	cancel
locate	coathook
meter	follow
moment	meatloaf
noticed	pantsuit
open	rowboat
robot	
soda	

The First Tortilla

Vowels *oo, ue, ew, ui*

oo			*ew*	*ue*	*ui*
bathroom	moo	spool	blew	blue	bruise
bloom	mood	spoon	brew	clue	cruise
boot	moon	stoop	chew	cue	fruit
broom	noon	too	crew	due	juice
classroom	pool	tool	drew	glue	nuisance
cool	proof	tooth	few	hue	recruit
food	raccoon	troop	flew	true	suit
goose	room	zoo	grew		
hoop	school	zoom	knew		
hoot	scoop		new		
loop	smooth		stew		
loose	snoop		threw		
	soon				

Spelling Words

boyhood
cowboy
daydream
downstairs
football
houseboat
oatmeal
outplay
railroad
rainbow
roadway
soybean

Selection Vocabulary

balance
canyons
coral
rattle
slivers
sway
whisper

Spiral Review

friend
love
move
pretty
school

Spelling Words

blue
clue
drew
flew
fool
fruit
juice
new
spoon
suit
too
true

Selection Vocabulary

awaken
cliffs
mountain
prize
rainbow
suffer
volcano

Spiral Review

around
enough
many
thought
took

Word Lists for Unit 5

Firefighter!

Suffixes *-ly, -ful, -er, -or, -ish*

-ly		**-ful**	thankful	rancher	editor
boldly	lightly	boastful	wonderful	reader	inventor
bravely	loudly	careful		singer	refrigerator
brightly	lovely	colorful	**-er**	storyteller	supervisor
carefully	proudly	eventful	computer	vacationer	
clearly	quietly	harmful	dancer	waiter	**-ish**
closely	smoothly	helpful	driver	writer	bookish
finally	softly	hopeful	farmer		childish
firmly	suddenly	joyful	firefighter	**-or**	fiftyish
fondly	sweetly	peaceful	gardener	actor	foolish
gently	tenderly	playful	hiker	calculator	selfish
gladly	tightly	powerful	leader	conductor	sheepish
harshly		restful	painter	creditor	
kindly		skillful	player	director	

Carl the Complainer

Prefixes *un-, re-, pre-, dis-*

un-	unpack	remake	**pre-**	disapprove
unable	unplug	repack	preflight	disconnect
unaware	unroll	repaint	preheat	disinfect
unclasp	unsafe	repave	preorder	dislike
undisturbed	unseen	replace	prepaid	dislocate
uneven	untie	replay	preread	displace
unfair	untrue	rerun	preschool	displease
unfold		rethink	preteen	disprove
unhappy	**re-**	reuse	pretest	distrust
unhook	redrew	rewind	preview	
unkind	refill	rewire		
unlatch	refold	rewrite	**dis-**	
unload	reheat		disagree	
unlock	relight		disappear	

Bad Dog, Dodger!

Silent Consonants: *kn, wr, gn, mb*

kn	**wr**	**gn**	**mb**
knee	wrap	design	climb
kneecap	wreath	gnat	comb
kneel	wreck	gnaw	crumb
knew	wren	gnome	dumb
knickers	wrench	gnu	lamb
knife	wrestle	resign	limb
knight	wriggle	sign	numb
knit	wringing		plumber
knob	wrinkle		thumb
knock	wrist		tomb
knot	write		
know	wrong		
knuckle	wrote		

Spelling Words

cheerful
fighter
graceful
hardly
helper
quickly
sailor
slowly
teacher
visitor
weekly
yearly

Selection Vocabulary

building
burning
masks
quickly
roar
station
tightly

High-Frequency Words

break
family
heard
listen
once
pull

Spelling Words

disagree
disappear
discolor
preheat
preschool
regroup
rerun
rewind
unlock
unpack
unplug
unsafe

Selection Vocabulary

annoy
complain
mumbles
P.M.
signature
shrugs

High-Frequency Words

become
enough
good-bye
nothing
people
stories
together

Spelling Words

climb
comb
gnat
knee
knob
knock
lamb
sign
wrap
wren
write
wrong

Selection Vocabulary

chased
chewing
dripping
grabbed
practice
treat
wagged

High-Frequency Words

above
enough
toward
whole
word

Word Lists for Unit 5
Horace and Morris but mostly Dolores

/f/ ph, gh, ck, ng

ph		gh	ck	ng
alphabet	phase	cough	duck	bang
autograph	pheasant	enough	hockey	clang
dolphin	phone	laugh	kick	ding
elephant	phony	rough	lack	fang
gopher	phooey	roughly	lock	gong
graph	photo	tough	sick	king
nephew	phrase		sock	lung
orphan	sphere		track	ping
phantom	telegraph		wreck	sang
	trophy			

The Signmaker's Assistant

Vowels aw, au, augh, al

aw		au	augh	
awful	paw	auto	caught	baseball
bawl	raw	because	daughter	call
brawny	saw	cause	haughty	chalk
claw	scrawl	fault	naughty	fall
crawl	shawl	haul	slaughter	false
draw	squawk	haunt	taught	malt
drawn	straw	jaunt		salt
fawn	thaw	launch		small
gnaw	yawn	laundry	al	talk
hawk		pause	all	taller
jaw	au	sauce	also	walk
law	applaud	sausage	always	wall
lawn	August	vault	bald	walnut
	author		ball	waltz

Spelling Words

backtrack	phone
clang	photo
cough	rough
duckling	ticket
enough	tough
graph	
laugh	

Selection Vocabulary

adventure
climbed
clubhouse
exploring
greatest
truest
wondered

High-Frequency Words

bought
people
pleasant
probably
scared
shall
sign

Spelling Words

August
auto
because
caught
chalk
draw
fault
launch
talk
taught
thaw
walk

Selection Vocabulary

afternoon
blame
idea
important
signmaker
townspeople

High-Frequency Words

behind
brought
door
everybody
minute
promise
sorry

Word Lists for Unit 6

Just Like Josh Gibson

Inflected Endings

added	cooking	happened	making	rides	stopping
beginning	cries	happiest	moved	rolling	streets
belonged	dancing	hardest	needed	rushed	talking
bigger	discovered	having	nicest	sadder	thanks
bounces	dropped	helped	nodded	sailed	thinking
braver	drumming	hoping	owned	scared	tied
called	excited	hopping	peeking	shouted	tries
carrying	fastest	hugged	picked	showed	used
changes	flies	hurried	places	singing	visits
chokes	floated	joking	plans	sleepiest	wanted
cleaned	friendlier	knows	pounds	smarter	watched
cleared	funnier	landed	prettiest	smiles	waving
climbed	glued	longest	replied	started	widest
closed	going	luckier	returns	stepped	wishes

Red, White, and Blue: The Story of the American Flag

Abbreviations

Days	Months	Titles
Sun.	Jan.	Dr.
Mon.	Feb.	Mr.
Tues.	Mar.	Mrs.
Wed.	Apr.	Ms.
Thurs.	Aug.	
Fri.	Sept.	**Roads**
Sat.	Oct.	Ave.
Sun.	Nov.	Rd.
	Dec.	St.

A Birthday Basket for Tía

Syllables -ion, -tion, -ture

ion/tion			ture	
action	fiction	potion	adventure	future
addition	fraction	recreation	capture	lecture
affection	location	section	creature	mixture
caption	lotion	station	culture	moisture
caution	mention	suction	feature	nature
celebration	motion	tuition	fixture	picture
creation	nation	vacation	fracture	puncture
edition	portion		furniture	sculpture
	position			vulture

Spelling Words

heavier
heaviest
lighter
lightest
liked
liking
planned
planning
skipped
skipping
tried
trying

Selection Vocabulary

bases
cheers
field
plate
sailed
threw

High-Frequency Words

guess
pretty
science
shoe
village
watch

Spelling Words

Aug.
Dec.
Dr.
Feb.
Jan.
Mr.
Mrs.
Ms.
Nov.
Oct.
Rd.
St.

Selection Vocabulary

America
birthday
flag
freedom
nicknames
stars
stripes

High-Frequency Words

answer
company
faraway
parents
picture
school
wash

Spelling Words

action
caution
feature
fixture
future
mixture
motion
nation
nature
picture
section
station

Selection Vocabulary

aunt
bank
basket
collects
favorite
present

High-Frequency Words

been
believe
caught
finally
tomorrow
whatever

Word Lists for Unit 6

Cowboys

Suffixes *-ness, -less, -able, -ible*

-ness			harmless	toothless	valuable
awareness	kindness	weakness	helpless	useless	washable
brightness	laziness	weariness	hopeless	worthless	
darkness	loneliness		jobless		**-ible**
emptiness	loudness	**-less**	joyless	**-able**	convertible
fairness	quickness	ageless	meatless	affordable	edible
fitness	redness	bottomless	painless	agreeable	flexible
fondness	rudeness	careless	pointless	breakable	horrible
friendliness	sadness	cloudless	restless	favorable	impossible
gentleness	sickness	colorless	sleepless	lovable	invisible
goodness	soreness	cordless	speechless	movable	possible
greatness	sweetness	countless	spotless	reasonable	terrible
happiness	tenderness	fearless	thankless	reliable	
illness	usefulness	flightless	thoughtless	reusable	
		friendless			

Grace for President

Prefixes *mis-, micro-, mid-, non-*

mis-		misspoke	**mid-**	midstream	nonproductive
misbehave	mislabel	misstep	midafternoon	midsummer	nonprofit
misbehavior	mislaid	mistreat	midair	midtown	nonsense
miscompute	mislead	mistype	midcircle	midway	nonskid
misconduct	misleading	misunderstood	midday	midweek	nonstop
miscopy	mismatch		midlife	midyear	nonviolence
misdeed	misplace	**micro-**	midline		
misdirect	misprint	microfilm	midnight	**non-**	
misfile	misquote	mircrophone	midpoint	nonexistent	
misfit	misread	microscope	midsentence	nonfiction	
misguided	misreport	microwave	midship	nonmetallic	
misinform	misshape		midsize	nonpoisonous	

Spelling Words

careless
darkness
fearless
fitness
goodness
helpless
kindness
sadness
sickness
thankless
useless
weakness

Selection Vocabulary

campfire
cattle
cowboy
galloped
herd
railroad
trails

High-Frequency Words

alone
buy
half
many
their
youngest

Spelling Words

midair
midday
midway
midweek
midyear
misbehave
misdeed
mislead
mismatch
misplace
misprint
mistake

Selection Vocabulary

assembly
election
microphone
rallies
slogan
speeches

High-Frequency Words

clothes
hours
money
neighbor
only
question
taught

Glossary of Reading Terms

This glossary includes academic language terms used with students as well as reading terms provided for your information and professional use.

abbreviation a shortened form of a word. *Dr.* is an abbreviation for *doctor*.

accuracy reading words in text without errors, an element of fluency

action verb a word that shows action

adjective a word that describes a person, place, or thing. An adjective tells how many, what kind, or which one.

adverb a word that tells how, when, or where something happens. Adverbs also tell how much or how little is meant. Adverbs often end in *-ly*.

affix a prefix, suffix, or inflected ending that is added to a base word to form a new word

alliteration the repetition of a consonant sound in a group of words, especially in poetry

allusion a word or phrase that refers to something else the reader already knows from history, experience, or reading

alphabetical order the arrangement of words according to the letters of the alphabet

animal fantasy a story about animals that talk and act like people

answer questions a reading strategy in which readers use the text and prior knowledge to answer questions about what they are reading

antecedent the noun or nouns to which a pronoun refers

antonym a word that means the opposite of another word

apostrophe punctuation (') that shows where letters have been left out in a contraction or that is used with *s* at the end of a noun to show possession

appositive a word or phrase that explains the word it follows

ask questions a reading strategy in which readers ask themselves questions about the text to help make sense of what they read

author a person who writes books, stories, poems, or plays

author's point of view the author's opinion on the subject he or she is writing about

author's purpose the reason the author wrote the text

autobiography a story that tells about a real person's life written by the person who lived it

automaticity the ability to read words or connected text automatically, with little or no attention to decoding

background knowledge the information and experience that a reader brings to a text

base word a word that can stand alone or take endings, prefixes, and suffixes

biography a story that tells about a real person's life. It is written by another person.

blend combine a series of sounds in sequence without pausing between them

cause why something happens

character a person, animal, or personalized object in a story

choral reading reading aloud in unison as a group

chronological order events in a selection, presented in the order in which they occurred

chunking a decoding strategy for breaking words into manageable parts to read them

classify and categorize put things, such as pictures or words, into groups

clause a group of words having a subject and predicate and used as part of a compound or complex sentence

climax the point in a story at which conflict is confronted

collective noun a noun that names a group of persons or things, such as *audience* or *herd*

colon punctuation (:) that may introduce a list or separate hours from minutes to show time

comma punctuation (,) that can be used, for example, to indicate a pause in a sentence or to separate items in a series

comparative adjective an adjective used to compare two people, places, or things. Add *-er* to most adjectives to make them comparative.

compare tell how things are the same

complete predicate all the words in the predicate

complete subject all the words in the subject

complex sentence a sentence made up of one independent clause and one or more dependent clauses

composition a short piece of written work

compound sentence a sentence that contains two or more independent clauses. The clauses are joined either by a comma and a conjunction or by a semicolon.

compound word a word made up of two or more short words

comprehension understanding of text being read—the ultimate goal of reading

comprehension strategy a conscious plan used by a reader to gain understanding of text. Comprehension strategies may be used before, during, or after reading.

conclusion a decision or opinion arrived at after thinking about facts and details and using prior knowledge

conflict the problem or struggle in a story

conjunction a word, such as *and, but,* and *or,* that connects words, phrases, clauses, or sentences

consonant any letter of the alphabet that is not a vowel

consonant blend two or more consecutive consonants, each of which is pronounced and blended with the other, such as *cl* in *clock*

consonant digraph two consecutive consonants, that stand for a single sound, such as *ch, sh, th.* Its pronunciation usually differs from the sound of either individual consonant.

context clue the words, phrases, or sentences near an unknown word that give the reader clues to the word's meaning

continuous sound a sound that can be sustained without distortion, such as /m/, /f/, and /s/

contraction a shorter word formed by combining two words. The omitted letters are replaced with an apostrophe.

contrast tell how things are different

cursive handwriting handwriting in which the letters are joined

declarative sentence a sentence that tells something and ends with a period

decode apply knowledge of sound-spellings and word parts to read a new word

definition the meaning of a word

dependent clause a clause that cannot stand alone as a sentence

details small pieces of information

dialect form of a language spoken in a certain region or by a certain group of people that differs from the standard form of that language

dialogue written conversation

diary a day-to-day record of one's activities and thoughts

digraph two letters that stand for a single sound

diphthong two consecutive vowels whose sounds are pronounced in immediate sequence within a syllable, such as *oi* in *noise*

direct object a noun or pronoun that follows an action verb and tells who or what receives the action of the verb

discussion talking something over with other people

draft the first attempt at a composition. A draft is a rough copy that usually requires revision and editing before publication.

drama a story written to be acted out for others

draw conclusions arrive at decisions or opinions after thinking about facts and details and using prior knowledge

edit the stage in the writing process when a draft is corrected for facts and such mechanical errors as grammar, punctuation, usage, and spelling

Glossary of Reading Terms

effect what happens as the result of a cause

elaborate add more detail to what has already been said or written

entry word the word being defined in a dictionary or glossary. It is printed in boldface type.

etymology an explanation of the origin and history of a word and its meaning

exaggeration a statement that makes something seem larger or greater than it actually is

exclamation mark punctuation (!) following a word, phrase, or sentence that was exclaimed, or spoken with strong feeling

exclamatory sentence a sentence that expresses strong feeling or surprise and ends with an exclamation mark

expository text text that tells facts about a topic

expression emotion put into words while reading or speaking

fable a story that teaches a lesson

fact piece of information that can be proved to be true

fairy tale a folk story with magical characters and events

fantasy a make-believe story that could never happen in the real world

fiction writing that tells about imaginary people, things, and events

figurative language the use of language that gives words a meaning beyond their usual definitions in order to add beauty or force

flashback an interruption in the sequence of events of a narrative to include an event that happened earlier

fluency the ability to read quickly, accurately, and with expression. Fluent readers can focus their attention on the meaning of the text.

folk tale a story that has been handed down over many years

foreshadowing the use of hints or clues about what will happen later in a story

generalize make a broad statement or rule after examining particular facts

gesture a meaningful movement of the hands, arms, or other part of the body. Gestures may be used instead of words or with words to help express an idea or feeling.

glossary an alphabetical list of words and their definitions, usually found at the back of a book

graphic organizer a drawing, chart, or web that illustrates concepts or shows how ideas relate to each other. Readers use graphic organizers to help them keep track of and understand important information and ideas as they read. Story maps, word webs, Venn diagrams, and K-W-L charts are graphic organizers.

graphic source a chart, diagram, or map within a text that adds to readers' understanding of the text

guide words the words at the top of a dictionary or glossary page that show the first and last entry words on that page

high-frequency words the words that appear most commonly in print. The one hundred most frequent words account for about 50 percent of printed words. They are often called *sight words* since automatic recognition of these words is necessary for fluent reading.

historical fiction realistic fiction that takes place in the past

homograph a word that is spelled the same as another word, but has a different meaning and history. The words may or may not be pronounced the same. *Bass,* meaning a low singing voice, and *bass,* meaning a fish, are homographs.

homophone a word that sounds the same as another word, but has a different spelling, meaning, and history. *Ate* and *eight* are homophones.

humor writing or speech that has a funny or amusing quality

humorous fiction a funny story about imaginary people and events

hyperbole an exaggerated statement not meant to be taken literally, such as *I'm so hungry I could eat a horse.*

idiom a phrase whose meaning differs from the ordinary meaning of the words. *A stone's throw* is an idiom meaning "a short distance."

illustrative phrase or sentence an example showing how an entry word in a dictionary may be used in a sentence or phrase. It is printed in italic type.

illustrator a person who draws the pictures to go with a selection

imagery the use of language to create beautiful or forceful pictures in the reader's mind

imperative sentence a sentence that gives a command or makes a request. It usually ends with a period.

indent to begin the first line of a paragraph farther in from the left margin than the other lines

independent clause a clause that can stand by itself as a sentence

index an alphabetical list of people, places, and things that are mentioned in a book. An index gives the page numbers where each of these can be found. It appears at the end of a book.

indirect object a noun or pronoun that shows to whom or for whom the action of the verb is done

inference conclusion reached on the basis of evidence and reasoning

inflected ending a letter or group of letters added to the end of a base word that does not change the part of speech of the base word. Inflected endings are *-s, -es, -ed, -ing, -er,* and *-est.*

inflection a grammatical change in the form of a word, usually by adding an ending

inform give knowledge, facts, or news to someone

informational text text that gives facts about real people, places and events or that gives instructions or directions

interjection a word that is used to express strong feeling, such as *Oh!*

interrogative sentence a sentence that asks a question and ends with a question mark

interview a face-to-face conversation in which someone responds to questions

intonation the rise and fall of a reader's or speaker's voice

introductory paragraph the first paragraph of a composition or piece of writing. It sets up what is to come in the composition.

introductory sentence the first sentence of the first paragraph in a composition or a piece of writing. It sets up what is to come in the paragraph.

irony a way of speaking or writing in which the ordinary meaning of the words is the opposite of what the speaker or writer is thinking; a contrast between what is expected and what actually happens

irregular verb a verb that does not add *-ed* to form the past tense

jargon the language of a special group or profession

legend an old story that tells about the great deeds of a hero

legible clear and easy to read

linking verb a verb that does not show action, such as *is, seem,* and *become*

literary elements the characters, setting, plot, and theme of a narrative text

literary nonfiction text that tells about a true event or a series of events as if it were a story

long vowel sound a vowel sound that is the same as the name of a vowel letter—*a, e, i, o,* and *u*

main idea the big idea that tells what a paragraph or a selection is mainly about; the most important idea of a text

media often, **the media** print and electronic sources such as newspapers, magazines, TV, radio, the Internet, and other such means of communication

Glossary of Reading Terms

metacognition an awareness of one's own thinking processes and the ability to monitor and direct them to a desired goal. Good readers use metacognition to monitor their reading and adjust their reading strategies.

metaphor a comparison that does not use *like* or *as,* such as *a heart of stone*

meter the pattern of beats or accents in poetry

modulation the variance of the volume, tone, or pitch of one's voice

monitor and clarify a comprehension strategy by which readers actively think about understanding their reading and know when they understand and when they do not. Readers use appropriate strategies to make sense of difficult words, ideas, or passages.

mood the atmosphere or feeling of a written work

moral the lesson or teaching of a fable or story

morpheme the smallest meaningful unit of language, including base words and affixes. There are three morphemes in the word *unfriendly—un, friend,* and *ly.*

motive the reason a character in a narrative does or says something

multiple-meaning word a word that has more than one meaning. Its meaning can be understood from the context in which it is used.

mystery a story about mysterious events that are not explained until the end, so as to keep the reader in suspense

myth an old story that often explains something about nature

narrative a story, made up or true, that someone tells or writes

narrator the character in a selection who tells the story

negative a word that means "no" or "not"

nonfiction writing that tells about real things, real people, and real events

noun a word that names a person, place, animal, or thing

onomatopoeia the use of words that sound like their meanings, such as *buzz* and *hum*

onset the part of a word or syllable that comes before the vowel. In the word *black, bl* is the onset. Also see *rime.*

opinion someone's judgment, belief, or way of thinking

oral rereading repeated reading of text until it can be read fluently

oral vocabulary the words needed for speaking and listening

outcome the resolution of the conflict in a story

pace (in fluency) the speed at which someone reads

paired reading reading aloud with a partner who provides help identifying words and other feedback. Also called *partner reading.*

paragraph a group of sentences about one main idea. Each paragraph begins on a new line and is indented.

paraphrase retell the meaning of a passage in one's own words

parentheses two curved lines ( ) used to set off words or phrases in text

participle a word formed from a verb and often used as an adjective or a noun

period the dot (.) that signifies the end of most sentences or shows an abbreviation, as in *Dec.*

personification a figure of speech in which human traits are given to animals or inanimate objects, as in *The sunbeam danced on the waves.*

persuade convince someone to do or to believe something

phoneme the smallest part of spoken language that makes a difference in the meaning of words. The word *sat* has three phonemes—/s/, /a/, and /t/.

phoneme blending orally combining a series of phonemes in sequence to form a word

phoneme isolation the ability to identify and pronounce an individual phoneme in a word

phoneme manipulation adding, deleting, or substituting phonemes in spoken words, for example, Say *fox* without the /f/: *ox*.

phonemic awareness one kind of phonological awareness. It includes the ability to hear individual sounds in words and to identify and manipulate them.

phonics the study of the relationship between sounds and their spellings

phonogram the part of a one-syllable word comprised of a vowel and all the letters that follow it, as *ack* in *back, crack, track, shack*. Words that share a phonogram are called a *word family*.

phonological awareness an awareness of the sounds that make up spoken language

photo essay a collection of photographs on one theme, accompanied by text

phrasing breaking text into natural thought units when reading

pitch degree of highness or lowness of a sound or of a speaker's voice

play a story that is written to be acted out for an audience

plot a series of related events at the beginning, middle, and end of a story; the action of a story

plural noun a noun that names more than one person, place, or thing

plural possessive noun a noun that shows there are two or more owners of something. Add an apostrophe to a plural noun ending in –*s* to make it a plural possessive noun.

poem an expressive, imaginative piece of writing often arranged in lines having rhythm and rhyme. In a poem, the patterns made by the sounds of the words have special importance.

possessive noun a noun that shows ownership or possession

possessive pronoun a pronoun that shows who or what owns or has something

pourquoi tale a type of folk story that explains why things in nature came to be. *Pourquoi* is a French word meaning "why."

predicate a word or group of words that tells what the subject is or does

predict tell what a selection might be about or what might happen in a text. Readers use text features and information to predict. They confirm or revise their predictions as they read.

prefix a word part added at the beginning of a base word to change its meaning or make another word, such as *un* in *unbutton*

preposition a word that shows the relationship of a noun or pronoun to another word. It is the first word in a prepositional phrase.

prepositional phrase a group of words that begins with a preposition and ends with a noun or pronoun

presentation something that is presented to an audience

preview look over a text before reading it

prewrite an initial stage in the writing process when topics may be brainstormed, ideas may be considered, and planning may occur

prior knowledge the information and experience that a reader brings to a text. Readers use prior knowledge to help them understand what they read.

procedural text a set of directions and graphic features telling how to do something

pronoun a word that can take the place of a noun or nouns

pronunciation key the explanation of the symbols used in a dictionary or glossary

pronunciation the letters and diacritical marks appearing in parentheses after an entry word in a dictionary that show how the word is pronounced

prop an item, such as an object, picture, or chart, used in a performance or presentation

proper noun a word that names a particular person, place, or thing. A proper noun begins with a capital letter.

Glossary of Reading Terms

punctuation the marks used in writing to separate sentences and their elements and to make meaning clear. Periods, commas, question marks, semicolons, and colons are punctuation marks.

question mark a punctuation mark (?) used at the end of a sentence to indicate a question

quotation marks the punctuation marks (" ") used to indicate the beginning and end of a speaker's exact words

reading vocabulary the words we recognize or use in print

realistic fiction a story of imaginary people and events that could happen in real life

r-controlled vowel sound the sound of a vowel immediately followed by r in the same syllable. Its sound is neither long nor short.

regular verb a verb that adds -ed to form the past tense

repetition the repeated use of some aspect of language

resolution the point in a story where the conflict is resolved

revise the stage in the writing process when a draft may be changed to improve such things as focus, ideas, organization, word choice, or voice

rhyme to end in the same sound(s)

rhythm a pattern of strong beats in speech or writing, especially in poetry

rime the part of a word or syllable that includes the vowel and any following consonants. In the word black, ack is the rime. Also see onset.

rising action the buildup of conflicts and complications in a story

root a word part, usually of Greek or Latin origin, that cannot stand alone, but is used to form a family of words. Trans in transfer and transportation is a root.

rubric a set of guidelines used to evaluate a product such as writing

run-on sentence two sentences written together without correct punctuation

salutation the words of greeting in a letter that address the person to whom the letter is being written

schwa the vowel sound in an unaccented syllable, such as the sound of a in above

science fiction a story based on science that tells what life in the future might be like

segment break a spoken word into its individual sounds

semantic map a graphic organizer, often a web, used to display words or concepts that are meaningfully related

semicolon punctuation (;) that indicates a pause between two clauses in a sentence

sensory language the use of words that help the reader understand how things look, sound, smell, taste, or feel

sentence a group of words that tells or asks something; asks a question; or makes a request, a command, or an exclamation

sequence the order of events in a selection or the order of the steps in which something is done

sequence words clue words such as first, next, then, and finally that signal the order of events in a selection

setting where and when a story takes place

short vowel sound the sound of a, e, i, o, and u as heard in bat, bet, bit, box, and but

simile a comparison that uses like or as, as in as busy as a bee

simple predicate the verb in the complete predicate

simple subject the main noun or pronoun in the complete subject

singular noun a noun that names one person, place, or thing

singular possessive noun a noun that shows there is one owner of something. Add an apostrophe and -s to a singular noun to make it a singular possessive noun.

sound boxes a graphic consisting of a row of boxes in which each box represents a single phoneme. A marker is placed in a box for each sound heard in a given word. Also called Elkonin boxes.

speech a public talk to a group of people made for a specific purpose

stanza a group of lines in a poem

statement a sentence that tells something. A statement ends with a period.

steps in a process the order of the steps in which something is done

stop sound a phoneme that can be said without distortion for only an instant. /b/, /k/, and /g/ are all stop sounds.

story map a graphic organizer used to record the literary elements and the sequence of events in a narrative text

story structure how the characters, setting, and events of a story are organized into a plot

subject a word or group of words that tells whom or what a sentence is about

subject-verb agreement when the subject and verb in a sentence work together, or agree. A sentence with a singular subject must have a verb that works, or agrees, with a singular subject.

suffix a word part added at the end of a word to change its meaning and part of speech, such as -*ly* in *friendly*

summarize give the most important ideas of what was read. Readers summarize important information in the selection to keep track of what they are reading.

superlative adjective an adjective used to compare three or more people, places, or things. Add -*est* to most adjectives to make them superlative.

supporting detail piece of information that tells about the main idea

syllable a word part that contains a single vowel sound

symbolism the use of one thing to suggest something else; often the use of something concrete to stand for an abstract idea

synonym a word with the same or nearly the same meaning as another word

table of contents list of chapters, articles, or stories in a book. It appears at the beginning of the book.

tall tale a story that uses exaggeration

tempo (in speaking) the speed at which someone speaks

text structure the organization of a piece of writing. Text structures of informational text include cause/effect, chronological, compare/contrast, description, problem/solution, proposition/support, and ask/answer questions.

theme the big idea or author's message in a story

think aloud an instructional strategy in which a teacher verbalizes his or her thinking to model the process of comprehension or the application of a skill

timed reading a method of measuring fluency by determining words correct per minute (WCPM)

title the name of a written work; a word or abbreviation that can come before the name of a person, such as *Dr.* or *Mrs.*

tone author's attitude toward the subject or toward the reader

topic the subject of a discussion, conversation, or piece of text

topic sentence the sentence that tells the main idea of a paragraph

verb a word that tells what something or someone does or is

visualize picture in one's mind what is happening in the text. Visualizing helps readers imagine the things they read about.

volume (in speaking) degree of loudness of a speaker's voice

vowel digraph two vowels together that stand for a single sound, such as *oa* in *boat* or *ea* in *leaf*

vowel the letters *a, e, i, o, u,* and sometimes *y*

WCPM words correct per minute; the number of words read correctly in one minute

word analysis decoding a word by using its parts, such as suffixes, prefixes, and syllables

word family a group of words that rhyme and share the same phonogram, such as *fill, still, will*

D'Nealian™ Cursive

a b c d e f g
h i j k l m n
o p q r s t u
v w x y z

A B C D E F G
H I J K L M N
O P 2 R S T U
V W X Y Z . , ' ?

1 2 3 4 5 6
7 8 9 10

D'Nealian™ Alphabet

a b c d e f g h i

j k l m n o p q r s t

u v w x y z

A B C D E F G

H I J K L M N O

P Q R S T U V

W X Y Z . , ' ?

1 2 3 4 5 6

7 8 9 10

Manuscript Alphabet

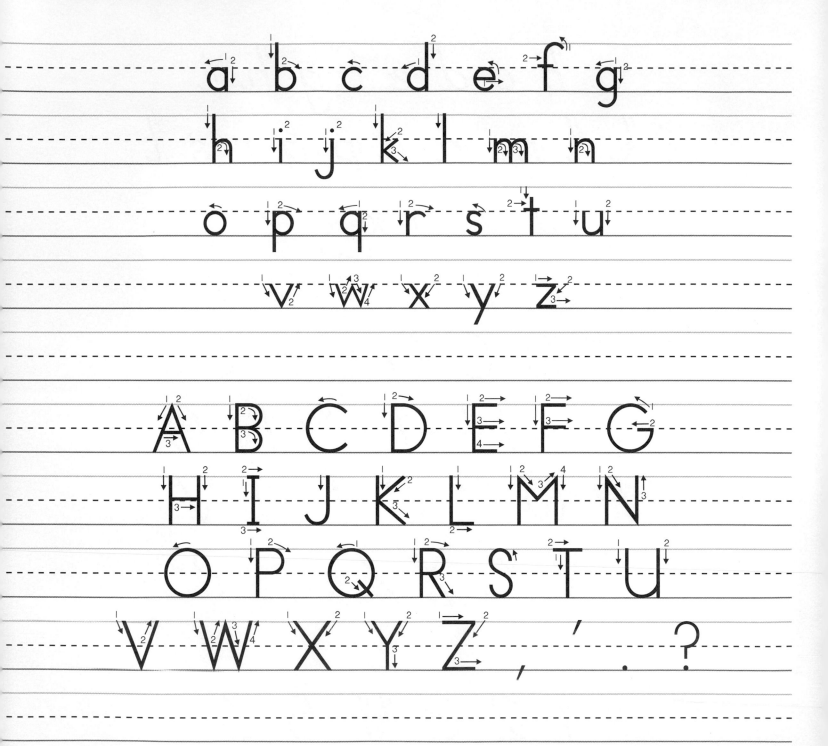

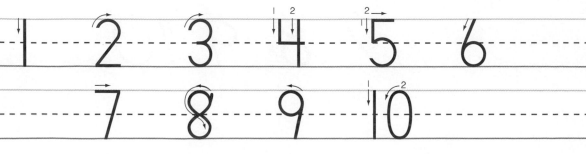

Reteach Lessons: Grade 2

Reteach Phonics

Reteach Comprehension

Reteach Phonics
Short Vowels: /e/ *ea*

1 Teach

Write *deck, sing, lock, luck, sick, man,* and *dust* on the board. Have volunteers read the words aloud and name the vowel sound in each. Help children understand that all the words have short vowel sounds.

Write *head* on the board. Frame *ea* and stretch out the vowel sound as you say *head.* Say: *The letters* ea *sometimes spell the short* e *sound.*

Write the following words on chart paper: *breath, clock, bread, thread, desk, ready, back, leather, sack, thick, tuck.* Read aloud each word. Invite a volunteer to circle the letter or letters for the short vowel sound in each word.

Remind children that when they see a word with the letters *ea,* they might try using both the long *e* sound and the short *e* sound when they sound out the word. They should choose the vowel sound that makes a word and that makes sense.

2 Practice

Write the following words on the board. Have a volunteer read each word. If the word has a short vowel sound, the child uses it in a sentence.

weather	**wheat**	**treat**	**spread**
black	**feather**	**king**	**drum**
crib	**thread**	**head**	**shock**

Then write *king* on the board. Have children make new words as you give the following instructions:

Change k *to* br. *Read the new word.* (bring)
Change ing *to* ead. *Read the new word.* (bread)
Change d *to* th. *Read the new word.* (breath)
Change br *to* f and *add* er *at the end. Read the new word.* (feather)
Change f *to* l. *Read the new word.* (leather)

Reteach Phonics
Long Vowels: vowel_e

① Teach

Write *plan* on the board. Ask children what vowel sound they hear in *plan*. (the short *a* sound) Below *plan*, write *plane*. Say the word, and have children repeat it. Explain that *plane* has the long *a* sound. Frame the letters *ane*. Identify the letters as V/C/e. Tell children that when a vowel is followed by a consonant and the letter *e*, the first vowel usually has its long vowel sound, and the *e* is silent.

Write *nice*, *rage*, and *nose* on the board. Ask children whether they hear a short vowel sound or a long vowel sound in each word. (long vowel sound) Point out the *e* at the end.

② Practice

Write these words on the board:

mad   **rid**   **bit**   **hop**   **us**

Have children read each word and identify the short vowel sound. Ask volunteers to come to the board and add a final *e* to each word. Have them read the new words and identify the long vowel sounds. Review the vowel/consonant/*e* rule.

Write this sentence on the board:

The snake chose a nice hole for its home.

Have children read the sentence aloud. Ask them to identify each long vowel sound and tell why the word has a long vowel sound.

Provide phonogram cards *ace*, *ake*, *ice*, *ime*, and letter cards *d*, *l*, *m*, *n*, *p*, and *t*. Have children use the cards to build words that have long vowel sounds and end in *e*. (*dice, dime, lace, lake, lice, lime, make, mice, mime, nice, pace, take, time*)

Record words children build on the board. Invite volunteers to use each word in a sentence.

Reteach Phonics
Consonant Blends

① Teach

Remind children that when they see two or three consonants together in a word, they should blend the consonant sounds together. Write *ride* and have children read the word. Then write *bride*. Say: *Listen as I blend this word.* (Blend the sounds of the word.) *Notice that you hear /b/ and /r/ blended together at the beginning of the word.*

Write *stump* and read the word. Say: *Notice /st/ at the beginning of the word and /mp/ at the end.*

Write these words on the board. Ask volunteers to read the words and circle the beginning and/or ending blends.

strap	**clamp**	**slip**	**stand**
smile	**crust**	**plank**	**greet**

② Practice

Display the following word cards, one at a time. Have children identify the letters for the initial and final consonant sounds in the words and read the words.

bride	strap	mask	pond
flop	camp	lost	send
land	tusk	strong	brake
string	bump	dust	flute

Have children work individually or in pairs to sort the word cards according to their beginning or ending blends. *(bride/brake; strap/string/strong; mask/tusk; pond/send/land; flop/flute; camp/bump; lost/dust)* Then have children name another word that begins or ends with each consonant blend.

Reteach Phonics
Inflected Endings
-s, -ed, -ing

① ## Teach

Write the sentences below on the board.

Tom <u>jumps</u>.
He is <u>jumping</u> now.
He <u>jumped</u> last week too.

Have the sentences read. Point out that *jump* is a base word. Adding an ending to a base word makes a new word. Have a child circle the endings in *jumps, jumping,* and *jumped*.

Explain that if a base word ends with a vowel followed by one consonant, the consonant is doubled before an ending is added. Demonstrate this by writing *hop, hopped,* and *hopping*. Identify the base word and endings. Point out the vowel and final consonant in *hop*. Ask which consonant was doubled before an ending was added. Tell children the *p* is not doubled before adding *-s*.

Write *hike, hikes, hiked,* and *hiking*. Explain that *hike* is the base word. Tell children that the final *e* is dropped before *-es, -ed,* or *-ing* is added.

② ## Practice

Create a chart as shown. Ask children to tell you which words will need to have the last consonant doubled before adding an ending.

	-ed	**-ing**
jump **pat** **rub** **ask**		

Have children take turns coming to the board and adding the endings to the words to complete the chart. Then review the sounds for *-ed* in *jumped* (/t/), *patted* (/ed/), and *rubbed* (/d/).

Reteach Phonics
Diphthongs /ou/
ou, ow

1 **Teach**

Write the following sentence on the board:

We found a brown mouse in our house in town.

Ask children to listen for /ou/ as you read the sentence, tracking the print. Have children underline each /ou/ word. Circle *ou* or *ow* in each /ou/ word. Help children conclude that the letters *ou* and *ow* can both spell /ou/.

2 **Practice**

Write the following words on the board:

found	**gown**	**clown**	**pound**
pout	**down**	**brown**	**out**

Give children these clues, and have them identify the /ou/ word that goes with each clue.

This is the opposite of in. (out)
This is the opposite of lost. (found)
This is a fancy dress. (gown)
You might do this if you are upset. (pout)
You do this with a hammer. (pound)
This is a funny person. (clown)
This is the opposite of up. (down)
This is a color. (brown)

Reteach Phonics
Diphthongs /oi/ *oi, oy*

① Teach

Write this sentence on the board and read it with children:

Troy had a noisy toy.

Say /oi/ and have children say the sound after you. Ask them to raise a hand each time they hear a word with /oi/ as you reread the sentence.

Have children underline each /oi/ word in the sentence. Point out that /oi/ can be spelled *oy* or *oi*.

② Practice

Display phonogram cards for *oil* and *oy*. Have children use letter cards for *b, c, f, j, R, s,* and *t* to build /oi/ words. (*boil, boy, coil, coy, foil, joy, Roy, soil, soy, toil, toy*) Have volunteers write each word on the board and circle the letters for /oi/.

Have children choose two /oi/ words and write a simple rhyming couplet.

Mike is such a happy boy.
He is always full of joy.

Reteach Phonics
Consonant Digraphs

1 Teach

Say: *The chick cheeped while the child changed channels. What sound is repeated?* (/ch/)

Write *chalk* on the board. Say the word and circle the letters *ch*. Explain that the letters for /ch/ are *ch*. Tell children that sometimes two consonants together spell one new sound. Touch *ch* and have children say /ch/ with you. Write the following words on the board:

ship	**thin**	**whale**	**catch**
with	**dash**	**each**	**child**

Have children read the words and circle the two or three consonants in each word that spell one sound *(sh, th, wh, ch, tch)*.

2 Practice

Have children suggest other words that begin or end with the same sounds as the words on the board. Add their words. Ask volunteers to circle the letters for the beginning or ending sound in each word.

Write the following sentences. Have children circle the digraphs and say the sounds for the digraphs.

Charlie fed each chicken so much food.
She will wash shells as shy people fish.
Thad hit his thumb with a thick stick.
Whales whistle while water whirls.
I will watch Mom strike the match.

Provide pictures of a whistle, a chicken, a shell, a thumb, and a match. On index cards, write these words: *while, whale, when, what, thirsty, bath, think, path, shape, wish, shirt, splash, chop, pinch, check, such, latch, patch, ditch, catch*. Have children place each card below the picture whose name begins or ends with the same digraph.

Reteach Phonics
r-Controlled
ar, or, ore, oar

1 Teach

Emphasize /är/ in this sentence: *It's not hard to see stars in the dark.*

Emphasize /ôr/ in this sentence: *Doris got boards at the store on a stormy morning.*

Ask children what vowel sound they heard repeated in each sentence.

Write *hard*, *stars*, and *dark* on the board. Tell children that /är/ is spelled *ar*. Underline *ar* in each word.

Repeat the routine for /ôr/ words in the second sentence. Tell children that /ôr/ can be spelled *or*, *ore*, or *oar*.

2 Practice

Have children work in small groups. Provide each group with a piece of poster board. Tell children to divide the poster into four columns and write one of these words at the top of each column: *dark, corn, shore, soar*. Have them circle the letters for /är/ or /ôr/ in each word.

Write the following words on index cards:

Have a child choose a word, read it aloud, identify /ôr/ or /är/, and tell the letters for that sound.

Children then find a word on their poster with the same sound–spelling and write the selected word in that column.

Reteach Phonics
Contractions
n't, 's, 'll, 'm

1 ## Teach

Remind children that a contraction is made by putting two words together and replacing one or more letters with an apostrophe. Write these word pairs on the board:

I am	**she is**	**you will**
I'm	**she's**	**you'll**

Have children read each contraction and tell what letter or letters have been replaced by the apostrophe. Write these sentences on chart paper and have them read:

I wasn't sure if I should or shouldn't.
He didn't know if he could or he couldn't.
She can't smile because she isn't happy.

Have children circle the contractions and tell what words are used to make the contractions.

2 ## Practice

Write the contractions below on the board. Invite children to write the two words that make each contraction. Help them identify the letter or letters replaced by the apostrophe.

isn't (is not)	**he'll (he will)**
aren't (are not)	**they'll (they will)**
doesn't (does not)	**we're (we are)**

Give groups the contraction cards *'ll, n't, 's,* and *'m* and word cards *I, he, she,* and *does* to use to build contractions. Tell them to make a list of the contractions they build. Invite groups to share their lists.

Reteach Phonics
Contractions *'re, 've, 'd*

1 ## Teach

Remind children that a contraction is made by putting two smaller words together and replacing a letter or letters with an apostrophe. Write the following word pairs and words in columns on the board:

you are	**I've**
they had	**they'd**
I have	**you're**

Ask children to draw a line from each word pair to its corresponding contraction. Have children circle the letter or letters in the word pair that are replaced by the apostrophe.

Then write the word *won't* on the board. Write the words *will not* below it. Explain that *won't* is an irregular contraction. Say: Won't *is the contraction for* will not.

2 ## Practice

Write the sentences below on the board. Have children rewrite each sentence using a contraction for the underlined words.

We <u>are</u> going home soon.
I <u>would</u> like to read that book.
I wish <u>she would</u> sit by me.
You <u>are</u> so nice.
I <u>have</u> never been late.
He <u>will not</u> ride with us.

Have children read their sentences aloud. Guide them to understand that using a contraction for the word pair does not change the meaning of the sentence.

Reteach Phonics
r-Controlled *er, ir, ur*

1 ## Teach

Write the following sentence and have it read.

Her family went to the circus on Thursday.

Remind children that when the letter *r* follows a vowel, the *r* affects the sound of the vowel. Have them underline the words with /ėr/. Explain that /ėr/ can be spelled by the letters *er*, *ir*, and *ur*. Circle those letters in the words *Her*, *circus*, and *Thursday*.

Write *enter, border,* and *after* and read the words aloud. Underline *er* at the end of each word. Tell children they can blend longer words with /ėr/ by dividing them into smaller parts. Explain that the words are usually divided between the two consonants. Have volunteers draw a line between the two syllables in each word and then blend them.

2 ## Practice

Write these sentences on the board:

A thirsty girl got dirt on her skirt.
A turtle turned in the surf.
He's certain to serve her dinner.

Ask children to read the sentences, find the words with /ėr/, and circle the letters for /ėr/.

Prepare the following word cards:

hurry   clever   birth   girl   herd

curly   first   church   germ   dirty

Have children work in pairs or small groups. Give a pile of cards to each group. Tell children to read and sort the words by their vowel patterns: *er, ir, ur.*

Reteach Phonics
Plurals *-s, -es, -ies*

1 Teach

Say: *The dogs bark at the big boxes.*

Ask children how many dogs and boxes they pictured—one or more than one. How did they know? Write these words on the board:

dog	box	puppy
dogs	boxes	puppies

Circle *-s* in *dogs* and *-es* in *boxes*. Remind children that *-s* or *-es* can be added to a noun to make it mean more than one. Explain that children can add *-s* to most nouns to make the plural form, but words that end in *s, ch, sh, tch, ss, x, z,* or *zz* add *-es*.

Explain that *puppies* means "more than one puppy." Circle *-ies* in *puppies*. Tell children that to form the plural of a noun ending in *y*, they change the *y* to *i* and add *-es*.

2 Practice

Write the following words on cards and give one or two to each child.

cherries   kittens   bushes

pencils   churches   lilies

Have each child read a word, identify the base word, and tell what ending was added: *-s, -es,* or changing the *y* to *i* and adding *-es*.

Write *-s, -es,* and *-ies* on the board, each at the top of a column. Write the words *baby, girl, peach, stamp, dish, penny, star, fox, book,* and *story* on cards. Have children choose a card and read the word. Then have them say the plural form of the word and write it in the correct column.

Reteach Phonics
Long *a*: *a*, *ai*, *ay*

① Teach

Remind children that a long vowel sound says the name of the vowel. Write *paint* and *way* on the board and read them with children. Ask what vowel sound they hear in each word. Frame *ai* in *paint* and *ay* in *way* and point out that the long *a* sound can be spelled *ai* or *ay*.

Write *paper*. Remind children to blend longer words by dividing them into syllables. Tell them that when a syllable ends with a single vowel, like *pa* in *paper*, the vowel sound is usually long. Blend *paper*.

② Practice

Write the sentences below on the board.

We paid to send the mail on the train.
I play every day in May.

Track the print with your finger as you read the sentences with children. Ask them to identify and underline the words that have the long *a* sound. Then invite volunteers to circle the letters for /ā/ in the words.

Pass out half-sheets of gray, white, and blue paper to each child. Have children draw a large raindrop and write *rain* on the white paper, write *gray* on the gray paper, and write *paper* on the blue paper.

Write the following words on the board and have them read.

bacon	label	baby	sail	away
stay	today	tail	table	favor
play	fail	ray	pain	wait

Have children sort the words according to the spelling pattern for long *a*, writing *ay* words on the gray paper, *ai* words on the raindrop, and *a* words on the blue paper.

Reteach Phonics
Long *e: e, ee, ea, y*

1 Teach

Remind children that a long vowel sound says the name of the vowel. Write the words *jeep* and *neat* on the board and say each word, stretching the long *e* sound. Point out that each word has the long *e* sound, but the letters for the vowel sound are different in each word. Circle *ee* in *jeep* and *ea* in *neat*.

Write the words *happy* and *be* on the board. Say each word, stretching the long *e* sound. Frame *y* in *happy* and explain that the letter for the long *e* sound is *y*. Then frame *e* in *be* and explain that the letter for the long *e* sound is *e*. Explain that when a vowel is the only vowel in a word, and it is at the end of the word, the vowel usually has its long sound, like *e* in *be*.

2 Practice

Write this rhyme on the board:

All three bees now agree.
Each wants to see a leafy tree.
The bees are as jolly as they can be
As they creep and feast under the tree.

Have children read the rhyme, identify each word that has the long *e* sound, and circle the letter or letters for long *e*.

Read aloud the riddles that follow. As children say each answer, write the word on the board. Have volunteers circle the letter or letters for the long *e* sound in each answer.

I'm what you do at night. What am I? (sleep)
I'm a word that means "you and me." What am I? (we)
I'm an animal that has long ears and a powder puff tail.
What am I? (bunny)
I'm where you go to build sand castles. What am I? (beach)

Reteach Phonics
Long *o: o, oa, ow*

① Teach

Remind children that a long vowel sound says the name of the vowel. Write this sentence and read it.

Local hero Joan knows how to hold a post and row a boat.

Ask children what long vowel sound they hear repeated in this silly sentence. Frame *Local, hero, Joan, hold, post, row,* and *boat.* Emphasize the long *o* sound as you say each word. Have children repeat each word. Underline the letters for the long *o* sound in each word. Have children identify how the long *o* sound is spelled in each word. For *hero* and *local,* remind them that a vowel usually has its long sound at the end of a word or syllable. For *hold* and *post,* remind them that words with *-old* or *-ost* usually have the long *o* sound.

② Practice

Tell children to fold a sheet of paper to make three columns and write one of the following at the top of each column: *o, oa, ow.* Tell children to choose at least one word from the silly sentence to write in each column.

o	oa	ow

Have children brainstorm other long o words to add. Then have them choose one word from each column to use in their own silly sentence to share with the rest of the group. They can write their silly sentence at the bottom of their paper, beginning it with an uppercase letter and ending it with proper punctuation.

Reteach Phonics
Compound Words

① Teach

Remind children that a compound word is made up of two small words joined together. Show word cards for *some* and *one*. Read each word separately. Then slide the cards together as you read *someone*. Repeat the routine with *cup* and *cake*, *no* and *where*.

② Practice

Write the following story on the board or chart paper:

> **Bees buzzed near their beehive, grasshoppers hopped, and sunflowers grew. Sunshine shone brightly that afternoon in our backyard. Then we heard thunder. "A thunderstorm is nearby!" I cried. We raced inside.**

Have the story read aloud. Help children identify and underline each compound word. Then have them draw a line to separate each compound into its two smaller words.

Create word cards for *airport, backpack, birthday, carpool, cowboy, flashlight, pancake, rainbow, starfish, sunrise, daylight,* and *watermelon*. Cut each compound word into its two smaller words and number the first word *1* and the second word *2*.

Distribute the cards to children, in no particular order. Have a child read a word card numbered *1*. Then ask which child has a word (numbered *2*) that could make a compound word when joined with the first word. Let the two children decide if the pairing works and then say their compound word for the group.

Reteach Phonics
Long *i: i, ie, igh, y*

1 ## Teach

Remind children that a long vowel sound says the name of the vowel. Write the following sentence on the board. Read it, emphasizing the long *i* words, and ask children what long vowel sound they hear repeated in the sentence.

A child behind me ate pie on a flight in the sky.

Repeat the words *child, behind, pie, flight,* and *sky* as you underline each one. Explain that each word has a different spelling for the long *i* sound. Frame the letter(s) for the long *i* sound in each word.

2 ## Practice

Write the following list on the board:

pie	**kind**	**fright**
high	**why**	**light**
mild	**sight**	**sky**
shy	**try**	**tie**
blind	**lie**	**find**

Create a four-column chart with *i, igh, y,* and *ie* as the headings. Have children sort the words according to the letters for the long *i* sound.

Reteach Phonics
Comparative Endings

1 Teach

Write the sentences below on the board:

Today is colder than yesterday.
Tomorrow will be the coldest day this week.

Point out the *-er* and *-est* endings. Explain that *-er* added to a word means "more," and *-est* means "most." Tell children they add *-er* to a word to compare two things and *-est* to compare three or more things.

Write the words *hot, hotter,* and *hottest.* Ask children what happens to *hot* when the endings are added. Remind them that when a base word ends with a short vowel sound and a consonant, the consonant is usually doubled before an ending is added.

Repeat with the words *little, littler,* and *littlest,* reminding children that when a base word ends in *e,* the *e* is dropped before an ending is added.

2 Practice

Create a chart as shown on chart paper.

base word	-er	-est
big	bigger	
	faster	
		slowest
wide		

Have children fill in the blanks in the chart and then select a word from the chart to finish each of these sentences:

The cat is the _____ animal of all.
The red car was _____ than the blue car.
The oak tree was the _____ tree in the yard.

Reteach Phonics
Syllables C + *le*

1 ## Teach

Write *dimple, purple,* and *cradle* on the board. Ask children what they notice about all three words. (They all end with *le*.) Point out that the letter before the *le* in each word is a consonant. Draw a line between the syllables in each word. Tell children they can blend two-syllable words with consonant + *le* by dividing them into smaller parts. Say: *We usually divide the word so that the consonant plus* le *makes up the last syllable of the word.*

Write this sentence on the board:

The girls giggle as they splash in the puddle.

Ask a child to read the sentence aloud and underline the words that end with consonant + *le*. Have another child draw a line between the syllables in each word.

2 ## Practice

Write the following words on the board. Ask children to read the words and erase any that do not end with consonant + *le*.

simple	**silly**	**whistle**	**sprinkle**
apple	**cable**	**cradle**	**number**
person	**title**	**puzzle**	**noble**

Then write *bundle* on the board. Have children make new words and read them as you give the following instructions:

Change nd *to* bb. *Read the new word.* (bubble)
Change bu *to* go. *Read the new word.* (gobble)
Change obb *to* igg. *Read the new word.* (giggle)
Change g *to* w. *Read the new word.* (wiggle)
Change igg *to* obb. *Read the new word.* (wobble)

Reteach Phonics
Vowels *oo, u*

1 Teach

Say this sentence: *I put the book on the table.* Ask children if they hear the same vowel sound in *put* and *book.* Tell them that the vowel sound in both words is /ù/.

Write the words *book* and *put.* Circle *oo* in *book* and *u* in *put* and tell children the letters for /ù/ in *book* and *put* are *oo* and *u.*

Have children point to a book each time you say a word that has /ù/: *look, full, bat, bull, book, hot, late, took, far, good, bush, shook, give, nook, hood.*

2 Practice

Write the sentences below on the board.

The good cook took a stick of wood.
It's hard to push or pull a full wagon.

Have the first sentence read aloud. Ask a child to underline each word that has /ù/. Repeat the routine with the second sentence.

Write *good* on the board and have it read. Have children follow these instructions to make and read new words:

Change g *to* w. *Read the new word.* (wood)
Change w *to* h. *Read the new word.* (hood)
Change d *to* k. *Read the new word.* (hook)
Change h *to* b. *Read the new word.* (book)
Change ook *to* ull. *Read the new word.* (bull)
Change b *to* p. *Read the new word.* (pull)
Change p *to* f. *Read the new word.* (full)

Reteach Phonics
Syllable Patterns

1 Teach

Ask children to tell what they know about reading words with more than one syllable. Remind children that all words in our language can be grouped into syllable types.

One syllable type is spelled with a consonant letter, then a vowel letter, then another consonant. Write the word *basket* on the board. Tell students, *The word* basket *has two syllables, which can be divided between the two consonants in the middle:* bas-ket. Model how to divide the word. Have children say the first syllable with you: /b/ /a/ /s/. Lead them to understand that the vowel in the syllable is short. Then say the second syllable together: /k/ /e/ /t/. Note the short vowel. Then read the two syllables together: *basket.*

Another is syllable type is spelled with a consonant letter and then a vowel. Write the word *tiger* on the board. Model how to divide the word after the first vowel. Have children say the first syllable with you: /t/ /i/. Lead them to understand that the vowel in the syllable is long. Then say the second syllable together: /g/ /er/. Read the two syllables together: *tiger.*

Remind students that words made up of other one-syllable words can be divided into syllables between those words. Write the word *playground* on the board. Model how to divide the word: *play-ground.* Read the two syllables together with children: *playground.*

2 Practice

Have children read the words *basket, tiger,* and *playground* with you. Then write the following words on the board. Have children volunteer to come to the board and mark where each word should be divided into syllables.

paper	**picnic**	**chapter**
boyhood	**frozen**	**downtown**
sailboat	**window**	**robot**
pencil	**oatmeal**	**soybean**

Reteach Phonics
Vowels *oo, ue, ew, ui*

1 Teach

Say: *We chew food and drink blue juice.*

Repeat the sentence as you stretch /ü/ in *chew, food, blue,* and *juice*. Ask children to identify the repeated vowel sound. Write the sentence on the board. Underline *ew* in *chew* and tell children these are the letters for /ü/ in *chew*. Repeat the routine for *oo* in *food*, *ue* in *blue*, and *ui* in *juice*.

Write the following words on the board. Help children use /ü/ as they blend each word.

stew	**true**	**tool**	**drew**
school	**fruit**	**blew**	**bruise**

2 Practice

Write these sentences on the board:

I don't have a clue where the fruit is.
The wind blew the crew.
She can float in the cool pool.

Have each sentence read aloud. Have children identify the /ü/ words and circle the letters for /ü/ in each word.

Have children think of as many /ü/ words as possible. Give them three minutes to write their lists. After time is up, have children share their lists. Write *oo, ue, ew,* and *ui* as column heads on the board. As children read their lists, write the words under the appropriate headings. Then have children circle the letters for /ü/ in the words.

Reteach Phonics
Suffixes
-ly, -ful, -er, -or

1 Teach

Write these suffixes on the board:

-ly   **-ful**   **-er**   **-or**

Say: *These suffixes can be added to the ends of base words. Sometimes they change the meaning of the base word or how the word is used. They always add a syllable to the base word.*

Write this sentence on the board with the words underlined as shown:

Our <u>teacher</u> talks <u>softly</u>, and she is a <u>wonderful</u> <u>actor</u>.

Tell children that each underlined word is made up of a base word and a suffix. Underline the base word *(teach, soft, wonder, act)* and circle the suffix in each.

Explain that when a word ends in a consonant followed by *y*, the *y* is changed to *i* before adding the suffix *-ly*. Write *happy* and *happily* on the board to demonstrate.

Tell children that the suffix *-ful* means "full of." Explain that when *-er* or *-or* is added to a word, the new word usually means "someone or something that _____."

2 Practice

Write the following words on the board:

peaceful	**quickly**	**sailor**
teacher	**careful**	**loudly**
slowly	**actor**	**rancher**

Have children underline the base word and circle the suffix in each. Then have them tell what each word means. Ask them to use each word in an oral sentence.

Reteach Phonics
Prefixes
un-, re-, pre-, dis-

① Teach

Write *dis-, un-, re-,* and *pre-* in a row on the board. Say: *These word parts are called prefixes. A prefix is added to the beginning of a base word. A prefix can change the meaning of the base word.*

Create a chart, writing the meaning above each prefix as shown.

"not, opposite of"		"again"	"before"
dis-	**un-**	**re-**	**pre-**

Explain that the prefixes *dis-* and *un-* can both mean "not" or "opposite of." Under *dis-* write *agree*, under *un-* write *true*, under *re-* write *write*, and under *pre-* write *view*. Help children add each prefix to the word under it. Write each new word. Have children explain what the base word means and how adding the prefix changes the meaning of the word.

② Practice

Write these words on the board. Ask children what was added to each base word in the first row to make the word in the second row.

play	**tie**	**connect**	**heat**
replay	**untie**	**disconnect**	**preheat**

Have children use each word pair in a sentence to show meaning.

Reteach Phonics
Silent Consonants

1 ## Teach

Write the sentences below on the board:

The knight will climb the ladder.
Can you write a sign?

Read the first sentence with children. Point out the word *knight* and have children repeat it. Frame *knight* and ask them what beginning sound *knight* has and what two consonants are at the beginning. (/n/, *kn*) Explain that when a word begins with *kn*, the *k* is silent.

Next, frame *climb*. Have children say it and listen for the ending sound. Ask what sound they hear at the end of *climb*. (/m/) Point out that the word ends with the letters *mb*. Tell children that when a word ends with *mb*, the *b* is silent.

Then read the second sentence with children. Point to *write*, have children identify the beginning sound and consonants, and ask them which consonant is silent. *(w)* Repeat the routine with *sign*. Explain that *w* can be silent when it comes before *r,* and *g* can be silent when it comes before *n.*

2 ## Practice

Write the rhyme below on the board.

Does a (gn)at have (kn)ees?
Can it (kn)ock on a door?
Can it (gn)aw on a cru(mb)
that it finds on the floor?
Can it (wr)iggle its (wr)ist?
Can it cli(mb) up a tree?
Can a (gn)at (wr)ap a box
and send it to me?

With children, read aloud the rhyme. Have them tell what sound each circled pair of letters spells.

Reteach Phonics
/f/ph, gh

1 Teach

Write this sentence on the board and read it with children:

The photo shows a girl laughing.

Say /f/ and have children raise a hand each time they hear a word with /f/ as you reread the sentence. Underline the words *photo* and *laughing* as children identify them. Circle *ph* in *photo* and *gh* in *laughing* and explain that these letters together usually spell /f/.

2 Practice

Write the rhymes below on the board.

**If you're strong and tough,
you'll laugh when things get rough.**

**My darling nephew Phil
won a trophy for his skill.**

Read aloud each rhyme, and have children repeat it. Ask children to identify the words that have /f/ and to circle the letters for /f/ in each word.

Reteach Phonics
Vowels
aw, au, augh, al

① Teach

Write this sentence on the board:

The naughty puppy paused when he saw a walnut drop from the tree.

Read the sentence aloud and underline the words *naughty*, *paused*, *saw*, and *walnut*. Say: *These four words have something in common: their vowel sound is /ȯ/.*

Have children say the words as you circle *augh*, *au*, *aw*, and *al*. Say: *The letter combinations* aw, au, augh, *and* al *usually spell /ȯ/.*

② Practice

Write the following words on self-stick notes: *paw, claw, toy, jaw, draw, straw, book, haunt, pause, because, town, launch, false, walk, talk, take, caught, catch, taught, daughter, band, luck.*

Have children take turns selecting a word and reading it aloud. If the word has /ȯ/, they should stick it to the board or chart paper. When all the /ȯ/ words have been identified, have children sort them into four groups according to the letters for /ȯ/. Have children read the words in each group.

Children can choose two or more /ȯ/ words to write sentences about a favorite toy, story, or movie.

Reteach Phonics
Inflected Endings

1 Teach

Write the following words on the board:

cries   cried   crying

lucky   luckier   luckiest

Read the words aloud. Explain that each word has a base word and an ending. Point to *cries* and ask children to name the base word. *(cry)* Write *cry* on the board. Ask how *cry* is changed before adding the ending. (*y* is changed to *i* before adding *-es*) Continue the routine with the other words.

Remind children that some base words have other spelling changes. Review doubling the final consonant, as in *hopped* and *hopping*, or dropping the final *e*, as in *raced* and *racing*.

Review with children how to decode words with endings. Tell them to cover the ending, read the base word, and then blend the base word and ending to read the whole word. Point out that sometimes they must break the base word into smaller parts to decode it.

2 Practice

Write the words and endings below on the board. Have pairs of children copy the words and endings on paper. Tell one child to write a word with the base word and one of the endings. Then have him or her pass the paper to a partner who adds a word with another ending. Tell children to continue until they have written all the new words.

try (-s, -ed, -ing)   big (-er, -est)
hope (-s, -ed, -ing)   wide (-er, -est)
stop (-s, -ed, -ing)   tiny (-er, -est)

Have children share their new words and point out the spelling changes.

Reteach Phonics
Abbreviations

1 ## Teach

Tell children that an abbreviation is a shortened form of a word or phrase. Explain that usually, but not always, it consists of a letter or group of letters taken from the longer word or phrase.

Write this sentence on the board:

We are going to the <u>doctor</u>'s office to see <u>Dr.</u> Smith.

Tell children that the two words that are underlined mean the same thing. Tell them that one is just an abbreviation of the other. Instead of writing the word *doctor* twice, we can use an abbreviation. *Dr.* is an abbreviation for the word *Doctor*.

There are many more words that can be abbreviated as well. Let the children know that when you abbreviate a word, you most often add a period to the end of the abbreviation.

2 ## Practice

Write these words on the board:

Avenue (Ave.)   **Senior (Sr.)**

Mister (Mr.)   **December (Dec.)**

January (Jan.)   **Junior (Jr.)**

Mistress (Mrs.)   **November (Nov.)**

Ask children to volunteer to go up to the board and write the abbreviation of each word. Then have them explain what each word means. Explain to children that almost every month of the year can be abbreviated, not just the ones listed on the board. Have children write sentences using the abbreviations.

Reteach Phonics
Syllables *-tion, -ture*

1 ## Teach

Say *go* as you clap one time. Explain that *go* is a word that has only one part. Then say *ba-by* as you clap twice. Explain that *baby* is a word that has two parts. Tell children that each word part is called a *syllable*.

Demonstrate using the word *hip/po/pot/a/mus*. Say: *When you see a long word that you don't know, you can break the word into syllables to make reading the word easier.*

Write the words *lotion* and *future* on the board. Read the words aloud and ask children how many syllables they hear in each word. Tell them that /shən/ is spelled *tion* in *lotion* and /chər/ is spelled *ture* in *future*.

2 ## Practice

Read these words together:

adventure	**action**	**furniture**
vacationer	**section**	**creature**
position	**lecture**	**pictures**

Make a three-column chart as shown below. As a class, decide how many syllables each word has and, therefore, under which number each word should be written. Show the word under the number divided into syllables.

2	3	4 or more
ac tion pic tures	ad ven ture	va ca tion er

Reteach Phonics
Suffixes *-ness, -less*

1 Teach

Write *-ness* and *-less* on the board. Say: *You know that suffixes are word parts that are added to the end of a word. The word parts* -ness *and* -less *are suffixes. The suffix* -ness *means "quality or condition of being _____." The suffix* -less *means "without."*

Write the words *dark* and *bottom*. Have children tell which suffix, *-ness* or *-less*, can be added to each word. Write the new words. Have children tell how many syllables each new word has. (*darkness* – 2, *bottomless* – 3) Repeat the routine with *happy* and *rest*. Point out that the *y* in *happy* is changed to *i* before adding *-ness*.

Guide children to understand that a suffix adds a syllable to the base word. Ask them what each new word means. Discuss how the meaning of the suffix affects the meaning of the base word.

2 Practice

Have children form new words by adding *-ness* or *-less* to the following base words. Remind children of any spelling changes that need to be made. Children should also write the number of syllables in each new word they make, such as *thoughtless* – 2, *gentleness* – 3.

thought	**quick**	**sad**
cord	**friendly**	**fear**
spot	**ill**	**sudden**
sick	**point**	**use**
bright	**gentle**	**pain**

Ask children to tell what each new word means.

Reteach Phonics
Suffixes *-able, -ible*

1 Teach

Write *-able* and *-ible* on the board. Say: *You know that suffixes are word parts that are added to the end of a word. The word parts -able and -ible are suffixes.*

Write the words *favor* and *convert* on the board. Have children tell which suffix, *-able* or *-ible*, can be added to each word. Write the new word. Volunteers can tell how many syllables the new word has. Repeat with the word *rely*. Point out that the *y* is changed to an *i* before adding the suffix *-able*. Repeat with the word *desire*. Point out that the *e* is deleted before adding the suffix *-able*.

2 Practice

Have children form new words by adding *-able* and *-ible* to these base words:

predict	**value**	**depend**
envy	**profit**	**collect**
imagine	**comfort**	**adore**
question	**vary**	**sense**

Ask children to tell what each new word means. Remind children of any spelling changes that need to be made. Children should write the number of syllables in each new word they make, such as *dependable – 4, sensible – 3*.

Reteach Phonics
Prefixes *mis-*, *mid-*

1 Teach

Write *place* and *week* on the board and *misplace* and *midweek* below them. Read the words aloud and ask children to tell what is the same and what is different about the word pairs. Say: *The word* misplace *has a word part at the beginning. That word part is called a prefix. The prefix changes the meaning of the base word,* place. *What does* place *mean? What does* misplace *mean?*

Repeat the routine with *week* and *midweek.* To help children with the meanings of *misplace* and *midweek,* explain that the prefix *mis-* means "bad or wrong" and the prefix *mid-* means "middle."

2 Practice

Write these words on the board.

type   stream   read   day   size   spoke

Give these clues and have volunteers add *mis-* or *mid-* to one of the words above to make a word that answers the clue.

This is the middle of the day. (midday)
If you read something wrong, you do this. (misread)
This is a car that isn't little or big. (midsize)
If you make a mistake while typing, you do this. (mistype)
If you said something wrong, you did this. (misspoke)
This is where you are if you are halfway across the stream. (midstream)

Have children tell why they chose the word they did.

Reteach Phonics
Prefixes *micro-, non-*

1 Teach

Write the words *scope* and *fiction* on the board and *microscope* and *nonfiction* below them. Read the words aloud and ask children to tell what is the same and what is different about the word pairs. Say: *The word* microscope *has a word part at the beginning. That word part is called a prefix. The prefix changes the meaning of the base word,* scope. *What does* scope *mean? What does* microscope *mean?*

Repeat the routine with *fiction* and *nonfiction*. To help children with the meanings of *microscope* and *nonfiction*, explain that the prefix *micro-* means "extremely small, tiny" and the prefix *non-* means "not."

2 Practice

Write these words on the board.

chip   stop   film   sense

Give these clues and have volunteers add *micro-* or *non-* to the words above to form a word that tells the answer.

This is a tiny photograph. (microfilm)
This is when you do not stop doing something. (nonstop)
This is a tiny chip. (microchip)
This is when you do not make any sense. (nonsense)

Have children tell you why they chose the word that they did.

Reteach
Comprehension
Character

❶ Teach

A character is a person or an animal in a story. A main character is the one the story is mostly about. Authors want their characters to seem like real people. When the characters are animals, sometimes they talk and act the way people do.

Readers learn about characters from what they say and do. Sometimes the author tells about what the characters are thinking, as well. Readers also learn about characters from the way others in the story feel about them and act toward them.

❷ Practice

Recall the fable "The Tortoise and the Hare." Ask: *Would you say that the Hare is slow, fair, or lazy? (lazy) Would you describe the Tortoise as steady, mean, or fast? (steady)*

Read the following description: *David's class is practicing for a program. David likes to sing, and he has a good voice, but he doesn't like to sing in front of others. He doesn't like to act in plays either.*

Ask: *Think of a word to describe David. (Possible response: shy) How do you imagine David will react when his teacher asks him to sing a solo? (Possible response: He will try to find some way to get out of it.)*

Reteach
Comprehension
Setting

① Teach

The setting of a story is where and when the story takes place. A setting may be real, or it may be imaginary. Sometimes a story takes place in several settings, one after another.

Sometimes an author will tell readers just what the setting is and use descriptive words to help readers see it. For example: *The barn was old and drafty. There was a strong smell of hay and of the animals who lived there. Usually there was a constant sound of animals going about their business, but now it was dark and quiet. The animals were asleep.*

Sometimes an author will let readers figure out for themselves what the setting is. For example: *Brenda slammed in the door and dropped her backpack and cell phone on the table. She looked in the refrigerator and took out a bottle of milk. Then she went to get a paper cup from a holder by the sink.*

Ask: *In what room of the house is the setting? (the kitchen) Is this story taking place in the past, present, or future? (probably the present)*

② Practice

Read the following story: *"This is so cool!" thought Zane as he zoomed across the bare, pitted surface with his jet pack. Second graders were allowed to leave early for Moon Base School. "When we were children on Earth," his father would always say, "we didn't have jet packs to get to school. We walked or took a bus."*

Ask: *Where does this story take place? How do you know? (Possible response: on the moon, because there is a bare, pitted surface, and Zane is going to Moon Base School)* Ask: *When does this story take place? How do you know? (Help children see that the story could not be set in the past and could not happen in the present because children cannot yet zip around the moon with jet packs. The story must be set in the future.)*

Reteach
Comprehension
Main Idea and Details

1 ## Teach

The main idea is the most important idea in a selection. The main idea usually tells what the writing is about. Explain that children should think about the whole paragraph or story when they are looking for the main idea. Usually the main idea will be in one sentence. Then details tell more about the main idea.

Read aloud the following paragraph. *Fido was a happy dog. He ate a big meal in the morning. He went for a walk in the afternoon. He had his bath once a month. He slept in a fluffy dog bed. He was sure that no dog could be happier.*

Write these sentence choices on the board. Ask children to think about Fido and the paragraph they just heard. Read each sentence aloud. Have children tell whether the sentence tells a detail or the main idea.

    a. Fido ate in the morning.
    b. Fido was a happy dog.
    c. Fido had a bath once a month.

Guide children in identifying *a* and *c* as details and *b* as the main idea. Explain that *a* and *c* are only small parts of the paragraph, but *b* tells what the paragraph is mostly about, so it is the main idea.

2 ## Practice

Recall nonfiction selections children have read. Assign small groups different selections. Have them look for a sentence that states the main idea of each selection. If the selection doesn't seem to have a stated main idea, have children tell what they think the main idea is and write it on the board. All groups can share their findings with the class.

Reteach
Comprehension
Details and Facts

1 Teach

Copy these sentences on the board. Read them aloud with students.

- A volcano is an opening in the earth where melted rock rises.
- There are at least 1,500 active volcanoes in the world.
- The best place to see volcanoes is Volcanoes National Park in Hawaii.
- Most volcanoes are shaped like mountains.
- A volcanic eruption is a thrilling sight.
- When they erupt, volcanoes are like angry giants.
- Volcanoes erupt rocks and lava, but also ashes and dangerous gases.

Ask: *What are all these sentences about? (volcanoes)* Say: *Volcanoes is the topic, and all these sentences are details about the topic. Details are small pieces of information. Often they can help you picture what you're reading about. But only some of these details are true.*

Go back and read each sentence again. Ask: *Is this a true sentence? How can we prove that it is true?* Explain that a piece of information that can be proven true is a *fact*. Other details may be about what someone thinks, or they may just be interesting pieces of information. Authors often use details and facts to support a point or to back up an opinion.

2 Practice

Have students work in small groups. Give each group one or more nonfiction books that students have read before. Have groups go through their books to find examples of facts—details that can be proven true. Have groups share their findings with the class. They should also tell *how* they would go about proving that a fact is true.

Reteach
Comprehension
Cause and Effect

1 ## Teach

Drop an object on a table. When the object makes a noise, tell children: *Because I dropped this, it made a loud noise. Why did it make a loud noise? (because you dropped it)*

Tell children that things that happen are often caused by other things. What happens is an *effect*. Why it happens is a *cause*. Explain that it's important to think about things that happen and why they happen in stories. Knowing why things happen helps readers understand what they mean.

Sometimes writers use clue words to point to causes and effects. Some clue words are *because, so, if, then,* and *since.*

2 ## Practice

Provide the following sentence stems on the board:

It was cold outside, so . . .
I did well on my test because . . .
Since you have a fever . . .
If you don't hear from your friend today then . . .
The bike had a flat tire, so . . .
The dog was barking because . . .

Have children work in pairs. Have them complete the sentences by supplying causes or effects. Then have them enter the causes and effects in a chart like the following:

Cause: Why did it happen?	Effect: What happened?

Children can think of more causes and effects as time allows.

Reteach
Comprehension
Author's Purpose

1 ## Teach

Explain that authors have various reasons for writing books and selections. They may want to tell a good story, give information, describe something, or convince a reader that something is important. Say: *When I read a book, I ask myself why the author wrote it. I know that the author must have had a purpose in mind. That helps me know how I should read it.*

Write the following titles on the board:

How to Grow Beautiful Flowers
The Three Little Pigs
Let's Recycle at Home
The Gingerbread Man
The First Astronomers

Read the titles aloud and ask children why they think the author wrote each selection. Discuss the authors' purposes. Guide children to understand that when they read a fiction story, they can read to be entertained. When they read nonfiction, they may need to read more carefully, in order to understand the information.

2 ## Practice

Show children the covers of fiction and nonfiction books that they have read. With children, read the titles and review the content of the books. Finally, ask why children think the author wrote each book. Help them give reasons to support their answers.

Continue by asking volunteers to describe books they have read recently. Have the rest of the class decide the author's purpose in each case.

Reteach
Comprehension
Compare and Contrast

1 ## Teach

Explain that to compare is to show how two or more things are alike. To contrast is to show how two or more things are different. Demonstrate by holding up two books and asking children how they are alike and different. *(Children may mention size, color, author, illustrations, fiction or nonfiction, and so on.)*

Tell children that authors often describe how things are alike or different in stories or in nonfiction. Sometimes they use clue words to signal likenesses and differences; for example: *like, both, alike, same, different, however, although, but, neither.* Write these words on the board and have children pronounce them and tell whether each signals a likeness or a difference.

2 ## Practice

Have children listen for clue words as you read this story:

Both Juan and Jamie are in the same grade. Juan goes to North School, but Jamie goes to West School. They both like sports, although neither plays on a team yet. Juan likes baseball, while Jamie prefers soccer. Both are just learning how to play. Unlike Juan, however, Jamie practices every day.

Explain how to use a Venn diagram to show likeness and differences: details about Juan go in one circle, details about Jamic go in the other circle, and details about both go in the section where the circles overlap.

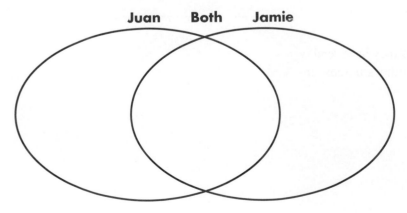

Juan   Both   Jamie

Reteach
Comprehension
Draw Conclusions

1 ## Teach

Explain that sometimes when children read a story, they can use details from the story along with what they already know from their own lives to figure out more about the characters or what is happening in the story.

For example, say: *Suppose I read this in a story: "'Oh Jane,' called her sister from the door to the garden, 'come out here and look at this beautiful rainbow!' Jane went to join her, not minding the wet grass."*

Model drawing a conclusion: *What does the story tell me? There is a rainbow, and the grass is wet. What do I know? That a rainbow sometimes happens after it rains. I know that light from the sun causes a rainbow. Now I can draw the conclusion that—in the story—it rained, but now the sun is shining. I am using information in the story plus what I know about real life to figure out more about the story.*

2 ## Practice

Have children work in small groups. Give each group one or more picture books (fiction and/or nonfiction). Have them find pictures that give information and then add information that they know from life to draw conclusions about what is happening in the book.

Invite groups to share their conclusions and their reasoning that led to each.

Reteach
Comprehension
Make Inferences

1 Teach

Explain to children that authors do not always tell everything about the characters or events in a story. When an author leaves out information about characters or events, readers can use clues in the story, along with their own experiences and knowledge, to make inferences, or reasonable guesses, about these characters or events. The same could be true about a friend, a family member, or even a pet! Sometimes, based on how well you know someone or his or her reaction to an event (the look on his or her face, for example), you might be able to guess the way that he or she is feeling at the time. That guess is also known as an *inference*: Something that you have *inferred* about someone else.

Describe an incident at a birthday party. Say: *A boy is opening a gift that he has just received. He opens the gift and is silent for a couple of minutes. He does not look up at anyone else in the room, nor does he say "thank you."*

What inference can we make from this description?

One inference would be that the boy is not very excited about the gift. We can make other inferences too: The gift might be something that he had not expected, or he might not want the gift at all. We can also infer the boy was so happy about the gift that he couldn't speak.

2 Practice

Describe another incident to gauge how well the children understand how to make inferences based on the lesson you just taught them. Say: *It is winter, and it is recess time. A girl goes outside without her jacket on. Her lips turn blue, and she starts to shiver.*

Ask the children to make an inference about the situation.

Have children choose a character from a book or story they read. Have children make inferences about their chosen character and share them with the class. Ask children to explain what clues led them to make each inference.

Reteach
Comprehension
Sequence

1 Teach

Explain that events in a story happen in a certain order. That order is called *sequence*. Remembering the events in order can help children remember the story. Often a story has clue words to help readers figure out the order of events. Write these clue words on the board and review them with children: *first, second, next, then, last, finally*.

Prepare a chart showing the "Jack and Jill" nursery rhyme. With children, read the rhyme aloud. Help children assign clue words to each line to tell the order of events. Clue words *then* and *next* are interchangeable, as are *last* and *finally*.

Help children recognize that the story would be different if the order of events were different.

2 Practice

Write the nursery rhyme "Little Miss Muffet" on sentence strips.

Little Miss Muffet sat on a tuffet, eating her curds and whey.
Along came a spider,
And sat down beside her,
And frightened Miss Muffet away.

Mix the order of the sentence strips. Invite children to place the strips in the correct order and give each a clue word. Then talk about how the story would be different if the order of events were different.

Have children recall other favorite nursery rhymes, such as "Hickory, Dickory, Dock!" and "Simple Simon," and have them assign clue words to each line.

Reteach
Comprehension
Fact and Opinion

1 ## Teach

Remind children that a fact is something that can be proved true
or false. *The sun is shining* is a fact. You can look out a window
and see if the sun is or is not shining. *It is a beautiful day* is an
opinion. An opinion cannot be proved true or false. It is what
someone thinks or feels.

2 ## Practice

Have children draw a capital *O* on a piece of paper and a
capital *F* on another piece of paper. Tell them you will say some
sentences. Ask them to listen to you say sentences. They should
try to figure out whether you are giving a fact or an opinion. If it
is an opinion, they should hold up the *O* paper. If it is a fact, they
should hold up the *F* paper.

Most birds can fly. (F)
Turtles are beautiful. (O)
Green is the best color. (O)
Red and yellow make orange. (F)
Bees can sting you. (F)
Winter is the prettiest time of year. (O)

Have children work in small groups to look through any selection
in any book they have read this school year. Have them write
down the title of the selection and one statement of fact and
one statement of opinion from the selection. Have them explain
how they decided which statement was a fact and which was
an opinion.

Reteach Comprehension
Plot

1 Teach

Explain that the plot of a story is what happens from the beginning to the end of a story. Tell children that remembering the important story events and the order in which they happen can help them keep track of the plot of the story. Use a simple story map to illustrate this.

Say: *When I read I try to think about what happens at the beginning, middle, and end. I can make a map of the story to help me remember. I will make a story map of* Goldilocks and the Three Bears.

> **Beginning**
> Goldilocks is hungry. She goes into an unfamiliar house in the woods.

> **Middle**
> Goldilocks finds food, a chair, and a bed that are just right. She goes to sleep.

> **End**
> When the bears come home, they are upset that someone has used their things. They scare Goldilocks away.

2 Practice

Have children work in small groups and give each group the name of a story they have read. Have groups make story maps showing the beginning, middle, and end of each story. Ask groups to share and discuss their story plots.

Reteach
Comprehension
Theme

① Teach

Review with children the fable "The Tortoise and the Hare." Retell or summarize the fable as necessary. Include a moral at the end, as usual. Then ask children to restate the moral or lesson of the fable. ("Slow and steady wins the race" or "A person who is slow and steady will win over a person who is fast but doesn't finish.") Explain that this moral is the *theme*, or big idea, of the fable. It is what the fable is all about.

Tell children that not all stories have morals stated in sentences at the end, as fables do. They can understand the big idea in such a story by asking:

- What is this story all about?
- What do the characters learn in the story?

Tell children that they can use something from their own lives to understand the theme, or big idea, of a story.

② Practice

Have children suggest titles of stories they have read and discuss with them what are the themes of these stories. Write the titles and themes on the board.

If children have trouble extracting a theme from any story, suggest that a theme is often a big idea about life that we get from reading a story. It may be helpful to model some big ideas about life, such as "It's always best to tell the truth" or "A true friend sticks with you no matter what."

Reteach Comprehension

Classify and Categorize

1 Teach

Explain that a group is a number of objects, people, or animals that are alike or that have something in common. Two other names for *group* are *class* and *category*. We can sort things into groups. We can also classify or categorize them.

To classify a number of things, think about how they are alike. Then put them into groups. Give each group a label that describes the things in it. For example, you might group *quarter, nickel, silver dollar, dime,* and *penny* under *Coins*.

2 Practice

Write the following animal names on the board.

deer	eagle	canary
cat	dog	gopher
guinea pig	squirrel	robin

Have children use a simple T-Chart (2-column chart) to classify them. Then ask: *Can you think of some other animals? How would you classify them?*

Pets	Wild Animals
cat	deer
guinea pig	eagle
dog	squirrel
canary	gopher
	robin

Reteach
Comprehension
Graphic Sources

1 Teach

Display a large picture of an animal, such as a deer. In the surrounding space, print labels, or the names of body parts, such as *forelegs, hind legs, back, tail, head, neck, antlers*. Have volunteers come up to draw lines from the labels to the body parts pictured.

Say: *We have created a* diagram, *which is one kind of* graphic source. Explain that graphic sources are ways of showing information visually, or in a way that you can see. Ask: *What did we do to turn this picture into a diagram? (added information in the form of labels, or names of body parts)*

Tell children that there are many kinds of graphic sources. In addition to pictures and diagrams, there are charts, graphs, time lines, and maps. Show examples of as many of these as possible. For each, ask: *What kinds of special information would you expect to get from this?*

Explain that when children read, they should first look through the story or article for graphics. They might help children understand what they read.

2 Practice

Have children draw pictures of common household articles that they use or else cut and paste pictures of such articles. Alternatively, they might draw themselves in their school clothes, with all their school paraphernalia. Then have children turn their pictures into diagrams by adding labels and callout lines. Tell them to be sure to title their diagrams.

Reteach
Comprehension
Steps in a Process

1 ## Teach

Explain that a *process* is a series of actions that are done to get a certain result. For example, to wash your hair, you put on shampoo, work up suds, and then rinse it. Have students suggest other simple processes and describe their steps. Write them on the board.

Tell children that when they read about the order in which something happens, they are following the steps in a process. Directions for making or doing something are also steps in a process.

Clue words such as *first, second, next, then,* and *finally* can help a reader keep these steps in order. Sometimes the steps are even numbered.

2 ## Practice

Refer to students' processes listed on the board. If you wish, add some of your own to the list, such as feeding a pet, making a peanut butter sandwich, or playing a DVD.

Give children Steps in a Process charts or have them make their own by drawing boxes and arrows. Have each child fill in a chart with the steps necessary for one of the processes listed. Tell them to be sure to title their charts. When they are finished, have volunteers share their charts with the class.

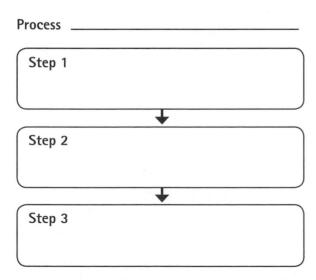

Process _____

| Step 1 |
↓
| Step 2 |
↓
| Step 3 |

Student Edition Glossary

agriculture • collar

Aa

astronaut

agriculture (ag ruh KUL cher) **Agriculture** is farming and growing crops. *NOUN*

armadillo (ar muh DIL oh) An **armadillo** is an animal that has a hard, bony covering. *NOUN*

astronaut (ASS truh nawt) An **astronaut** is a person who has been trained to fly in a spacecraft. While in space, **astronauts** repair space stations and do experiments. *NOUN*

Bb

brave (BRAYV) If you are **brave,** you are not afraid: The **brave** girl pulled her little brother away from the burning leaves. *ADJECTIVE*

Cc

cactus

cactus (KAK tuhss) A **cactus** is a plant with sharp parts but no leaves: Most **cactuses** grow in very hot, dry areas of North and South America. Many have bright flowers. *NOUN*

chiles (CHIL ayz) **Chiles** are a green or red pepper with a hot taste. *NOUN*

climate (KLY mit) **Climate** is the kind of weather a place has. *NOUN*

collar (KOL er) A **collar** is a band that is put around the neck of a dog or other pet. **Collars** can be made of leather or plastic. *NOUN*

518

college • drooled

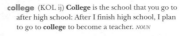

coyote

college (KOL ij) **College** is the school that you go to after high school: After I finish high school, I plan to go to **college** to become a teacher. *NOUN*

cousins (KUH zins) Your **cousins** are the children of your aunt or uncle. *NOUN*

coyote (ky OH tee *or* KY oht) A **coyote** is a small animal that looks something like a wolf: **Coyotes** have light yellow fur and bushy tails. *NOUN*

creature (KREE chur) A **creature** is a living being: Many **creatures** live in the forest. *NOUN*

Dd

desert

dangerous (DAYN jer uhss) Something that is **dangerous** is not safe: Skating on thin ice is **dangerous.** *ADJECTIVE*

delicious (di LISH uhss) When something is **delicious,** it tastes or smells very good: The cookies were **delicious.** *ADJECTIVE*

desert (DEZ ert) A **desert** is a place without water or trees but with a lot of sand. It is usually hot. *NOUN*

drooled (DROOLD) To **drool** is to let saliva run from the mouth like a baby sometimes does: The dog **drooled** when it saw the bone. *VERB*

519

electricity • gravity

Ee

electricity (i lek TRISS uh tee) **Electricity** is a kind of energy that makes light and heat. **Electricity** also runs motors. **Electricity** makes light bulbs shine, radios and televisions play, and cars start. *NOUN*

envelope (EN vuh lohp) An **envelope** is a folded paper cover. An **envelope** is used to mail a letter or something else that is flat. *NOUN*

excitement (ek SYT muhnt) **Excitement** happens when you have very strong, happy feelings about something that you like. *NOUN*

experiment (ek SPEER uh ment) An **experiment** is a test to find out something: We do **experiments** in science class. *NOUN*

Ff

fault (FAWLT) If something is your **fault,** you are to blame for it. *NOUN*

Gg

gnaws (NAWZ) When an animal **gnaws,** it is biting and wearing away by biting: The brown mouse **gnaws** the cheese. *VERB*

grateful (GRAYT fuhl) If you are **grateful** for something, you are thankful for it. *ADJECTIVE*

gravity (GRAV uh tee) **Gravity** is the natural force that causes objects to move toward the center of the Earth. **Gravity** causes objects to have weight. *NOUN*

520

greenhouse • laboratory

greenhouse (GREEN howss) A **greenhouse** is a building with a glass or plastic roof and sides. A **greenhouse** is kept warm and full of light for growing plants. *NOUN*

greenhouse

groaned (GROHND) To **groan** is to make a low sound showing that you are in pain or are unhappy about something: We all **groaned** when it started to rain during recess. *VERB*

Hh

harsh (HARSH) To be **harsh** is to be rough, unpleasant, and unfriendly: The **harsh** weather made us stay indoors. *ADJECTIVE*

honest (ON ist) Someone who is **honest** does not lie, cheat, or steal. *ADJECTIVE*

hurricanes (HUR uh kains) A **hurricane** is a violent storm with strong winds: The Florida **hurricanes** blew the roofs off many houses. *NOUN*

Jj

justice (JUHS tis) **Justice** happens when things are right and fair. *NOUN*

Ll

laboratory (LAB ruh tor ee) A **laboratory** is a room where scientists work and do experiments and tests. *NOUN*

521

Glossary

lanterns • musician

lantern

lanterns (LAN ternz) **Lanterns** are portable lamps with coverings around them to protect them from wind and rain. *NOUN*

lawyer (LOI er) A **lawyer** is someone who is trained to give people advice about the law. A **lawyer** helps people when they go to court. *NOUN*

lazy (LAY zee) If a person is **lazy**, he or she does not want to work hard or to move fast: The **lazy** cat lay on the rug all day. *ADJECTIVE*

luckiest (LUHK ee est) The **luckiest** person is the one who has had the best fortune. *ADJECTIVE*

Mm

meadow (MED oh) A **meadow** is a piece of land where grass grows: There are sheep in the **meadow.** *NOUN*

mill (MIL) A **mill** is a building in which grain is ground into flour or meal. *NOUN*

monsters (MON sterz) **Monsters** are make-believe people or animals that are scary. In stories, some **monsters** are friendly, and others are not: Dragons are **monsters.** *NOUN*

musician (myoo ZISH uhn) A **musician** is a person who sings, plays, or writes music. *NOUN*

522

narrator • resources

Nn

narrator (NAIR ayt or) A **narrator** is a person who tells a story or play. In a play, a **narrator** keeps the action moving. *NOUN*

noticed (NOH tisd) To **notice** means to see something or become aware of it: The boys **noticed** a strange smell near the cave. *VERB*

Pp

parents (PAIR ents) Your **parents** are your mother and father. *NOUN*

persimmons

persimmons (puhr SIM uhns) **Persimmons** are round yellow and orange fruits about the size of plums. *NOUN*

photograph (FOH tuh graf) A **photograph** is a picture you make with a camera. *NOUN*

promise (PROM iss) If you make a **promise** to do something, you are giving your word that you will do it. *NOUN*

Rr

relatives (REL uh tivs) Your **relatives** are the people who belong to the same family as you do: Your mother, sister, and cousin are all your **relatives.** *NOUN*

resources (REE sor sez) **Resources** are things people need and use, such as food, water, and building materials. *NOUN*

523

Glossary

robbers • smudged

robots

robbers (ROB ers) **Robbers** are people who rob or steal: The police chased the bank **robbers.** *NOUN*

robot (ROH bot *or* ROH BUHT) A **robot** is a machine that is run by a computer. **Robots** help people do work. **Robots** can look like people. *NOUN*

Ss

scarce (SKAIRSS) If something is **scarce**, it is hard to find because there is so little of it: Empty seats were **scarce** at the sold-out show. *ADJECTIVE*

scarcity (SKAIR suh tee) **Scarcity** happens when there is not enough of something for everyone who wants it: Dry weather damaged the farmers' crops and caused a **scarcity** of corn. *NOUN*

shivered (SHIV erd) To **shiver** is to shake with cold, fear, or excitement: I **shivered** in the cold wind. *VERB*

shuttle (SHUHT uhl) A **shuttle** is a spacecraft with wings, which can orbit the Earth, land like an airplane, and be used again. *NOUN*

slipped (SLIPT) When you **slip**, you slide suddenly and unexpectedly: She **slipped** on the ice. *VERB*

smudged (SMUDJD) If something is **smudged**, it is marked with a dirty streak. *ADJECTIVE*

524

snorted • weave

snuggled

snorted (SNOR ted) To **snort** means to breathe noisily through the nose: Her brother **snorted** when he laughed. *VERB*

snuggled (SNUHG uhld) To **snuggle** is to lie closely and comfortably together; cuddle: The kittens **snuggled** together in the basket. *VERB*

Tt

telescope (TEL uh skohp) A **telescope** is something you look through to make things far away seem nearer and larger: We looked at the moon through a **telescope.** *NOUN*

tortillas (tor TEE uhs) **Tortillas** are thin, flat, round breads usually made of cornmeal. *NOUN*

trash

trade-off (TRAYD off) You make a **trade-off** when you give up one thing you want for something else you want even more. *NOUN*

trash (TRASH) **Trash** is anything of no use or that is worn out. **Trash** is garbage or things to be thrown away. *NOUN*

Ww

wad (WOD) A **wad** is a small, soft ball or chunk of something: She threw a **wad** of paper in the wastebasket. *NOUN*

weave (WEEV) To **weave** is to form threads into cloth. *VERB*

525

Student Edition
Glossary

Aa

adventure (ad VEN cher) An **adventure** is an exciting or unusual thing to do: Riding a raft down the river was a great **adventure**. *NOUN*

afternoon (af ter NOON) The **afternoon** is the part of the day between morning and evening: On Saturday we played all **afternoon**. *NOUN*

America (uh MAIR uh kuh) **America** is another name for North **America**. Some people use the name **America** to mean the United States. *NOUN*

annoy (uh NOI) To **annoy** is to bother or make someone feel upset or angry: Please do not **annoy** others by talking during the movie. *VERB*

assembly (uh SEM blee) An **assembly** is a group of people gathered for some purpose: The principal spoke to the school **assembly**. *NOUN*

aunt (ANT *or* AHNT) Your **aunt** is your father's sister, your mother's sister, or your uncle's wife. *NOUN*

awaken (uh WAY ken) To **awaken** is to wake up: Birds **awaken** me each morning. *VERB*

Bb

balance (BAL ens)

1. **Balance** is a steady condition or position: The gymnast lost her **balance** and fell. *NOUN*

2. To **balance** something is to put or keep something in a steady or stable condition: She **balanced** a basketball on her finger. *VERB*

530

bank[1] (BANGK) A **bank** is a place where people keep their money: My brother has a **bank** for nickels and pennies. *NOUN*

bank[2] (BANGK) The **bank** of a river or lake is the ground beside it: He fished from the **bank**. *NOUN*

bases (BAY sez)

1. A **base** is the bottom of something: The metal **bases** of the floor lamps might scratch the floor. *NOUN*

2. A **base** is also an object in some games: After hitting a home run, the player ran the **bases**. *NOUN*

basket (BASS kit)
1. A **basket** is something to carry or store things in: **Baskets** are made of straw, plastic, or other materials. *NOUN*

2. In basketball a **basket** is used as a goal: The **basket** is made of a metal ring with a net hanging from it. *NOUN*

basket

birthday (BERTH day) A **birthday** is the day that a person was born or something was started: Our country's **birthday** is July 4th. *NOUN*

blame (BLAYM) To **blame** is to hold someone responsible for something bad or wrong. *VERB*

building (BIL ding) A **building** is something that has been built: A **building** has walls and a roof. Schools, houses, and barns are **buildings**. *NOUN*

building

531

bumpy (BUHM pee) If something is **bumpy**, it is rough or has a lot of bumps: This sidewalk is too **bumpy** to skate on. *ADJECTIVE*

burning (BERN ing) **Burning** means to be on fire: The campers enjoyed watching the **burning** logs. *ADJECTIVE*

Cc

campfire (KAMP fyr) A **campfire** is an outdoor fire used for cooking or staying warm. *NOUN*

canyons (KAN yuhnz) A **canyon** is a narrow valley with high steep sides, sometimes with a stream at the bottom: There are many **canyons** to visit in the western states of America. *NOUN*

cattle (KAT uhl) **Cattle** are animals raised for their meat, milk, or skins: Cows and bulls are **cattle**. *NOUN PLURAL*

chased (CHAYST) When you **chase** someone or something, you run after it: The children **chased** the ball down the hill. *VERB*

cheers (CHEERZ) When you **cheer**, you call out or yell loudly to show you like something: She **cheers** for her team. *VERB*

chewing (CHOO ing) When you **chew** something, you crush it with your teeth: He was **chewing** the nuts. *VERB*

clearing (KLEER ing) A **clearing** is an open space of land in a forest: We came to a **clearing** on our nature walk through the forest. *NOUN*

chewing

532

cliffs (KLIFZ) A **cliff** is a very steep, rocky slope: Climbers must be very careful on **cliffs**. *NOUN*

climbed (KLYMD) When you **climb**, you go up something, usually by using your hands and feet: The children **climbed** into the bus. *VERB*

clubhouse (KLUB HOWSS) A **clubhouse** is a building used by a group of people joined together for some special reason. *NOUN*

collects (kuh LEKTS) If you **collect** things, you bring them together or gather them together: The student **collects** the crayons. *VERB*

complain (kuhm PLAYN) To **complain** is to say that you are unhappy about something: Some people **complain** about the weather. *VERB*

coral (KOR uhl) The hard substance formed from the skeletons of tiny sea animals is **coral**: Many islands in the Pacific Ocean started as large piles of living and dead **coral**. *NOUN*

cowboy (KOW boi) A **cowboy** is a person who works on a cattle ranch: **Cowboys** also take part in rodeos. *NOUN*

crashed (KRASHD) To **crash** is to fall, hit, and be damaged with force and a loud noise: The car **crashed** into a stop sign. *VERB*

cowboy

533

238

Glossary

dripping • freedom

Dd

dripping (DRIP ing) When something **drips**, it falls in drops: The rain was **dripping** on the roof. *VERB*

Ee

election (i LEK shuhn) An election is an act of choosing by vote: In our city we have an election for mayor every two years. *NOUN*

exploring (ek SPLOR ing) When you are **exploring**, you are traveling to discover new areas: Astronauts are **exploring** outer space. *VERB*

Ff

favorite (FAY vuhr it)
1. Your **favorite** thing is the one you like better than all the others: What is your **favorite** color? *ADJECTIVE*
2. A **favorite** is a person or thing that you like very much: Pizza is a **favorite** with me. *NOUN*

field (FEELD) A **field** is a piece of land used for a special purpose: The football **field** needs to be mowed. *NOUN*

flag (FLAG) A **flag** is a piece of colored cloth with stars or other symbols on it: Every country and state has its own **flag**. *NOUN*

flag

freedom (FREE duhm) **Freedom** is not being under someone else's control or rule. *NOUN*

534

fruit • harvest

fruit

fruit (FROOT) **Fruit** is the part of a tree, bush, or vine that has seeds in it and is good to eat: Apples, oranges, and strawberries are **fruit**. *NOUN*

Gg

galloped (GAL uhpt) To **gallop** is to run very fast: The horse **galloped** down the road. *VERB*

grabbed (GRABD) When you **grab** something, you take it suddenly: The dog **grabbed** the bone. *VERB*

grains (GRAYNZ) **Grains** are tiny pieces or particles: There are millions of **grains** of sand on the beach. *NOUN*

greatest (GRAYT est) If something is the **greatest**, it is the best and most important: He thought it was the **greatest** book he had ever read. *ADJECTIVE*

Hh

harvest (HAR vist)
1. A **harvest** is the ripe crops that are picked after the growing season is over: The corn **harvest** was poor after the hot, dry summer. *NOUN*
2. When you **harvest**, you gather in the crops and store them: We **harvest** the apples in late fall. *VERB*

535

Glossary

herd • mumbles

herd (HERD) A **herd** is a group of the same kind of animals: We saw a **herd** of cows when we drove through the country. *NOUN*

herd

Ii

idea (eye DEE uh) An **idea** is a thought or plan: The class had different **ideas** on how to spend the money. *NOUN*

important (im PORT uhnt) Something that is **important** has a lot of meaning or worth: Learning to read is **important**. *ADJECTIVE*

Mm

masks (MASKS) **Masks** are coverings that hide or protect your face: The firefighters wear **masks** to help them breathe. *NOUN*

materials (muh TIR ee uhlz) **Materials** are what a thing is made from or used for: Wood and steel are building **materials**. *NOUN*

microphone (MY kruh fon) A **microphone** is an electrical device that makes your voice sound louder: People who work in television and radio stations use a **microphone**. *NOUN*

mountain (MOWN tuhn) A **mountain** is a very high hill. Some people enjoy climbing **mountains** in their free time. *NOUN*

mumbles (MUHM buhls) Someone who **mumbles** speaks too quietly to be heard clearly: When John **mumbles,** I can't understand what he is saying. *VERB*

536

nicknames • practice

Nn

nicknames (NIK naymz) **Nicknames** are names used instead of real names: Ed is a **nickname** for Edward. *NOUN*

Pp

particles (PAR tuh kuhls) **Particles** are very tiny pieces: The table had **particles** of dust on top. *NOUN*

perfect (PER fikt) When something is **perfect**, it is without any faults or mistakes. Larry had a **perfect** spelling test. *ADJECTIVE*

plate (PLAYT)
1. A **plate** is a dish that is almost flat and is usually round: We eat food from **plates**. *NOUN*
2. A **plate** is a hard rubber slab that a baseball player stands beside to hit the ball. *NOUN*

P.M. (PEE EM) These letters stand for *post meridiem*, which means "after midday." **P.M.** refers to the time between noon and 11:59 at night.

pond (POND) A **pond** is a body of still water that is smaller than a lake: My neighbor has a duck **pond** in his backyard. *NOUN*

practice (PRAK tiss) A **practice** is a training session: Coach says that to play the game, you must go to **practice**. *NOUN*

537

Student Edition
Glossary

present

present¹ (PREZ uhnt) Another word for **present** is *here*. If you are **present**, you are not absent: Every member of the class is **present** today. *ADJECTIVE*

present² (PREZ uhnt) A **present** is a gift. A **present** is something that someone gives you or that you give someone: His uncle sent him a birthday **present**. *NOUN*

prize (PREYEZ) A **prize** is something you win for doing something well: **Prizes** will be given for the best stories. *NOUN*

Qq

quickly (KWIK lee) **Quickly** means in a short time: When I asked him a question, he answered **quickly**. *ADVERB*

Rr

railroad (RAYL rohd) A **railroad** is a system of trains, tracks, stations, and other property run by a transportation company: The cattle pens were near the **railroad** tracks. *NOUN*

rainbow

rainbow (RAYN bo) A **rainbow** is a curved band of many colors in the sky. A **rainbow** often appears when the sun shines right after it rains. *NOUN*

rallies (RAL eez) **Rallies** are meetings of many people for a specific purpose: We all attended the **rallies** in support of the candidate for President. *NOUN*

rattle (RAT uhl) To **rattle** is to make short, sharp sounds: The wind made the door **rattle**. *VERB*

roar (ROR) A **roar** is a loud, deep sound: The **roar** of the lion frightened some people at the zoo. *NOUN*

root (ROOT) The **root** is the part of a plant that grows underground: A plant gets food and water through its **roots**. *NOUN*

Ss

sailed (SAYLD) When something **sails**, it travels on the water or through the air: The ball **sailed** out of the ballpark. *VERB*

seeps (SEEPS) When something **seeps**, it soaks through or passes through an opening very slowly in small amounts: Water **seeps** into our basement after heavy rains. *VERB*

shrugs (SHRUHGZ) To **shrug** is to raise your shoulders briefly to show that you are not interested or do not know: Every time I ask my brother if he wants to play, he just **shrugs**. *VERB*

signature (SIG nuh chur) Your **signature** is the way you sign your name: Each student needed a parent's **signature** on the permission slip. *NOUN*

signmaker (SYN mayk er) A **signmaker** makes marks or words on a sign that give information or tell you what to do or not to do. *NOUN*

slivers (SLIV uhrz) A **sliver** is a long, thin piece that has been split off or broken off. He ate a **sliver** of cheese before dinner. *NOUN*

slogan (SLO guhn) A **slogan** is a word or phrase used by a business, political party, or any group to make its purpose known: "Lunch served in 30 minutes or it's free" was the restaurant's **slogan**. *NOUN*

smooth (SMOOTH) When something is **smooth**, it has an even surface. Something that is **smooth** is not bumpy or rough: The road was very **smooth**. *ADJECTIVE*

soil¹ (SOIL) **Soil** is the top layer of the Earth. **Soil** is dirt: Our garden has such rich **soil** that almost anything will grow in it. *NOUN*

soil² (SOIL) If you **soil** something, you make it dirty: The dust will **soil** her white gloves. *VERB*

soil

speeches (SPEECH es)

1. **Speech** is the act of talking: People express their thoughts by **speech**. *NOUN*

2. A **speech** is a formal talk to a group of people: The President gave an excellent **speech**. *NOUN*

spilling (SPIL ing) To **spill** is to let something fall out or run out of its container: Dad knocked the saltshaker over, **spilling** salt on the table. *VERB*

splashing (SPLASH ing) To **splash** is to cause liquid to fly about and get others wet: The swimmers are **splashing** each other with water. *VERB*

splashing

stars (STARZ)

1. **Stars** are the very bright points of light that shine in the sky at night: On a clear night, the **stars** are very bright. *NOUN*

2. **Stars** are shapes that have five or six points. I drew **stars** on the paper. *NOUN*

station (STAY shuhn) A **station** is a building or place used for a special reason: The man went to the police **station**. *NOUN*

stripes (STRYPS) **Stripes** are long, narrow bands of color: Our flag has seven red **stripes** and six white **stripes**. *NOUN*

substances (SUHB stan sez) A **substance** is something that has weight and takes up space: Solids, liquids, and powders are examples of **substances**. *NOUN*

suffer (SUHF ur) To **suffer** is to have or feel pain, grief, or injury: She **suffered** a broken leg while skiing. *VERB*

sway (SWAY) To **sway** is to swing or cause to swing back and forth, side to side, or to one side: The dancers **sway** to the music. *VERB*

Glossary

texture • truest

Tt

threw

texture (TEKS chur) **Texture** is the look and feel of something, especially its roughness or smoothness. *NOUN*

threw (THROO) When you **threw** something, you sent it through the air: She **threw** the ball back to him. *VERB*

tightly (TYT lee) When something is tied **tightly**, it is firmly tied: The rope was tied **tightly** around the ladders on the truck. *ADVERB*

townspeople (TOWNZ pee puhl) **Townspeople** are the men, women, and children who live in a village or town: The **townspeople** enjoyed the fair. *NOUN*

trails (TRAYLZ) **Trails** are paths across fields or through the woods: Two **trails** led to the river. *NOUN*

traveled (TRAV uhld) To **travel** is to go from one place to another: He **traveled** in Europe this past summer. *VERB*

treat (TREET) A **treat** is a gift of food, drink, a free ticket, or the like: She gave us **treats** on the last day of school. *NOUN*

truest (TROO ist) To be **true** is to be faithful and loyal: She is the **truest** friend I have. *ADJECTIVE*

542

vine • wondered

Vv

vine (VYN) A **vine** is a plant that grows along the ground. Some **vines** climb up walls and fences: Pumpkins, melons, and grapes grow on **vines**. *NOUN*

vine

volcano (vol KAY no) A **volcano** is a cone-shaped hill or mountain that has an opening through which lava, rock fragments, and gas are forced out from the Earth's crust: They feared the **volcano** would erupt. *NOUN*

Ww

wagged (WAGD) To **wag** is to move from side to side or up and down: The dog **wagged** her tail. *VERB*

whisper (WIS puhr) To **whisper** is to speak very softly and gently: Children **whisper** secrets to each other. *VERB*

wondered (WUHN derd) When you **wondered** about something, you wanted to know about it: He **wondered** what time it was. *VERB*

543

Scope and Sequence

Reading

Concepts About Print	Pre-K	K	1	2	3	4	5	6
Hold book right side up, turn pages correctly, move from front to back of book	•	•	•					
Identify parts of a book and their functions (front cover, title page/title, back cover, page numbers)	•	•	•					
Identify information that different parts of a book provides (title, author, illustrator)	•	•	•	•				
Know uppercase and lowercase letter names and match them	•	•	•					
Know the order of the alphabet	•	•	•					
Demonstrate one-to-one correspondence between oral words and printed words		•	•					
Identify and distinguish between letters, words, and sentences	•	•	•					
Recognize distinguishing features of a paragraph		•	•					
Recognize environmental print		•	•		•			
Track print (front to back of book, top to bottom of page, left to right on line, sweep back left for next line)		•	•					
Recognize first name in print	•	•	•					

Phonological and Phonemic Awareness	Pre-K	K	1	2	3	4	5	6
Phonological Awareness								
Identify and produce rhyming words in response to an oral prompt	•	•	•					
Distinguish rhyming pairs of words from nonrhyming pairs	•	•						
Track and represent changes in simple syllables and words with two and three sounds as one sound is added, substituted, omitted, or changed		•	•					
Count each syllable in a spoken word		•	•					
Segment and blend syllables in spoken words		•						
Segment and blend onset and rime in one-syllable words		•	•					
Recognize and produce words beginning with the same sound	•	•	•					
Phonemic Awareness								
Identify and isolate initial, final, and medial sounds in spoken words	•	•	•	•				
Blend sounds orally to make words or syllables		•	•	•				
Segment a word or syllable into sounds		•	•					
Count sounds in spoken words or syllables and syllables in words		•	•	•				
Manipulate sounds in words (add, delete, and/or substitute phonemes)	•	•	•	•				
Distinguish long- and short-vowel sounds in orally stated single-syllable words				•				

Decoding and Word Recognition	Pre-K	K	1	2	3	4	5	6
Read simple one-syllable and high-frequency (sight) words		•T	•T	•T	•			
Phonics								
Understand and apply the *alphabetic principle* that spoken words are composed of sounds that are represented by letters; as letters change, so do sounds	•	•	•					
Know sound-letter relationships and match sounds to letters		•T	•T	•				
Generate sounds from letters and blend those sounds to decode		•	•T	•T	•T			
Consonants, consonant blends, and consonant digraphs			•T	•T	•T			
Short and long vowels			•T	•T	•T			
r-controlled vowels; vowel digraphs; diphthongs; common vowel patterns			•T	•T	•T			
Phonograms/word families		•	•	•				

• instructional opportunity   T tested in standardized test format

Decoding and Word Recognition *continued*	Pre-K	K	1	2	3	4	5	6
Word Structure								
Decode multisyllabic words with common word parts and spelling patterns		•	•T	•T	•T	•T	•T	•T
Base words and inflected endings; plurals			•T	•T	•T	•T	•T	•T
Contractions and compound words			•T	•T	•T	•T	•T	•T
Prefixes and suffixes			•T	•T	•T	•T	•T	•T
Greek and Latin roots						•	•	•
Apply knowledge of syllabication rules to decode words			•T	•T	•T	•T	•T	•T
Recognize common abbreviations			•	•	•			
Decoding Strategies								
Blending strategy: Apply knowledge of sound-letter relationships to decode unfamiliar words		•	•	•	•			
Apply knowledge of word structure to decode unfamiliar words		•	•	•	•	•	•	•
Use context along with sound-letter relationships and word structure to decode		•	•	•	•	•	•	•
Self-monitor accuracy of decoding and self-correct			•	•	•	•	•	•
Fluency								
Read aloud grade level text fluently with accuracy, comprehension, appropriate pace/rate; with expression/intonation (prosody); with attention to punctuation and appropriate phrasing			•T	•T	•T	•T	•T	•T
Practice fluency in a variety of ways, including choral reading, partner/paired reading, Readers' Theater, repeated oral reading, and tape-assisted reading		•	•	•	•	•	•	•
Work toward appropriate fluency goals by the end of each grade			•	•	•	•	•	•
Read regularly and with comprehension in independent-level material		•	•	•	•	•	•	•
Read silently for increasing periods of time		•	•	•	•	•	•	•
Vocabulary and Concept Development	Pre-K	K	1	2	3	4	5	6
Recognize and understand selection vocabulary		•	•	•T	•T	•T	•T	•T
Understand content-area vocabulary and specialized, technical, or topical words			•	•	•	•	•	•
Word Learning Strategies								
Develop vocabulary through direct instruction, concrete experiences, reading, listening to text read aloud	•	•	•	•	•	•	•	•
Use knowledge of word structure to figure out meanings of words			•	•T	•T	•T	•T	•T
Use context clues for meanings of unfamiliar words, multiple-meaning words, homonyms, homographs			•	•T	•T	•T	•T	•T
Use grade-appropriate reference sources to learn word meanings	•	•	•	•	•T	•T	•T	•T
Use picture clues to help determine word meanings	•	•	•	•	•			
Use new words in a variety of contexts	•	•	•	•	•	•	•	•
Create and use graphic organizers to group, study, and retain vocabulary			•	•	•	•	•	•
Monitor expository text for unknown words or words with novel meanings by using word, sentence, and paragraph clues to determine meaning						•	•	•
Extend Concepts and Word Knowledge								
Academic language	•	•	•	•	•	•	•	•
Classify and categorize	•	•	•	•	•	•	•	•
Abbreviations			•	•	•			•
Antonyms and synonyms			•	•T	•T	•T	•T	•T
Prefixes and suffixes			•	•	•	•	•	•T

• instructional opportunity   **T** tested in standardized test format

Vocabulary and Concept Development *continued*	Pre-K	K	1	2	3	4	5	6
Homographs and homophones				•	•T	•T	•T	•T
Multiple-meaning words			•	•T	•T	•T	•T	•T
Related words and derivations					•	•	•	•
Compound words			•	•	•		•	•
Figurative language and idioms				•	•	•	•	•
Descriptive words (location, size, color, shape, number, ideas, feelings)	•	•	•	•				
High-utility words (shapes, colors, question words, position/directional words, and so on)	•	•	•	•				
Time and order words	•	•	•	•	•	•	•	•
Word origins: etymologies/word histories; words from other languages, regions, or cultures						•	•	•
Adages and sayings							•	
Analogies						•	•	•
Reading Comprehension	**Pre-K**	**K**	**1**	**2**	**3**	**4**	**5**	**6**
Comprehension Strategies								
Predict and set purpose to guide reading	•	•	•	•	•	•	•	•
Use background knowledge before, during, and after reading	•	•	•	•	•	•	•	•
Monitor and clarify by using fix-up strategies to resolve difficulties in meaning: adjust reading rate, reread and read on, seek help from references sources and/or other people, skim and scan		•	•	•	•	•	•	•
Inferring		•	•	•	•	•	•	•
Questioning before, during, and after reading	•	•	•	•	•	•	•	•
Visualize—use mental imagery		•	•	•	•	•	•	•
Summarize text		•	•	•	•	•	•	•
Recall and retell stories	•	•	•	•	•	•	•	•
Important ideas (nonfiction) that provide clues to an author's meaning			•	•	•	•	•	•
Text structure (nonfiction—such as cause/effect, chronological, compare/contrast, description)	•		•	•	•	•	•	•
Story structure (fiction—such as plot, problem/solution)	•		•	•	•	•	•	•
Create and use graphic and semantic organizers, including outlines, notes, summaries					•	•	•	•
Use strategies flexibly and in combination				•	•T	•T		•
Comprehension Skills								
Author's purpose			•T	•T	•T	•T	•T	•T
Author's viewpoint/bias							•T	•T
Categorize and classify	•	•	•	•				
Cause and effect		•	•T	•T	•T	•T	•T	•T
Compare and contrast		•	•T	•T	•T	•T	•T	•T
Draw conclusions and make inferences		•	•T	•T	•T	•T	•T	•T
Facts and details		•	•T	•T	•	•	•	•T
Fact and opinion (statements of fact and opinion)			•T	•T	•T	•T	•T	•T
Follow directions/steps in a process	•	•	•	•	•	•	•	•
Generalize					•T	•T	•T	•

• instructional opportunity   **T** tested in standardized test format

Reading Comprehension *continued*	Pre-K	K	1	2	3	4	5	6
Graphic sources (illustrations, photos, maps, charts, graphs, font styles, etc.)		•	•	•	•	•T	•T	•T
Main idea and supporting details		•T	•T	•T	•T	•T	•T	•T
Paraphrase				•	•	•	•	•
Persuasive devices and propaganda					•	•	•	•
Realism/fantasy	•	•T	•T					
Sequence of events	•	•T	•T	•T	•T	•T	•T	•T
Higher Order Thinking Skills								
Analyze				•	•	•	•	•
Analyze text with various organizational patterns					•	•	•	•
Describe and connect the essential ideas, arguments, and perspectives of a text				•	•	•	•	•
Evaluate and critique ideas and text				•	•	•	•	•
Draw inferences, conclusions, or generalizations; support them with textual evidence and prior knowledge	•	•T	•T	•T	•T	•T	•T	•T
Make judgments about ideas and texts				•	•	•	•	•
Hypothesize					•	•	•	•
Make connections (text to self, text to text, text to world)	•	•	•	•	•	•	•	•T
Organize and synthesize ideas and information				•	•	•	•	•T

Literary Response and Analysis	Pre-K	K	1	2	3	4	5	6
Genre and Its Characteristics								
Identify types of everyday print materials (storybooks, poems, newspapers, signs, labels)	•	•	•	•	•	•	•	•
Recognize characteristics of a variety of genre	•	•	•	•	•	•	•	•
Distinguish common forms of literature		•	•	•	•	•	•	•
Identify characteristics of literary texts, including drama, fantasy, traditional tales		•	•	•	•	•	•	•
Identify characteristics of nonfiction texts, including biography, interviews, newspaper articles		•	•	•	•	•	•	•
Identify characteristics of poetry and song, including nursery rhymes, limericks, blank verse	•	•	•	•	•	•	•	•
Literary Elements and Story Structure								
Character	•	•T	•T	•T	•T	•T	•T	•T
Recognize and describe traits, actions, feelings, and motives of characters		•	•	•	•	•	•	•
Analyze characters' relationships, changes, and points of view		•	•	•	•	•	•	•
Analyze characters' conflicts				•	•	•	•	•
Analyze the effect of character on plot and conflict						•	•	•
Plot and Plot Structure	•	•T	•T	•T	•T	•T	•T	•T
Beginning, middle, end	•	•	•	•	•			
Goal and outcome or problem and solution/resolution		•	•	•	•	•	•	•
Rising action, climax, and falling action/denouement; setbacks						•	•	•
Setting	•	•T	•T	•T	•T	•T	•T	•T
Relate setting to problem/solution		•	•	•	•	•	•	•
Explain ways setting contributes to mood						•	•	•
Theme				•T	•T	•T	•T	•T

• instructional opportunity   **T** tested in standardized test format

Literary Response and Analysis *continued*	Pre-K	K	1	2	3	4	5	6
Use Literary Elements and Story Structure	•	•	•	•	•	•	•	•
Analyze and evaluate author's use of setting, plot, character, and compare among authors				•	•	•	•	•
Identify similarities and differences of characters, events, and settings within or across selections/cultures		•	•	•	•	•	•	•
Literary Devices								
Dialect						•	•	•
Dialogue and narration	•		•	•	•	•	•	•
Identify the speaker or narrator in a selection		•	•	•	•	•	•	•
Exaggeration/hyperbole				•	•	•	•	•
Figurative language: idiom, jargon, metaphor, simile, slang				•	•	•	•	•
Flashback						•	•	•
Foreshadowing				•	•	•	•	•
Formal and informal language				•	•	•	•	•
Humor				•	•	•	•	•
Imagery and sensory words			•	•	•	•	•	•
Mood				•	•	•	•	•
Personification						•	•	•
Point of view (first-person, third-person, omniscient)					•	•	•	•
Puns and word play				•	•	•	•	•
Sound devices and poetic elements	•	•	•	•	•	•	•	•
Alliteration, assonance, onomatopoeia	•	•	•	•	•	•	•	•
Rhyme, rhythm, repetition, and cadence	•	•	•	•	•	•	•	•
Word choice		•	•	•	•	•	•	•
Symbolism							•	•
Tone						•	•	•
Author's and Illustrator's Craft								
Distinguish the roles of author and illustrator	•	•	•	•				
Recognize/analyze author's and illustrator's craft or style				•	•	•	•	•
Evaluate author's use of various techniques to influence readers' perspectives						•	•	•
Literary Response								
Recollect, talk, and write about books	•	•	•	•	•	•	•	•
Reflect on reading and respond (through talk, movement, art, and so on)	•	•	•	•	•	•	•	•
Ask and answer questions about text	•	•	•	•	•	•	•	•
Write about what is read			•	•	•	•	•	•
Use evidence from the text to support opinions, interpretations, or conclusions		•	•	•	•	•	•	•
Support ideas through reference to other texts and personal knowledge				•	•	•	•	•
Locate materials on related topic, theme, or idea				•	•	•	•	•
Make connections: text to self, text to text, text to world			•	•	•	•	•	•
Offer observations, react, speculate in response to text				•	•	•	•	•

• instructional opportunity   **T** tested in standardized test format

Literary Response and Analysis *continued*

	Pre-K	K	1	2	3	4	5	6
Literary Appreciation/Motivation								
Show an interest in books and reading; engage voluntarily in social interaction about books	•	•	•	•	•	•	•	•
Choose text by drawing on personal interests, relying on knowledge of authors and genres, estimating text difficulty, and using recommendations of others	•	•	•	•	•	•	•	•
Read a variety of grade-level-appropriate narrative and expository texts		•	•	•	•	•	•	•
Read from a wide variety of genres for a variety of purposes		•	•	•	•	•	•	•
Read independently		•	•	•	•	•	•	•
Establish familiarity with a topic		•	•	•	•	•	•	•
Cultural Awareness								
Comprehend basic plots of classic tales from around the world					•	•	•	•
Compare and contrast tales from different cultures				•	•	•	•	•
Develop attitudes and abilities to interact with diverse groups and cultures	•	•	•	•	•	•	•	•
Connect experiences and ideas with those from a variety of languages, cultures, customs, perspectives	•	•	•	•	•	•	•	•
Compare language and oral traditions (family stories) that reflect customs, regions, and cultures		•	•	•	•	•	•	•
Recognize themes that cross cultures and bind them together in their common humanness		•	•	•	•	•	•	•

Language Arts

Writing	Pre-K	K	1	2	3	4	5	6
Concepts About Print for Writing								
Write uppercase and lowercase letters		•	•					
Print own name and other important words	•	•	•					
Write using pictures, some letters, some phonetically spelled words, and transitional spelling to convey meaning	•	•	•					
Write consonant-vowel-consonant words		•	•					
Dictate messages or stories for others to write	•	•	•					
Create own written texts for others to read; write left to right on a line and top to bottom on a page	•	•	•					
Participate in shared and interactive writing	•	•	•					
Traits of Writing								
Focus/Ideas		•	•	•	•	•	•	•
State a clear purpose and maintain focus; sharpen ideas		•	•	•	•	•	•	•
Use sensory details and concrete examples; elaborate			•	•	•	•	•	•
Delete extraneous information			•	•	•	•	•	•
Use strategies, such as tone, style, consistent point of view, to achieve a sense of completeness						•	•	•
Organization		•	•	•	•	•T	•T	•T
Use graphic organizers to group ideas	•	•	•	•	•	•	•	•
Write coherent paragraphs that develop a central idea and have topic sentences and facts and details				•	•	•	•	•
Use transitions to connect sentences and paragraphs and establish coherence			•	•	•	•	•	•

• instructional opportunity   **T** tested in standardized test format

247

Writing *continued*	Pre-K	K	1	2	3	4	5	6
Select an organizational structure, such as comparison and contrast, categories, spatial order, climactic order, based on purpose, audience, length							•	•
Organize ideas in a logical progression, such as chronological order or order of importance	•	•	•	•	•	•	•	•
Write introductory, supporting, and concluding paragraphs					•	•	•	•
Use strategies of note-taking, outlining, and summarizing to impose structure on composition drafts					•	•	•	•
Write a multi-paragraph paper				•	•	•	•	•
Voice			•	•	•	•	•	•
Develop personal, identifiable voice and an individual tone/style			•	•	•	•	•	•
Maintain consistent voice and point of view						•	•	•
Use voice appropriate to audience, message, and purpose						•	•	•
Word Choice		•	•	•	•T	•T	•T	•T
Use clear, precise, appropriate language		•	•	•	•	•	•	•
Use figurative language and vivid words			•	•	•	•	•	•
Use sensory details, imagery, characterization				•	•	•	•	•
Select effective vocabulary using word walls, dictionary, or thesaurus		•	•	•	•	•	•	•
Sentences		•	•	•	•T	•T	•T	•T
Combine, elaborate, and vary sentences	•	•	•	•	•T	•T	•T	•T
Write topic sentence, supporting sentences with facts and details, and concluding sentence			•	•	•	•	•	•
Use correct word order		•	•	•	•	•	•	•
Conventions		•	•	•	•T	•T	•T	•T
Use correct spelling and grammar; capitalize and punctuate correctly		•	•	•	•	•	•	•
Correct sentence fragments and run-ons				•	•	•	•	•
Use correct paragraph indentation			•	•	•	•	•	•

The Writing Process

	Pre-K	K	1	2	3	4	5	6
Prewrite using various strategies	•	•	•	•	•	•	•	•
Develop first drafts of single- and multiple-paragraph compositions		•	•	•	•	•	•	•
Revise drafts for varied purposes, including to clarify and to achieve purpose, sense of audience, improve focus and coherence, precise word choice, vivid images, and elaboration		•	•	•	•	•	•	•
Edit and proofread for correct conventions (spelling, grammar, usage, and mechanics)		•	•	•	•	•	•	•
Publish own work	•	•	•	•	•	•	•	•

Writing Genres

	Pre-K	K	1	2	3	4	5	6
Narrative writing (such as personal narratives, stories, biographies, autobiographies)	•	•	•T	•T	•T	•T	•T	•T
Expository writing (such as comparison and contrast, problem and solution, essays, directions, explanations, news stories, research reports, summaries)		•	•	•T	•T	•T	•T	•T
Descriptive writing (such as labels, captions, lists, plays, poems, response logs, songs)	•	•	•T	•T	•T	•T	•T	•T
Persuasive writing (such as ads, editorials, essays, letters to the editor, opinions, posters)		•	•	•T	•T	•T	•T	•T
Notes and letters (such as personal, formal, and friendly letters, thank-you notes, and invitations)		•	•	•	•	•	•	•

• instructional opportunity   T tested in standardized test format

Writing *continued*	Pre-K	K	1	2	3	4	5	6
Responses to literature			•	•	•	•	•	•
Writing Habits and Practices								
Write on a daily basis	•	•	•	•	•	•	•	•
Use writing as a tool for learning		•	•	•	•	•	•	•
Write independently for extended periods of time			•	•	•	•	•	•
Penmanship								
Gain increasing control of penmanship, including pencil grip, paper position, posture, stroke	•	•	•	•	•			
Write legibly, with control over letter size and form; letter slant; and letter, word, and sentence spacing		•	•	•	•	•	•	•
Write lowercase and uppercase letters	•	•	•	•	•	•	•	•
Manuscript	•	•	•	•	•	•	•	•
Cursive					•	•	•	•
Write numerals	•	•	•					

Written and Oral English Language Conventions	Pre-K	K	1	2	3	4	5	6
Grammar and Usage in Speaking and Writing								
Sentences								
Correct word order in written sentences		•	•	•				
Types (declarative, interrogative, exclamatory, imperative)	•	•	•T	•T	•T	•T	•T	•T
Structure (complete, incomplete, simple, compound, complex, compound-complex)	•	•	•	•T	•T	•T	•T	•T
Parts (subjects/predicates: complete, simple, compound; phrases; clauses)			•	•T	•T	•T	•T	•T
Fragments and run-on sentences		•	•	•	•	•	•	•
Combine and rearrange sentences; use appositives, participial phrases, adjectives, adverbs, and prepositional phrases			•	•	•	•	•	•
Transitions and conjunctions to connect ideas; independent and dependent clauses			•	•	•	•	•	•
Varied sentence types and sentence openings to present effective style						•	•	•
Parts of speech: nouns (singular and plural), verbs and verb tenses, adjectives, adverbs, pronouns and antecedents, conjunctions, prepositions, interjections, articles		•	•	•T	•T	•T	•T	•T
Contractions			•	•T	•T	•T	•T	•T
Usage								
Subject-verb agreement		•	•	•T	•T	•T	•T	•T
Pronoun agreement/referents			•	•	•T	•T	•T	•T
Misplaced modifiers							•	•
Misused words						•		•
Negatives; avoid double negatives						•	•	•
Mechanics in Writing								
Capitalization (first word in sentence, proper nouns and adjectives, pronoun *I*, titles, months, days of the week, holidays, and so on)	•	•	•T	•T	•T	•T	•T	•T
Punctuation (period, question mark, exclamation mark, apostrophe, comma, quotation marks, parentheses, colon, and so on)		•	•T	•T	•T	•T	•T	•T

• instructional opportunity   **T** tested in standardized test format

Written and Oral English Language Conventions *continued*	Pre-K	K	1	2	3	4	5	6
Spelling								
Spell independently by using pre-phonetic knowledge, knowledge of letter names, sounds of the alphabet	•	•	•T	•	•	•	•	•
Consonants: single, double, blends, digraphs, silent letters, and unusual consonant spellings		•	•T	•T	•T	•T	•T	•T
Vowels: short, long, *r*-controlled, digraphs, diphthongs, less-common vowel patterns, schwa		•	•T	•T	•T	•T	•T	•T
Use knowledge of word structure to spell					•	•		
Base words and affixes (inflections, prefixes, suffixes), possessives, contractions, and compound words			•	•T	•T	•T	•T	•T
Greek and Latin roots, syllable patterns, multisyllabic words				•	•	•	•	•
Spell high-frequency, irregular words		•T	•T	•	•	•	•	•
Spell frequently misspelled words correctly, including homophones or homonyms				•	•	•	•	•
Use meaning relationships to spell						•	•	•

Listening and Speaking	Pre-K	K	1	2	3	4	5	6
Listening Skills and Strategies								
Listen to a variety of presentations attentively and politely	•	•	•	•	•	•	•	•
Self-monitor comprehension while listening, using a variety of skills and strategies, e.g., ask questions	•	•	•	•	•	•	•	•
Listen for a purpose								
For enjoyment and appreciation	•	•	•	•	•	•	•	•
To expand vocabulary and concepts	•	•	•	•	•	•	•	•
To obtain information and ideas	•	•	•	•	•	•	•	•
To follow oral directions	•	•	•	•	•	•	•	•
To answer questions and solve problems	•	•	•	•	•	•	•	•
To participate in group discussions	•	•	•	•	•	•	•	•
To identify and analyze the musical elements of literary language	•	•	•	•	•	•	•	•
To gain knowledge of one's own culture, the culture of others, and the common elements of cultures	•	•	•	•	•	•	•	•
To respond to persuasive messages with questions or affirmations						•	•	•
Determine purpose of listening				•	•	•	•	•
Recognize formal and informal language				•	•	•	•	•
Connect prior experiences to those of a speaker	•	•	•	•	•	•	•	•
Listen critically to distinguish fact from opinion and to analyze and evaluate ideas, information, experiences		•	•	•	•	•	•	•
Paraphrase, retell, or summarize information that has been shared orally				•	•	•	•	•
Evaluate a speaker's delivery; identify tone, mood, and emotion					•	•	•	•
Interpret and critique a speaker's purpose, perspective, persuasive techniques, verbal and nonverbal messages, and use of rhetorical devices; draw conclusions							•	•
Speaking Skills and Strategies								
Speak clearly, accurately, and fluently, using appropriate delivery for a variety of audiences, and purposes; sustain audience interest, attention	•	•	•	•	•	•	•	•
Use proper intonation, volume, pitch, modulation, and phrasing		•	•	•	•	•	•	•
Speak with a command of standard English conventions	•	•	•	•	•	•	•	•
Use appropriate language for formal and informal settings	•	•	•	•	•	•	•	•

• instructional opportunity   **T** tested in standardized test format

Listening and Speaking *continued*

	Pre-K	K	1	2	3	4	5	6
Use visual aids to clarify oral presentations	•	•	•	•	•	•	•	•
Organize ideas and convey information in a logical sequence or structure with a beginning, middle, and end and an effective introduction and conclusion			•	•	•	•	•	•
Support opinions with detailed evidence and with visual or media displays					•	•	•	•
Emphasize key points to assist listener						•	•	•
Speak for a purpose								
To ask and answer questions	•	•	•	•	•	•	•	•
To give directions and instructions	•	•	•	•	•	•	•	•
To retell, paraphrase, or explain information	•	•	•	•	•	•	•	•
To communicate needs and share ideas and experiences	•	•	•	•	•	•	•	•
To describe people, places, things, locations, events, and actions		•	•	•	•	•	•	•
To participate in conversations and discussions	•	•	•	•	•	•	•	•
To express an opinion	•	•	•	•	•	•	•	•
To recite poems or songs or deliver dramatic recitations, interpretations, or performances	•	•	•	•	•	•	•	•
To deliver oral responses to literature	•	•	•	•	•	•	•	•
To deliver presentations or oral reports (narrative, descriptive, persuasive, problems and solutions, and informational based on research)	•	•	•	•	•	•	•	•
Stay on topic; maintain a clear focus	•	•	•	•	•	•	•	•
Support spoken ideas with details and examples		•	•	•	•	•	•	•
Use appropriate verbal and nonverbal elements (such as facial expression, gestures, eye contact, posture)	•	•	•	•	•	•	•	•

Viewing/Media

	Pre-K	K	1	2	3	4	5	6
Interact with and respond to a variety of media for a range of purposes	•	•	•	•	•	•	•	•
Compare and contrast print, visual, and electronic media				•	•	•	•	•
Analyze media						•	•	•
Evaluate media			•	•	•	•	•	•
Recognize bias and propaganda in media message						•	•	•
Recognize purpose and persuasion in media messages			•	•	•	•	•	•

Research Skills

Understand and Use Graphic Sources

	Pre-K	K	1	2	3	4	5	6
Advertisement			•	•	•	•	•	•
Chart/table	•	•	•	•	•	•	•	•
Diagram/scale drawing			•	•	•	•	•	•
Graph (bar, circle, line, picture)			•	•	•	•	•	•
Illustration, photograph, caption, label	•	•	•	•	•	•	•	•
Map/globe		•	•	•	•	•	•	•
Poster/announcement	•	•	•	•	•			•
Schedule						•	•	•
Sign	•	•	•	•	•		•	•
Time line				•	•	•	•	•

• instructional opportunity   **T** tested in standardized test format

Understand and Use Reference Sources	Pre-K	K	1	2	3	4	5	6
Know and use organizational features and parts of a book to locate information	•	•	•	•	•	•	•	•
Use alphabetical order			•	•	•	•	•	•
Understand purpose, structure, and organization of reference sources (print, electronic, media, Internet)	•	•	•	•	•	•	•	•
Almanac						•	•	•
Atlas				•	•	•	•	•
Card catalog/library database				•	•	•	•	•
Picture Dictionary		•	•	•				
Dictionary/glossary				•	•T	•T	•T	•T
Encyclopedia				•	•	•	•	•
Magazine/periodical				•	•	•	•	•
Newspaper and newsletter				•	•	•	•	•
Readers' Guide to Periodical Literature						•	•	•
Technology (on- and offline electronic media)		•	•	•	•	•	•	•
Thesaurus				•	•	•	•	•
Study Skills and Strategies	**Pre-K**	**K**	**1**	**2**	**3**	**4**	**5**	**6**
Adjust reading rate			•	•	•	•	•	•
Clarify directions	•	•	•	•	•	•	•	•
Outline				•	•	•	•	•
Skim and scan			•	•	•	•	•	•
SQP3R					•	•	•	•
Summarize		•	•	•	•	•	•	•
Take notes, paraphrase, and synthesize			•	•	•	•	•	•
Use graphic and semantic organizers to organize information		•	•	•	•	•	•	•
Test-Taking Skills and Strategies	**Pre-K**	**K**	**1**	**2**	**3**	**4**	**5**	**6**
Understand the question, the vocabulary of tests, and key words			•	•	•	•	•	•
Answer the question; use information from the text (stated or inferred)	•	•	•	•	•	•	•	•
Write across texts				•	•	•	•	•
Complete the sentence				•	•	•	•	•
Technology/New Literacies	**Pre-K**	**K**	**1**	**2**	**3**	**4**	**5**	**6**
Non-Computer Electronic Media								
Audiotapes/CDs, videotapes/DVDs	•	•	•	•	•	•	•	•
Computer Programs/Services: Basic Operations and Concepts								
Use accurate computer terminology	•	•	•	•	•	•	•	•
Create, name, locate, open, save, delete, and organize files		•	•	•	•	•	•	•
Use input and output devices (such as mouse, keyboard, monitor, printer, touch screen)	•	•	•	•	•	•	•	•
Use basic keyboarding skills		•	•	•	•	•	•	•
Responsible Use of Technology Systems and Software								
Work cooperatively and collaboratively with others; follow acceptable-use policies	•	•	•	•	•	•	•	•
Recognize hazards of Internet searches					•	•	•	•
Respect intellectual property					•	•	•	•

• instructional opportunity   **T** tested in standardized test format

Technology/New Literacies *continued*	Pre-K	K	1	2	3	4	5	6
Information and Communication Technologies:								
Information Acquisition								
Use electronic Web (nonlinear) navigation, online resources, databases, keyword searches				•	•	•	•	•
Use visual and nontextual features of online resources	•	•	•	•	•	•	•	•
Internet inquiry				•	•	•	•	•
Identify questions				•	•	•	•	•
Locate, select, and collect information				•	•	•	•	•
Analyze information				•	•	•	•	•
Evaluate electronic information sources for accuracy, relevance, bias					•	•	•	•
Understand bias/subjectivity of electronic content (about this site, author search, date created)					•	•	•	•
Synthesize information					•	•	•	•
Communicate findings				•	•	•	•	•
Use fix-up strategies (such as clicking *Back, Forward,* or *Undo;* redoing a search; trimming the URL)					•	•	•	•
Communication								
Collaborate, publish, present, and interact with others		•	•	•	•	•	•	•
Use online resources (e-mail, bulletin boards, newsgroups)				•	•	•	•	•
Use a variety of multimedia formats				•	•	•	•	•
Problem Solving								
Use technology resources for solving problems and making informed decisions					•	•	•	•
Determine when technology is useful		•	•	•	•	•	•	•

The Research Process	Pre-K	K	1	2	3	4	5	6
Identify topics; ask and evaluate questions; develop ideas leading to inquiry, investigation, and research		•	•	•	•	•	•	•
Choose and evaluate appropriate reference sources		•	•	•	•	•	•	•
Locate and collect information including using organizational features of electronic text	•	•	•	•	•	•	•	•
Take notes/record findings		•	•	•	•	•	•	•
Combine and compare information				•	•	•	•	•
Evaluate, interpret, and draw conclusions about key information		•	•	•	•	•	•	•
Paraphrase and summarize information		•	•	•	•	•	•	•
Make an outline				•	•	•	•	•
Organize content systematically		•	•	•	•	•	•	•
Communicate information		•	•	•	•	•	•	•
Write and present a report		•	•	•	•	•	•	•
Include citations					•	•	•	•
Respect intellectual property/avoid plagiarism						•	•	•
Select and organize visual aids		•	•	•	•	•	•	•

• instructional opportunity   **T** tested in standardized test format

Pacing

BACK TO SCHOOL!

UNIT 1

	WEEK 1	WEEK 2	WEEK 3	WEEK 4	WEEK 5	WEEK 6	WEEK 7	WEEK 8
Phonics	Short Vowels	Long Vowels CVCe	Consonant Blends	Inflected Endings	Consonant Digraphs		*r*-Controlled *ar, or, ore, oar*	Contractions
High-Frequency Words	*someone, somewhere, friend, country, beautiful, front*	*everywhere, live, work, woman, machines, move, world*	*couldn't, love, build, mother, bear, father, straight*	*water, eyes, early, animals, full, warm*	*together, very, learn, often, though, gone, pieces*	Cumulative Review	*family, once, pull, listen, heard, break*	*laugh, great, you're, either, certainly, second, worst*
Comprehension Skill	Character and Setting	Main Idea	Character and Setting	Main Idea	Facts and Details		Cause and Effect	Author's Purpose
Comprehension Strategy	Monitor and Clarify	Text Structure	Story Structure	Important Ideas	Predict and Set Purpose		Summarize	Text Structures
Fluency	Appropriate Rate	Read with Accuracy	Accuracy and Appropriate Rate	Attend to Punctuation	Read with Expression/ Intonation		Accuracy and Appropriate Rate	Read with Expression/ Intonation

Where the "Cumulative Review" column falls it is WEEK 6. UNIT 2 spans WEEK 7 and WEEK 8.

UNIT 4

	WEEK 19	WEEK 20	WEEK 21	WEEK 22	WEEK 23	WEEK 24	WEEK 25	WEEK 26
Phonics	Syllables C + *le*	Vowels *oo, u* (as in book)	Diphthongs *ou, ow* /ou/; *oi, oy* /oi/	Syllables CV, CVC	Vowels *oo, ue, ew, ui* (as in moon)		Suffixes *-ly, -ful, -er, -ish, -or*	Prefixes *un-, re-, pre-, dis-*
Comprehension Skill	Draw Conclusions	Sequence	Fact and Opinion	Plot and Theme	Plot and Theme	Cumulative Review	Fact and Opinion	Cause and Effect
Comprehension Strategy	Background Knowledge	Important Ideas	Questioning	Visualize	Monitor and Clarify		Important Ideas	Visualize
Vocabulary Strategy/Skill	Context Clues/ Multiple-Meaning Words	Context Clues/ Antonyms	Word Structure/ Suffixes	Context Clues/ Multiple-Meaning Words	Word Structure/ Prefixes		Word Structure/ Suffixes	Dictionary/ Unfamiliar Words
Fluency	Accuracy and Appropriate Rate	Read with Accuracy	Appropriate Phrasing	Character-ization	Read with Expression/ Intonation		Read with Accuracy	Accuracy and Appropriate Rate

Where the "Cumulative Review" column falls it is WEEK 24. UNIT 5 spans WEEK 25 and WEEK 26.

IT'S TEST TIME!

How do I cover all the skills before the test?

This chart shows the instructional sequence from Scott Foresman Reading Street.
You can use this pacing guide as is to ensure you're following a comprehensive scope
and sequence, or you can adjust the sequence to match your school/district focus
calendar, curriculum map, or testing schedule.

UNIT 3

WEEK 9	WEEK 10	WEEK 11	WEEK 12	WEEK 13	WEEK 14	WEEK 15	WEEK 16	WEEK 17	WEEK 18
r-Controlled er, ir, ur	Plurals	Long a: a, ai, ay	Cumulative Review	Long e: e, ee, ea, y	Long o: o, oa, ow	Compound Words	Long i: i, ie, igh, y	Comparative Endings	Cumulative Review
enough, toward, above, ago, word, whole	people, sign, shall, bought, probably, pleasant, scared	door, behind, brought, minute, promise, sorry, everybody		science, shoe, won, guess, village, pretty, watch	picture, school, answer, wash, parents, company, faraway	today, whatever, caught, believe, been, finally, tomorrow	their, many, alone, buy, half, youngest, daughters	only, question, clothes, money, hours, neighbor, taught	
Facts and Details	Cause and Effect	Compare and Contrast		Author's Purpose	Draw Conclusions	Compare and Contrast	Sequence	Fact and Opinion	
Background Knowledge	Story Structure	Inferring		Questioning	Visualize	Summarize	Predict and Set Purpose	Inferring	
Read with Appropriate Phrasing	Express Character-ization	Accuracy		Read with Appropriate Rate	Accuracy and Appropriate Rate	Express Character-ization	Attend to Punctuation	Read with Expression and Intonation	

UNIT 6

WEEK 27	WEEK 28	WEEK 29	WEEK 30	WEEK 31	WEEK 32	WEEK 33	WEEK 34	WEEK 35	WEEK 36
Silent Consonants	ph, gh/f/, ck, ng	Vowels aw, au, augh, al	Cumulative Review	Inflected Endings	Abbreviations	Syllables -tion, -ture, -ion	Suffixes -ness, -less, -able, -ible	Prefixes mis-, mid-, micro-, non-	Cumulative Review
Plot and Theme	Character and Setting	Main Idea		Compare and Contrast	Author's Purpose	Draw Conclusions	Sequence	Facts and Details	
Background Knowledge	Story Structure	Inferring		Monitor and Clarify	Summarize	Questioning	Text Structure	Predict and Set Purpose	
Dictionary/ Classify and Categorize	Word Structure/ Compound Words	Word Structure/ Suffixes		Context Clues/ Homophones	Context Clues/ Multiple-Meaning Words	Context Clues/words from other languages	Context Clues/ Unfamiliar Words	Dictionary/ Multiple-Meaning Words	
Read with Expression/ Intonation	Express Character-ization	Appropriate Phrasing		Accuracy and Appropriate Rate	Read with Accuracy	Appropriate Phrasing	Accuracy and Appropriate Rate	Appropriate Phrasing	

WHEN IS YOUR STATE TEST?

Pacing

BACK TO SCHOOL!

UNIT 1 / UNIT 2

	WEEK 1	WEEK 2	WEEK 3	WEEK 4	WEEK 5	WEEK 6 Cumulative Review	WEEK 7	WEEK 8
Speaking, Listening, and Viewing	Why We Speak/Why We Listen	Be a Good Speaker/Listen Attentively	Recognize Purposes of Media	Narrate in Sequence	Dramatize		Give and Follow Directions	Explain Purposes of Media
Research and Study Skills	Media Center/ Library	Reference Sources	Personal Sources	Parts of a Book	Maps		Notes	Timeline
Grammar	Sentences	Subjects	Predicates	Statements and Questions	Commands and Exclamations		Nouns	Proper Nouns
Weekly Writing; Trait of the Week	Personal Narrative/ Conventions	Expository Paragraph/ Sentences	Realistic Story/ Organization	Brief Report/ Word Choice	Play Scene/ Conventions		Narrative Nonfiction/ Voice	Biography/ Focus/Ideas
Writing	Keyboarding/Personal Narrative							

UNIT 4 / UNIT 5

	WEEK 19	WEEK 20	WEEK 21	WEEK 22	WEEK 23	WEEK 24 Cumulative Review	WEEK 25	WEEK 26
Speaking, Listening, and Viewing	Media Techniques	Make an Announcement	Speak Well	Media Techniques	Give an Oral Summary		Identify Cultural Characteristics in Media	Give a Demonstration
Research and Study Skills	Thesaurus	Personal Sources	Diagram	E-mail	Natural and Personal Sources		Online Directory	Bar Graph
Grammar	Adjectives and Our Senses	Adjectives for Number, Size, and Shape	Adjectives That Compare	Adverbs That Tell When and Where	Adverbs That Tell How		Pronouns	Singular and Plural Pronouns
Weekly Writing; Trait of the Week	Friendly Letter/ Organization	Expository Nonfiction/ Word Choice	Short Expository Report/ Sentences	Narrative Poem/ Voice	Thank-You Note/ Focus/Ideas		Narrative Nonfiction/ Word Choice	Realistic Story/ Organization
Writing	E-Newsletter/Description							

IT'S TEST TIME!

UNIT 3

WEEK 9	WEEK 10	WEEK 11	WEEK 12	WEEK 13	WEEK 14	WEEK 15	WEEK 16	WEEK 17	WEEK 18
Ask and Answer Questions	Explain Purposes of Media	Give and Follow Directions	Cumulative Review	Make Introductions	Solve Problems	Summarize Information	Give a Description	Describe Media Technique	Cumulative Review
Chapter Headings	Encyclopedia	Read a Web Page		Picture-Graph	Newspaper and Periodicals	Interview	Alphabetized Index	Search Internet	
Singular and Plural Nouns	Plural Nouns That Change Spelling	Possessive Nouns		Verbs	Verbs with Singular and Plural Nouns	Verbs for Past, Present, and Future	More About Verbs	Verbs: *Am, Is, Are, Was,* and *Were*	
Expository Nonfiction/ Word Choice	Fairy Tale/ Organization	Folk Tale/ Sentences		Animal Fantasy/ Voice	Friendly Letter/ Focus/Idea	Narrative Poem/ Conventions	Realistic Story/ Word Choice	Review/ Organization	

Electronic Pen Pal/Directions   Story Starters/Compare and Contrast Essay

UNIT 6

WEEK 27	WEEK 28	WEEK 29	WEEK 30	WEEK 31	WEEK 32	WEEK 33	WEEK 34	WEEK 35	WEEK 36
Listen for Facts and Opinions	Maintain Focus in a Narrative Presentation	Speak to Your Audience	Cumulative Review	Use Vocabulary to Express Ideas	Evaluate Ads	Listen to a Description	Identify Conventions	Listen for Speaker's Purpose	Cumulative Review
Online Reference Sources	Tables	Evaluate Online Sources		Globe	Chart	Interview a Natural Source	Schedules	Interview a Natural Source	
Using *I* and *Me*	Different Kinds of Pronouns	Contractions		Capital Letters	Quotation Marks	Prepositions	Commas	Commas in Compound Sentences	
Journal Entry/Voice	Animal Fantasy/ Conventions	Humorous Story/ Sentences		Realistic Story/ Organization	Descriptive Poem or Song/ Voice	Invitation or Letter/ Sentences	Compare-Contrast Text/ Focus/Ideas	Persuasive Statement/ Word Choice	

Community Interview/Persuasive Letter   Blogging/Research Report

WHEN IS YOUR STATE TEST?

Student Progress Report: Grade 2

Name _____

This chart lists the skills taught in this program. Record your child's progress toward mastery of the skills covered in this school year here. Use the chart below to track the coverage of these skills.

Skill	Date	Date	Date	Date	Date
Distinguish features of a sentence.					
Decode multisyllabic words by applying letter-sound correspondences of single letters.					
Decode words with consonant blends.					
Decode words with consonant digraph.					
Decode words with vowel digraphs and diphthongs.					
Use common syllable patterns to decode words with closed syllables.					
Use common syllable patterns to decode words with open syllables.					
Use common syllable patterns to decode words with final stable syllables.					
Use common syllable patterns to decode words with a silent "e" at the end.					
Use common syllable patterns to decode words with r-controlled vowels.					
Use common syllable patterns to decode words with vowel digraphs and diphthongs.					
Decode words with common spelling patterns.					
Read words with common prefixes and suffixes.					
Identify and read abbreviations.					
Identify and read contractions.					

Skill	Date	Date	Date	Date	Date
Identify and read at least 300 high-frequency words from a commonly used list.					
Monitor accuracy of decoding.					
Use ideas to make and confirm predictions.					
Ask relevant questions, clarify text, locate facts and details about texts, and support answers with evidence.					
Establish a purpose for reading and monitor comprehension.					
Read aloud grade-level appropriate text with fluency and comprehension.					

Skill	Date	Date	Date
Use prefixes and suffixes to determine the meaning of words.			
Use context to determine the meaning of unfamiliar words or multiple-meaning words.			
Identify and use antonyms and synonyms.			
Alphabetize a series of words and use a dictionary or a glossary to find words.			
Identify themes in well-known fables, legends, myths, or stories.			
Compare the characters, settings, and plots in traditional and contemporary folktales.			
Describe how rhyme, rhythm, and repetition create images in poetry.			
Identify the elements of dialogue and use them in informal plays.			

Skill	Date	Date	Date
Describe similarities and differences in the plots and settings of works by the same author.			
Describe main characters in works of fiction, including their traits, motivations, and feelings.			
Distinguish between fiction and nonfiction.			
Recognize that some words and phrases have literal and non-literal meanings.			
Read independently for a sustained period of time and paraphrase texts.			
Identify the topic and explain the author's purpose for writing.			
Students should be able to identify the main idea in a text and distinguish it from the topic.			
Locate the facts that are clearly stated in a text.			
Describe the order of events or ideas in a text.			
Use text features to locate specific information.			
Follow written multi-step directions.			
Use graphic features to interpret text.			
Recognize different purposes of media.			
Describe techniques that are used to create media messages.			
Identify the conventions of writing for different kinds of media and the Internet.			

Skill	Date	Date	Date
Plan a first draft by generating ideas for writing.			
Develop drafts and put ideas in order through sentences.			
Revise drafts by adding or deleting words, phrases, or sentences.			
Edit drafts for grammar, punctuation, and spelling using a teacher-developed rubric.			
Publish and share writing with others.			
Write brief stories that include a beginning, middle, and end.			
Write short poems that convey sensory details.			
Write brief nonfiction compositions about topics of interest to them.			
Write short letters.			
Write brief comments on literary or informational texts.			
Write persuasively on issues that are important to the student.			
Understand and use verbs (past, present, and future) in when reading, writing, and speaking.			
Understand and use nouns (singular/plural, common/ proper) when reading, writing, and speaking.			
Understand and use adjectives when reading, writing, and speaking.			
Understand and use adverbs when reading, writing, and speaking.			

Skill	Date	Date	Date
Understand and use prepositions and prepositional phrases when reading, writing, and speaking.			
Understand and use pronouns when reading, writing, and speaking.			
Understand and use time-order transition words when reading, writing, and speaking.			
Use complete sentences with correct subject-verb agreement.			
Distinguish among declarative and interrogative sentences.			
Write legibly and leave appropriate margins for readability.			
Use capitalization for proper nouns.			
Use capitalization for months and days of the week.			
Use capitalization for the salutation and closing of a letter.			
Recognize and use ending punctuation in sentences.			
Recognize and use apostrophes and contractions.			
Recognize and use apostrophes and possessives.			
Match sounds to letters to construct unknown words.			
Spell words with complex consonants.			
Spell words with r-controlled vowels.			
Spell words with long vowels.			
Spell words with vowel digraphs and diphthongs.			
Spell high-frequency words from a commonly used list.			

Skill	Date	Date	Date
Spell base words with inflectional endings.			
Spell simple contractions.			
Use resources to find correct spellings.			
Generate topics for research and ask questions about the topics.			
Determine relevant sources to use to answer questions.			
Gather evidence from sources and experts.			
Use text features in reference works to locate information.			
Record basic information in simple visual formats.			
Revise the topic as a result of answers to initial research questions.			
Create a visual display to show the results of research.			
Listen attentively and ask relevant questions.			
Follow, restate, and give oral instructions.			
Share information and ideas about the topic and speak at an appropriate pace.			
Follow rules for discussion.			
Set a purpose for reading.			
Ask literal questions of text.			
Monitor and adjust comprehension.			

Skill	Date	Date	Date
Make inferences about text using textual evidence to support understanding.			
Retell important events in stories in logical order.			
Make connections to own experiences, to ideas in other texts, and to the larger community.			

English/Language Arts and Cross-Disciplinary Connections

Grade 2

English/Language Arts Standards

Writing

Compose a variety of texts that demonstrate clear focus, the logical development of ideas in well-organized paragraphs, and the use of appropriate language that advances the author's purpose. • Determine effective approaches, forms, and rhetorical techniques that demonstrate understanding of the writer's purpose and audience. • Generate ideas and gather information relevant to the topic and purpose, keeping careful records of outside sources. • Evaluate relevance, quality, sufficiency, and depth of preliminary ideas and information, organize material generated, and formulate thesis. • Recognize the importance of revision as the key to effective writing.	U1W1, U1W2, U1W3, U1W4, U1W5, U2W1, U2W2, U2W3, U2W4, U2W5, U3W1, U3W2, U3W3, U3W4, U3W5, U4W1, U4W2, U4W3, U4W4, U4W5, U5W1, U5W2, U5W3, U5W4, U5W5, U6W1, U6W2, U6W3, U6W4, U6W5

Reading

Locate explicit textual information and draw complex inferences, analyze, and evaluate the information within and across texts of varying lengths. • Use effective reading strategies to determine a written work's purpose and intended audience. • Use text features and graphics to form an overview of informational texts and to determine where to locate information. • Identify explicit and implicit textual information including main ideas and author's purpose. • Draw and support complex inferences from text to summarize, draw conclusions, and distinguish facts from simple assertions and opinions. • Analyze the presentation of information and the strength and quality of evidence used by the author, and judge the coherence and logic of the presentation and the credibility of an argument. • Analyze imagery in literary texts. • Evaluate the use of both literal and figurative language to inform and shape the perceptions of readers. • Compare and analyze how generic features are used across texts. • Identify and analyze the audience, purpose, and message of an informational or persuasive text. • Identify and analyze how an author's use of language appeals to the senses, creates imagery, and suggests mood. • Identify, analyze, and evaluate similarities and differences in how multiple texts present information, argue a position, or relate a theme.	U1W1, U1W2, U1W3, U1W4, U1W5, U2W1, U2W2, U2W5, U3W1, U3W2, U3W3, U3W5, U4W1, U4W2, U4W3, U4W4, U4W5, U5W1, U5W2, U5W3, U5W4, U5W5, U6W1, U6W2, U6W3, U6W4, U6W5
Understand new vocabulary and concepts and use them accurately in reading, speaking, and writing. • Identify new words and concepts acquired through study of their relationships to other words and concepts. • Apply knowledge of roots and affixes to infer the meanings of new words. • Use reference guides to confirm the meanings of new words or concepts.	U1W2, U1W3, U1W5, U2W1, U2W3, U2W4, U2W5, U3W1, U3W2, U3W3, U3W4, U3W5, U4W1, U4W2, U4W3, U4W4, U4W5, U5W1, U5W2, U5W3, U5W4, U5W5, U6W1, U6W2, U6W3, U6W4, U6W5

Describe, analyze, and evaluate information within and across literary and other texts from a variety of cultures and historical periods. • Read a wide variety of texts from American, European, and world literatures. • Analyze themes, structures, and elements of myths, traditional narratives, and classical and contemporary literature. • Analyze works of literature for what they suggest about the historical period and cultural contexts in which they were written. • Analyze and compare the use of language in literary works from a variety of world cultures.	U1W1, U1W2, U1W3, U1W4, U1W5, U2W1, U2W2, U2W3, U2W4, U2W5, U3W1, U3W2, U3W3, U3W4, U3W5, U4W1, U4W2, U4W3, U4W4, U4W5, U5W1, U5W2, U5W3, U5W4, U5W5, U6W1, U6W2, U6W3, U6W4, U6W5
Explain how literary and other texts evoke personal experience and reveal character in particular historical circumstances. • Describe insights gained about oneself, others, or the world from reading specific texts. • Analyze the influence of myths, folktales, fables, and classical literature from a variety of world cultures on later literature and film.	U1W1, U1W2, U1W3, U1W4, U1W5, U2W1, U2W2, U2W3, U2W4, U2W5, U3W1, U3W2, U3W3, U3W4, U3W5, U4W1, U4W2, U4W3, U4W4, U4W5, U5W1, U5W2, U5W3, U5W4, U5W5, U6W1, U6W2, U6W3, U6W4, U6W5

Speaking

Understand the elements of communication both in informal group discussions and formal presentations (e.g., accuracy, relevance, rhetorical features, and organization of information). • Understand how style and content of spoken language varies in different contexts and influences the listener's understanding. • Adjust presentation (delivery, vocabulary, length) to particular audiences and purposes.	U1W2, U1W5, U2W1, U2W5, U3W1, U4W2, U5W2, U5W5, U6W3, U6W5
Develop effective speaking styles for both group and one-on-one situations. • Participate actively and effectively in one-on-one oral communication situations. • Participate actively and effectively in group discussions. • Plan and deliver focused and coherent presentations that convey clear and distinct perspectives and demonstrate solid reasoning.	U1W4, U2W2, U2W4, U3W2, U3W3, U3W4, U4W1, U4W2, U4W4, U4W5, U5W2, U5W3, U5W4, U6W2, U6W5

Listening

Apply listening skills as an individual and as a member of a group in a variety of settings (e.g., lectures, discussions, conversations, team projects, presentations, interviews). • Analyze and evaluate the effectiveness of a public presentation. • Interpret a speaker's message; identify the position taken and the evidence in support of that position. • Use a variety of strategies to enhance listening comprehension (e.g., focus attention on message, monitor message for clarity and understanding, provide verbal and nonverbal feedback, note cues such as change of pace or particular words that indicate a new point is about to be made, select and organize key information).	U1W1, U1W2, U1W4, U2W2, U2W3, U2W4, U2W5, U4W2, U5W2, U5W3, U5W4, U6W1, U6W3, U6W5
Listen effectively in informal and formal situations. • Listen critically and respond appropriately to presentations. • Listen actively and effectively in one-on-one communication situations. • Listen actively and effectively in group discussions.	U1W1, U1W2, U1W4, U2W2, U2W3, U2W4, U2W5, U4W1, U4W2, U4W4, U5W2, U5W3, U5W4, U6W1, U6W3, U6W5

Research

Formulate topic and questions. • Formulate research questions. • Explore a research topic. • Refine research topic and devise a timeline for completing work.	U1W1, U1W2, U1W3, U1W4, U1W5, U2W1, U2W2, U2W3, U2W4, U2W5, U3W1, U3W2, U3W3, U3W4, U3W5, U4W1, U4W2, U4W3, U4W4, U4W5, U5W1, U5W2, U5W3, U5W4, U5W5, U6W1, U6W2, U6W3, U6W4, U6W5
Select information from a variety of sources. • Gather relevant sources. • Evaluate the validity and reliability of sources. • Synthesize and organize information effectively. • Use source material ethically	U1W1, U1W2, U1W3, U1W4, U1W5, U2W1, U2W2, U2W3, U2W4, U2W5, U3W1, U3W2, U3W3, U3W4, U3W5, U4W1, U4W2, U4W3, U4W4, U4W5, U5W1, U5W2, U5W3, U5W4, U5W5, U6W1, U6W2, U6W3, U6W4, U6W5
Produce and design a document. • Design and present an effective product. • Use source material ethically.	U1W1, U1W2, U1W3, U1W4, U1W5, U2W1, U2W2, U2W3, U2W4, U2W5, U3W1, U3W2, U3W3, U3W4, U3W5, U4W1, U4W2, U4W3, U4W4, U4W5, U5W1, U5W2, U5W3, U5W4, U5W5, U6W1, U6W2, U6W3, U6W4, U6W5

Cross-Disciplinary Standards

Key Cognitive Skills

Intellectual curiosity • Engage in scholarly inquiry and dialogue. • Accept constructive criticism and revise personal views when valid evidence warrants.	U1W1, U1W2, U1W3, U1W4, U1W5, U2W1, U2W2, U2W3, U2W4, U2W5, U3W1, U3W2, U3W3, U3W4, U3W5, U4W1, U4W2, U4W3, U4W4, U4W5, U5W1, U5W2, U5W3, U5W4, U5W5, U6W1, U6W2, U6W3, U6W4, U6W5
Reasoning • Consider arguments and conclusions of self and others. • Construct well-reasoned arguments to explain phenomena, validate conjectures, or support positions. • Gather evidence to support arguments, findings, or lines of reasoning. • Support or modify claims based on the results of an inquiry.	U1W1, U1W2, U1W3, U1W4, U1W5, U2W1, U2W2, U2W3, U2W4, U2W5, U3W1, U3W2, U3W3, U3W4, U3W5, U4W1, U4W2, U4W3, U4W4, U4W5, U5W1, U5W2, U5W3, U5W4, U5W5, U6W1, U6W2, U6W3, U6W4, U6W5
Problem solving • Analyze a situation to identify a problem to be solved. • Develop and apply multiple strategies to solving a problem. • Collect evidence and data systematically and directly relate to solving a problem.	U2W5, U3W2, U3W3
Academic behaviors • Self-monitor learning needs and seek assistance when needed. • Use study habits necessary to manage academic pursuits and requirements. • Strive for accuracy and precision. • Persevere to complete and master tasks.	U1W1, U1W2, U1W3, U1W4, U1W5, U2W1, U2W2, U2W3, U2W4, U2W5, U3W1, U3W2, U3W3, U3W4, U3W5, U4W1, U4W2, U4W3, U4W4, U4W5, U5W1, U5W2, U5W3, U5W4, U5W5, U6W1, U6W2, U6W3, U6W4, U6W5
Work habits • Work independently. • Work collaboratively.	U1W1, U1W2, U1W3, U1W4, U1W5, U2W1, U2W2, U2W3, U2W4, U2W5, U3W1, U3W2, U3W3, U3W4, U3W5, U4W1, U4W2, U4W3, U4W4, U4W5, U5W1, U5W2, U5W3, U5W4, U5W5, U6W1, U6W2, U6W3, U6W4, U6W5

Academic integrity

- Attribute ideas and information to source materials and people.
- Evaluate sources for quality of content, validity, credibility, and relevance.
- Include the ideas of others and the complexities of the debate, issue, or problem.
- Understand and adhere to ethical codes of conduct.

U4W4, U5W4, U5W5, U6W4

Foundational Skills

Reading across the curriculum

- Use effective prereading strategies.
- Use a variety of strategies to understand the meanings of new words.
- Identify the intended purpose and audience of the text.
- Identify the key information and supporting details.
- Analyze textual information critically.
- Annotate, summarize, paraphrase, and outline texts when appropriate.
- Adapt reading strategies according to structure of texts.
- Connect reading to historical and current events and personal interest.

U1W1, U1W2, U1W3, U1W4, U1W5, U2W1, U2W2, U2W3, U2W4, U2W5, U3W1, U3W2, U3W3, U3W4, U3W5, U4W1, U4W2, U4W3, U4W4, U4W5, U5W1, U5W2, U5W3, U5W4, U5W5, U6W1, U6W2, U6W3, U6W4, U6W5

Writing across the curriculum

- Write clearly and coherently using standard writing conventions.
- Write in a variety of forms for various audiences and purposes.
- Compose and revise drafts.

U1W1, U1W2, U1W3, U1W4, U1W5, U2W1, U2W2, U2W3, U2W4, U2W5, U3W1, U3W2, U3W3, U3W4, U3W5, U4W1, U4W2, U4W3, U4W4, U4W5, U5W1, U5W2, U5W3, U5W4, U5W5, U6W1, U6W2, U6W3, U6W4, U6W5

Research across the curriculum

- Understand which topics or questions are to be investigated.
- Explore a research topic.
- Refine research topic based on preliminary research and devise a timeline for completing work.
- Evaluate the validity and reliability of sources.
- Synthesize and organize information effectively.
- Design and present an effective product.
- Integrate source material.
- Present final product.

U1W1, U1W2, U1W3, U1W4, U1W5, U2W1, U2W2, U2W3, U2W4, U2W5, U3W1, U3W2, U3W3, U3W4, U3W5, U4W1, U4W2, U4W3, U4W4, U4W5, U5W1, U5W2, U5W3, U5W4, U5W5, U6W1, U6W2, U6W3, U6W4, U6W5

Technology

- Use technology to gather information.
- Use technology to organize, manage, and analyze information.
- Use technology to communicate and display findings in a clear and coherent manner.
- Use technology appropriately.

U2W2, U3W5, U4W4, U5W1, U5W3, U5W5

Science Connections on Reading Street

Grade 2

Science, Technology, and Society

Interactions between innovations and science • Recognize how scientific discoveries are connected to technological innovations.	U1W2
History of science • Understand the historical development of major theories in science. • Recognize the role of people in important contributions to scientific knowledge.	U1W2, U3W1, U3W5

Cross-Disciplinary Themes

Change over time/equilibrium • Recognize patterns of change. • Use computer models, applications and simulations.	U4W2, U4W3, U4W5

Biology

Systems and homeostasis • Know that organisms possess various structures and processes (feedback loops) that maintain steady internal conditions. • Describe, compare, and contrast structures and processes that allow gas exchange, nutrient uptake and processing, waste excretion, nervous and hormonal regulation, and reproduction in plants, animals, and fungi; give examples of each.	U1W5, U3W3, U4W2, U5W3
Ecology • Identify Earth's major biomes, giving their locations, typical climate conditions, and characteristic organisms present in each. • Know patterns of energy flow and material cycling in Earth's ecosystems. • Understand typical forms of organismal behavior. • Know the process of succession.	U1W3, U1W4

Earth and Space Sciences

Sun, Earth, and moon system • Understand interactions among the sun, Earth, and moon. • Possess a scientific understanding of the formation of the Earth and moon.	U1W2, U1W3

Environmental Science

Earth systems • Recognize the Earth's systems. • Know the major features of the geosphere and the factors that modify them. • Know the major features of the atmosphere. • Know the major features of the hydrosphere. • Be familiar with Earth's major biomes. • Describe the Earth's major biogeochemical cycles.	U1W4, U4W5

Human practices and their impacts	U3W5, U4W2
<ul><li>Describe the different uses for land (land management).</li><li>Understand the use and consequences of pest management.</li><li>Know the different methods used to increase food production.</li><li>Understand land and water usage and management practices.</li><li>Understand how human practices affect air, water, and soil quality.</li></ul>	

Social Studies Connections on Reading Street

Grade 2

Analysis, Synthesis and Evaluation of Information

Research and methods • Use established research methodologies. • Explain how historians and other social scientists develop new and competing views of past phenomena. • Gather, organize and display the results of data and research. • Identify and collect sources.	U1W1, U1W2, U1W3, U1W4, U1W5, U2W1, U2W2, U2W3, U2W4, U2W5, U3W1, U3W2, U3W3, U3W4, U3W5, U4W1, U4W2, U4W3, U4W4, U4W5, U5W1, U5W2, U5W3, U5W4, U5W5, U6W1, U6W2, U6W3, U6W4, U6W5
Critical listening • Understand/interpret presentations (e.g., speeches, lectures, less formal presentations) critically.	U1W1, U1W2, U1W4, U2W2, U2W3, U2W4, U2W5, U4W2, U5W2, U5W3, U5W4, U6W1, U6W3, U6W5

Effective Communication

Clear and coherent oral and written communication • Use appropriate oral communication techniques depending on the context or nature of the interaction. • Use conventions of standard written English.	U1W1, U1W2, U1W3, U1W4, U1W5, U2W1, U2W2, U2W3, U2W4, U2W5, U3W1, U3W2, U3W3, U3W4, U3W5, U4W1, U4W2, U4W3, U4W4, U4W5, U5W1, U5W2, U5W3, U5W4, U5W5, U6W1, U6W2, U6W3, U6W4, U6W5

Index

H

I

Logs, strategy response

activate prior knowledge, **2.3v1:** 388h

background knowledge, **2.1v1:** 58h, **2.1v2:** 120h, **2.2v1:** 254h, 269a, **2.4v1:** 28a, 43a, 62a, 77a, **2.5v1:** 198a, 264a, 279a

genre, **2.1v1:** 88h, **2.2v1:** 224h, **2.2v2:** 284h, 303a, 320h, **2.3v1:** 424h, **2.3v2:** 486h, **2.4v2:** 128a, 145a, **2.5v2:** 332a, **2.6v2:** 466a, 489a

important ideas, **2.1v2:** 141a, **2.5v1:** 213a

inferring, **2.2v2:** 337a, **2.3v2:** 509a, **2.5v2:** 349a

monitor and clarify, **2.1v1:** 26h, 45a, **2.3v1:** 407a, **2.4v2:** 162a, 179a, **2.6v1:** 368a, 383a

predict and/or set purpose, **2.1v2:** 156h, 175a, **2.3v2:** 458h, 471a, **2.5v1:** 230a, **2.5v2:** 296a, **2.6v1:** 400a, 419a, **2.6v2:** 504a, 521a

questioning, **2.3v1:** 354h, 373a, **2.4v1:** 92a, 111a, **2.6v1:** 434a, 449a

summarize, **2.2v1:** 192h, 209a, **2.3v1:** 445a, **2.6v1:** 419a

text/story structure, **2.1v1:** 73a, 105a, **2.2v1:** 241a, **2.5v2:** 315a, **2.6v2:** 489a

visualize, **2.5v1:** 249a

M

Magazine article. *See* Genres.

Magazine/periodical (as reference source). *See* Reference sources.

Main idea

details and, **2.1v1:** 48h, 48–49, 49a, 57a, 58h, 64–65, 66–67, 68–69, 73a, 76–77, 78–79, 81b, 81f, 94–95, 104h, CL10–CL11, **2.1v2:** 119a, 120h, 122–123, 126–127, 130–131, 136–137, 141a, 146–147, 149b, 149f, IR23–IR24, IR43–IR44, CL8–CL9, **2.2v2:** 301a, **2.4v1:** 109a, **2.4v2:** 166–167, 178h, **2.5v2:** 318–319, 320–321, 328a, 328–329, 332a, 338–339, 342–343, 344–345, 349a, 357b, 357f, IR53–IR54, CL10–CL11, **2.6v2:** 476–477, 488h

topic and, **2.2v1:** 247c, **2.6v1:** 417b, 425c

See also Oral language, listening comprehension.

Making connections. *See* Connections, making.

Map/globe. *See* Graphic sources.

Mapping selections. *See* Graphic and semantic organizers, types.

Mass media. *See* Media literacy.

Mechanics (of English grammar and writing). *See* Apostrophe, Capitalization, Comma, Exclamation mark, Period, Question mark, Quotation marks.

Media. *See* Media literacy.

Media center/library. *See* Reference sources.

Media literacy

kinds of media

advertising/billboards, **2.4v1:** 51f, 53a, **2.6v1:** 423f, 424–425, 425a

audiotapes, **2.2v2:** 311f, **2.3v2:** 515e

CD-ROM, **2.1v1:** 43g, **2.4v1:** 51f

DVD, **2.4v1:** 51f, **2.4v2:** 151e

illustrations/photographs, **2.1v1:** 76h, **2.4v1:** 109b, **2.4v2:** 151e, 152–153

Internet, **2.2v1:** 245f, 247a, 272h, 272–275, **2.2v2:** 335f, **2.3v2:** 507g, 515e, 516–517, 517a, **2.4v1:** 51f, 52–53, 53a, **2.4v2:** 151e, 152–153, **2.6v1:** 424–425, 452h, 452–455

magazines, **2.1v1:** 43g, 113a, **2.2v1:** 245f, 247a, **2.2v2:** 313a, **2.4v1:** 51f, 52–53, 53a, **2.4v2:** 151e, 152–153, **2.5v2:** 318h, 318–321, **2.6v1:** 424–425, 425a

newspapers, **2.1v1:** 43g, **2.2v1:** 245f, 247a, **2.2v2:** 311f, 312–313, 313a, **2.3v2:** 515e, 516–517, 517a, **2.4v1:** 53a, **2.4v2:** 151e, 152–153, **2.6v1:** 424–425, 425a

radio, **2.1v1:** 111e, 113a, **2.2v2:** 245f, 247a, 311f, 312–313, 313a, **2.3v2:** 515e, 516–517, 517a, **2.4v1:** 51f, 52–53, 53a

stage production, **2.2v2:** 311f, 312–313, 313a

television news, **2.2v2:** 245f, 247a, **2.3v2:** 515e, 516–517, 517a

television/videos/films, **2.1v1:** 111e, 113a, **2.2v2:** 245f, 311f, 312–313, 313a, **2.3v2:** 515e, 516–517, 517a, **2.4v1:** 51f, 52–53, 53a, **2.4v2:** 151e, 152–153

video game, **2.6v2:** 493f, 494–495, 495a

purposes of media

entertainment, **2.1v1:** 111e, 112–113, 113a, **2.2v1:** 245f, 246–247, 247a, **2.2v2:** 311f, 312–313, 313a, **2.6v2:** 493f, 494–495, 495a

information, **2.1v1:** 111e, 112–113, 113a, **2.2v1:** 245f, 246–247, 247a, **2.2v2:** 245f, 247a, 311f, 312–313, 313a, **2.3v2:** 515e, 516–517, 517a

persuasion, **2.1v1:** 113a, **2.2v2:** 311f, 312–313, 313a, **2.4v1:** 51f, 52–53, 53a, **2.6v1:** 423f, 424–425, 425a

responding to media

evaluation of, **2.2v2:** 311f, 312–313, 313a, **2.4v1:** 51f, 53a, 151e, **2.6v1:** 423f, 494–495, 495a

oral, **2.1v1:** 111e, 245f, **2.2v2:** 311f, 312–313, 313a

written, **2.1v1:** 111e

techniques of media

audial, **2.3v1:** 515e, 516–517, 517a, **2.4v1:** 51f, 52–53, 53a

culture, characteristics of, **2.5v1:** 219e, 220–221, 221a

graphics, **2.4v2:** 151e, 152–153

visual, **2.3v2:** 515e, 516–517, 517a, **2.4v2:** 151e, 152–153

written conventions, **2.6v2:** 493f, 494–495, 495a

Metacognition. *See* Monitor and clarify, Self-check.

Metaphor. *See* Figurative language, Literary terms.

Modeling. Teacher modeling and think-alouds are presented throughout Skills/Strategies in Context lessons and After Reading lessons.

Monitor and clarify

adjust reading rate, **2.4v2:** 182–183, 184–185, **2.6v1:** 386–387

ask questions, **2.1v1:** 26h, 30–31, 38–39, 42–43, 48–49, 49a, CL14–CL15, **2.2v1:** 214–215, **2.2v2:** IR13, IR15, **2.4v2:** 158–159, 162a, 164–165, 166–167, 176–177, 182–183, IR55, **2.6v1:** 264–265, 364–365, 386–387, **2.6v2:** IR15

background knowledge, **2.1v1:** 48–49, **2.2v1:** 272–273

read on, **2.1v1:** CL14–CL15, **2.2v1:** 212–213, **2.6v1:** 386–387, 388–389, CL14–CL15

reread, **2.1v1:** 26h, 30–31, 38–39, 42–43, 45a, 48–49, 49a, 110–111, CL14–CL15, **2.1v2:** IR13, IR15, **2.2v1:** 214–215, **2.2v2:** 306–307, **2.4v1:** 30–31, 38–39, **2.4v2:** 158–159, 162a, 166–167, 176–177, 179a, 182–183, 184–185, IR53, IR55, **2.6v1:** 364–365, 368a, 372–373, 383a, 386–387, CL14–CL15, **2.6v2:** IR13, IR15

seek help from others, **2.1v1:** CL14–CL15, **2.6v1:** CL14–CL15

seek help from reference sources, **2.1v1:** CL14–CL15, **2.4v2:** 164–165

use graphic sources, **2.6v1:** 368a, 372–373

use illustrations, **2.1v1:** CL14–CL15, **2.4v1:** 184–185, **2.6v1:** 286–287, **2.6v2:** IR13

use text features, **2.1v1:** CL14–CL15, **2.6v1:** 286–287, CL14–CL15

visualize, **2.1v1:** 48–49

See also Graphic and semantic organizers, Self-check.

Oral vocabulary development

Organizing information

P

Paired reading. *See* Fluency, reading; Oral reading ability.

Paraphrase. *See* Summarize.

Parents. *See* School-home connection.

Parts of a book

Penmanship. *See* Handwriting.

Period

Index

Index

W

Web. *See* Graphic and semantic organizers, types.

Web site. *See* Genres; Technology, new literacies.

Word analysis

Word attack skills. *See* Context clues for meaning, Dictionary/glossary, Phonics/decoding, Vocabulary development, Vocabulary strategies, Word analysis.

Word choice. *See* Literary terms, Writing traits.

Word identification. *See* Context clues for meaning, Dictionary/glossary, Vocabulary strategies, Word analysis.

Word reading. *See* Fluency, reading.

Words from other languages. *See* Vocabulary strategies.

Word study. *See* Context clues for meaning, Dictionary/glossary, Vocabulary development, Vocabulary strategies, Word analysis.

Writing assessment. *See* Assessment.

Writing forms/products